T0329929

MISRECOGNITIONS

MISRECOGNITIONS

PLOTTING CAPITAL IN THE VICTORIAN NOVEL

BEN PARKER

CORNELL UNIVERSITY PRESS

Ithaca and London

First published 2024 by Cornell University Press

Library of Congress Cataloging-in-Publication Data

Names: Parker, Ben (Benjamin W.), author.
Title: Misrecognitions : plotting capital in the Victorian
    novel / Ben Parker.
Description: Ithaca [New York] : Cornell University Press,
    2024. | Includes bibliographical references and index.
Identifiers: LCCN 2023032687 (print) | LCCN 2023032688
    (ebook) | ISBN 9781501774072 (hardcover) |
    ISBN 9781501774089 (epub) | ISBN 9781501774096 (pdf)
Subjects: LCSH: Recognition in literature. | Capitalism in
    literature. | English literature—19th century—History
    and criticism.
Classification: LCC PN56.R33 P37 2024 (print) |
    LCC PN56.R33 (ebook) | DDC 820.9/008—dc23/eng
    /20230831
LC record available at https://lccn.loc.gov/2023032687
LC ebook record available at https://lccn.loc.gov
    /2023032688

Like one who dreams he is being harmed,
And even as he dreams, wishes it may be a dream,
So that he longs for what is, as if it were not . . .
    —Dante, *Inferno*

CONTENTS

ACKNOWLEDGMENTS

Ludwig Wittgenstein ends the preface to his *Philosophical Investigations* by saying, "I should have liked to produce a good book. It has not turned out that way." Along those lines, I feel I owe the following people something better than attaching their names to the work in front of you, but it is all I have, and without their support and criticism, writing it would simply not have been possible.

My earliest gratitude is to Nicholas Dames and Bruce Robbins, advisors for the original dissertation research. Many friends played a role in my writing and thinking—as readers, as interlocutors, as models of discernment and integrity: Spencer Bastedo, Nico Baumbach, Anna Clark, Anne Diebel, Merve Emre, Cassandra Guan, Anjuli Raza Kolb, Yumi Lee, Andy Liu, Piper Marshall, Meg McDermott, Matt Moss, Golnar Nikpour, Zach Samalin, Jeanette Samyn, and Wendy Xin. Christine Smallwood deserves a special note, as something like Agamemnon in this catalog of heroes. During the writing of the book, Genevieve Yue brought a warm intelligence to every query and countless drafts.

I have been very lucky to find excellent colleagues at Brown. Amanda Anderson, Tim Bewes, Stuart Burrows, Jacques Khalip, Marc Redfield, and Ellen Rooney all gave valuable advice on different parts of the book. David Miller's friendship and advice at the start of the book meant the world to me. Jay Bernstein helped to clarify the Hegelian dimension of my reading of Henry James. Toward the end of the process, Anna Kornbluh and an anonymous reader for the press urged me to fully take on the most important questions—once more into the breach! Mahinder Kingra, my editor at Cornell University Press, was a champion for the best version of this book.

It is not possible to state what I owe to my parents, Ray and Mary Jean. My father has, I believe, read every page of this book with (so to speak) a red pencil in hand. My mother shows up on more pages than she perhaps knows. All through the writing of the book, my own daughter has belonged, in the words of Simone Weil, to a "precarious, touching world" of family, nearness, and concern. My love to Harriet.

MISRECOGNITIONS

Introduction
Capital's Plot Hole

Victorian novels have frequently been criticized
for their implausible and labyrinthine plots. Critics have especially lamented
their reliance on recognition scenes: the reunions and identifications that all too
conveniently tie everything together at the end. The plots of Victorian novels are
notoriously littered with such scenes. Orphans are claimed by their next of kin,
concealed spouses make untimely appearances from upper floors, and Red-
Headed Leagues and Speckled Bands are at length apprehended. No other aspect of Victorian fiction has been so consistently cried down as these moments of
belated discovery. Just to mention these scenes is to invite a vast critical groan
over their labored machinations, for being at once clumsy and artificial. Typical
of these objections is George Orwell bemoaning the "awful Victorian 'plot'"
that mars novelistic form with a "crossword puzzle of coincidences, intrigues,
murders, disguises, buried wills, long-lost brothers, etc. etc."[1]

Victorian recognition scenes have also been indicted for their complicity in
ideological closure. Closure here is understood as a strategy of containment, or
forced reconciliation. The creaky apparatus and plot scaffolding of recognition
scenes thus turn out to play a load-bearing role in supporting ideological coherence. Thus, for Roland Barthes, the "hermeneutic code" of nineteenth-century
fiction—culminating in recognition scenes that decipher a text's enigmas and
disclose its hidden truths—closes down, finalizes, arrests, fixes, and terminates
meaning, all in the name of "a return to order."[2] D. A. Miller reads Victorian

recognition scenes in a Foucauldian light, as a ruse of power, effecting a panopticon-like social control.[3] In Miller's account, recognition scenes are a feint or cover that attempts to localize and confine the effects of surveillance. The recourse to enlightenment, revelation, and nomination in recognition scenes permits the novel to manage, displace, and hedge its implications in a diffuse disciplinary apparatus.

This book offers a defense of recognition scenes in novelistic plots. They are not the regrettable contrivances they are often made out to be. I do not find them to be unnecessary, Byzantine contraptions, designed to rig up an unearned finality. Neither should they be condemned outright for accomplishing the resolution or binding of ideological energies, or for weaving ever tighter the warp and woof of power. I argue instead that Victorian recognition scenes, in novels by Charles Dickens, Anthony Trollope, and Henry James, mount a narrative critique of the social relations structured by capital. These recognition scenes plot out what Gillian Rose calls the "social and historical forms of misrecognition" in capitalism.[4] Victorian novels frequently install capital as a site of opacity and misdirection, where financialized abstractions are translated into plots of mystery and disclosure. The formal structures of Victorian recognition scenes allow us to trace capital's own hidden ramifications and disguised relations. They reveal the inversions of agency and temporality that are repressed in capitalist production—specifically, how capital conceals, obscures, and misrepresents subjectivity. In the story I am telling, this critique attains its greatest scope in James's *The Portrait of a Lady*, only to at last come undone in the solutions of the Sherlock Holmes stories at the close of the Victorian period.

An illustration of how the Victorian novel might critique the misrecognitions of capital by locating the constitutive moments of subjectivity within the detours and blind spots of capital can be found in Dickens's *Great Expectations*. The central misrecognition in the plot is Pip mistaking the identity of his benefactor. The problem, in other words, is that he does not know where his money is coming from. The actual source of his expectations is the unseen labor of the convict Magwitch, who has become a sheep farmer in Australia. The real origin of Pip's expectations is therefore in colonial primitive accumulation. But Pip—on little evidence—jumps to the conclusion that the money is coming from Miss Havisham. He is ecstatic to imagine that he has been arbitrarily hailed by her, as if by providential election, even as he senses that he is being drawn into her grievances as a mere convenience. This is for me the great poignancy of the novel. For his expectations are really Magwitch's outlandish tribute to Pip's childhood kindness. But Pip instead yokes his life to the shriveled, faded ruins (and undiminished rancor) of Satis House. He locates the meaning of his expectations where it would be most meaningless and barren. What is eventually devastating for Pip is not to learn that he does *not* deserve the money, but to learn that he *does*.

Pip's selfhood is totally bound up with this misperception of the origins of his fortune. He takes the spectacle of decay and wasting consumption of Satis House to be the basis of his fortune. A profitable brewery once operated there but has long been deserted; capital stands idle. Nothing is produced there any longer, and the visible trappings of wealth are left to molder. The great bridecake laid out for Miss Havisham's wedding stands rotting, a vast form overhung with cobwebs and inhabited by spiders. Time itself has been arrested; all the clocks are stopped at twenty minutes to nine. The very name, Satis, should tell us not to expect new value to spring forth from this exhausted place. In his self-misrecognition, Pip identifies himself with the same cessation of time, the denial or enforced ignorance of the past belonging to the dead capital that rules over Satis House.

Hardly anything touching on Pip's inner being is not overturned when Magwitch arrives at Pip's door to announce that he is the unknown benefactor: "All the truth of my position came flashing on me; and its disappointments, dangers, disgraces, consequences of all kinds, rushed in in such a multitude that I was borne down by them and had to struggle for every breath I drew."[5] The recognition scene confronts Pip with the real determinants of his expectations, which have been concealed by the form of commodity production. The commodity is Pip. For Magwitch exults in Pip as a particularly valuable item available on the market. He sees himself as the "owner of . . . a brought-up London gentleman," just as one might own "stock or land" (306). In the person of the weather-beaten and grimy sheep farmer, Pip discovers the hitherto-concealed source of his income and genteel position. The origin of his expectations, kept so long from view, is the large-scale dynamic of colonial capital. Well might Pip compare his own crisis to the inexorable, rigged apparatus in "the Eastern story": the long-prepared quarrying, hauling, and tunneling which dropped a massive stone slab on the sultan (297). For Pip's fate is such another unsuspected outcome of distant labors. His own personhood is a gentrified means of hiding that form of labor and profit.

Pip has been produced as a commodity—a thing of purchase and sale—all behind his back. He is revealed to be, in the clerk Wemmick's expression, only so much "portable property" (184). The real determinants of his expectations and position are repressed by the anonymity of the money-form of capital. The first time Magwitch gives money to Pip, the paper notes still reek of the commodity. They "seemed to have been on terms of the warmest intimacy with all the cattle markets in the county" (73). But Pip's expectations effectively launder the money. As Marx observed, "The capitalist knows that all commodities . . . however badly they may smell, are in faith and truth money."[6] Magwitch's fortune now reappears as "clean and new" banknotes, unmarked by any origin (303). The money that Pip draws on freely, which has passed through all the stages of being capital, represses the materiality of its production: Magwitch's rough, hard living, and the dust he ate. It is this misrecognition in capital itself (its dissemblance in the produced commodity) that permitted the confusion of origins. The money, detached from its origin in the sweat and grime of work, can be misread as if it were bestowed by Miss Havisham's magic wand. When Pip relocates the providential meaning of his elevation back behind the decrepit facade of Satis House, he projects on its frozen relics a false animation, as if they were possessed of new generative powers. The enchantment that altered Pip from blacksmith's apprentice to London gentleman, as in a fairy tale—really derived from unseen labor—is thus misrecognized when it is imagined to originate from the desolate, living ruin of Miss Havisham's dead capital.

Victorian recognition scenes thus plot out the constitutive misrecognition of subjectivity by way of its entanglements and mediations within capital. By misrecognition, I mean not just an error or wrong perception, but a structure of representation where the subject mistakes its own role and position in setting up its world. The work of the subject in erecting an external world is no longer perceived or is disavowed; this work is projected instead as the doing of the representation itself, with no involvement from the subject. Misrecognitions in this sense are failures to locate one's agency and activity as they take shape outside oneself—especially long-standing disavowals of how meanings and purposes go awry, donning forms that one refuses to own as one's own life.

This is where Hegel comes in, with Marx following closely behind. Subjectivity in Hegel is a misrepresentation, an illusory determination of substance *as* subject.[7] For Marx, these determinations occur preeminently in the commodity-form and its attendant misrecognitions.[8] As Hegel describes this form of misrecognition in *The Phenomenology of Spirit*, it is a "shattered" self-relation, an "unhappy consciousness"; subjectivity comes upon the traces of its desire and history only to blindly "nullify this certification of its own being."[9] We find the same structure in Jacques Lacan's theorization of the mirror stage and in Louis Althusser's scene of ideological interpellation.[10] "The unconscious," Lacan writes, "is made up of what the subject essentially misrecognizes [*méconnaît*] in his structuring image . . . those captivations . . . which were unassimilable to the symbolic development of his history."[11]

Recognition scenes overturn the misrecognitions through which characters give an account of themselves and make sense of their lives. They restore absent mediations, slot isolated fragments into meaningful order, and strip away the spurious agency projected on illusory actors. Characters confront the abasement of their origins, or experience the dissolution of their self-images when unseen past involvements finally come to light. The most affecting recognition scenes are the site of an important truth: that structures of selfhood are frequently defenses against (or evasions of) painful histories, even against time itself as a degradation. It is humiliating to lose our grand illusions about how we came into being. For this reason, recognition scenes often leave their people destitute, denuded. They are moments of existential exposure, revealing the utter lack of a safety net, and an ongoing blindness to loss, which may just be intolerable. What is illuminated by recognition scenes may only be the unending humiliation of agency; subjectivity finds itself unmade, dispersed, annulled within its own history.

The concept of misrecognition provides a meeting point between narrative and social forms. In what follows, I engage with Marx's critique of political economy not as an account of capital's outward being, but of subjectivity's immanent historicity of misprision within capital. The schisms that are internal to capital are also induced in the structure of subjectivity itself.[12] Capital is made out of the subjectivity it appropriates through the commodification of abstract time, so that subjectivity is plotted as its own absence. This means a formalist reading not of Marx's *Capital*, but of capital as narrative form. Marx analyzes capitalist production as a drama of disguised relations and mystifications.[13] He takes us into the "hidden abode of production."[14] Where Marx comes closest to Hegel's notion of misrecognition is his interpretation of the commodity, which demonstrates, as Rose puts it, how "substance is ((mis)-represented as) subject, how necessary illusion arises out of productive activity."[15] My methodological starting point, therefore, is to locate Marx's theory of subjectivity and its misrecognitions in his commodity analysis—that is, in the production of value and surplus-value—rather than in ideology.[16] The crucial point for my purposes is that the historically determinate social relations in capitalism are mediated by the material form of their misrecognition, by the commodity-form of value. As the bearer of value, the commodity masquerades as the very absence of the social plot that constitutes it.

What emerges across this study is that the "awful plot" that is supposed to spoil the Victorian novel is so convoluted because it retraces the contradictory and obscure circuit of capital. Note that Samuel Johnson defines "plot" as "an artful involution of affairs, unraveled at last by some unsuspected means."[17] As much as any tortuous plot, the capitalist production of value entails such "involutions": disguised relationships, the misattribution of agency, and the separation of subjects' roles from the circumstances of their formation.[18] Like the Count of Monte Cristo, capital seems to have no backstory. Its grubby origins are hidden from view. When capital steps forward as the self-unfolding of autonomous value, it sheds any antecedents or prior determinations. The real process of appropriating surplus-value from wage labor in commodity production does not show up anywhere in the glistening increase that capital appears to accrue to itself as its own doing. Marx's critique of political economy is as an attempt to furnish the plot of capital's real divagations, the social and historical dimensions of its formation. *Capital* allows us to discern capital's hidden *Bildung*, and what is occluded in its "interiority." Marx's critique thus functions like a recognition scene, uncovering the secrets and concealed ramifications of capital's inner processes.

Capital is erected on a misrecognition of its constitutive social relations. It presents us with a "bewitched, distorted, and upside-down world" that must be disenchanted.[19] Specifically, the commodity-form of value is a material misrecognition, "a social hieroglyphic" in which the constitutive social activity behind the products of labor becomes indecipherable.[20] Value in all of its incarnations always appears as something without a past, cut off from the social, material, and historical circumstances of its formation. The real story of capital—the inner processes of surplus-value accumulation—is missing from its apparent result. The work of subjectivity within the interior of capital is misrecognized as the work of capital itself. There are two aspects of misrecognition here. On one hand, capital appears as self-begot, self-raised, independent of labor's subjective, value-positing role. On the other hand, subjectivity never glimpses its own involvement in capital, and so appears to itself as autonomous and uncontaminated by the "other scene" of grimy material production.

The misrecognitions at work in capitalist production and accumulation amount to a "plot hole." We say that a story has a plot hole if there is some unaccountable gap in its narrative causality. It is as if its gears do not all line up. The rods and pistons of plot are turning, but these inner workings somehow do not add up. A plot hole means that incidents have come unglued from the sequence of causes, so that the pretended logic of events only belies their specious or empty forward procession. Like a conclusion pulled out of thin air, disconnected from what had come before, the final result of capitalist accumulation (more surplus-value) omits the inner causality leading up to it.

The misprision of capital's temporality as vacant, as comprising a plot hole, occurs not in ideology but in capital's material production and reproduction. Capital unfolds behind the backs of its social actors, but this is not because of an accidental oversight or because the real determinants of production wear a cap of invisibility.[21] Rather, misrecognition, the elision of its inner history, is built into capital's most basic categories. Going on within capitalist production at all times is a hidden drama of secrecy, concealments, reversals, and misrecognitions. The hiding from view of the processes and relations that constitute capital is itself a material result, alongside the industrial yield. Capital produces not only commodities, but also the absence of its real determinations from its reified and fetishistic appearances. In particular, the inner processes of capital not only appropriate subjectivity qua the value-positing activity of social labor purchased as a commodity, but that appropriation further vanishes from, cannot be discerned in, the constituted value of its product.

This cover-up does not occur after the fact. It is not as though the crime of capitalist exploitation first takes place, and then the blood is mopped up later. The crime, so to speak, is in the mopping up. All the moves and positions internal to capitalist production occur in and through the commodity-form of value that conceals them. The social relation that valorizes capital is one dialectical moment, which occurs concurrently with the moment of its cancelation in the commodity. Analyzing capital as a narrative form, then, allows us to see that capital's missing causality, its plot hole, is not a sheer absence of process and relation. It is the very narrative closure imposed by capital, tying everything neatly together, which suppresses the plot of capital's formation. The temporal inversions involved in capital's appropriation of surplus-value also render their absence from the finished form of capital. For this reason, I cannot agree with Fredric Jameson that plot is only one of the "unavoidable false problems" belonging to the narrative projection of ideology.[22] I contend instead that capital's plotting is a starting point for immanent critique, where the blind thoroughfares and dislocations of novelistic plot can be translated back into temporal entanglements within capital itself.

Reading capital in terms of misrecognized subjectivity allows us to see what is going on in the form of the Victorian novel, especially its plotting of recognition scenes. By subjectivity I mean the interminable process of working out and revising the terms under which what one is doing counts as meaningful. It is the ongoing but undecidable construction of agency and identity as a history, together with its blind spots. To be a subject is to pose oneself as taking a hand in one's own becoming—but any self-ascriptions about one's position in one's own history are themselves (nonfinal) moves within that history. There is no subjectivity that is not always already entangled, misrecognized. No pure or original subjectivity can be cleanly extricated, as by a rescue operation. Subjectivity's obscured view of its own conditions is therefore built-in, a feature rather than a glitch. Misrecognition is constitutive, not subtractable.

I take novelistic form in turn to be structured by this constitutive misrecognition of subjectivity—its dislocations, divisions, disguises, and secret returns.

Subjectivity as we find it in the novel is internally barred, or denied access to its own origins. It is separated from its foundational moment, or held asunder from the place of its ongoing definition, which seems to be other than and outside of subjectivity. It cannot get a hold of itself as subjectivity. In other words, subjectivity finds itself out of place, as something unrecognizable, nonsubjective, unmediated. (Here my account of the novel departs from the most enduring and indeed unsurpassed account, Georg Lukács's *The Theory of the Novel*. For Lukács, the novelistic world is *alien to* meaning.[23] The contrary view defended in this book is that meaning is *alienated in* the world of the novel.) The novelistic self is defined, and its meanings are constructed, from the outside rather than from within. There are specific historical, social, and ontological conditions for a subject having a purposeful identity and the capacity to get it right about his or her own reasons, commitments, and self-interpretations. Novels show how those conditions get separated from, or put out of reach of, the hero's work of self-definition. The possibility of the right meaning or the locus of values for a coherent life project are found elsewhere, are somehow not immediately available to the hero.

Recognition scenes foreground this problematic in the novel, by plotting the discovery of subjectivity within its dislocated, nonsubjective form as a climactic revelation. An immediate externality, a bare feature of the world, opens up to reveal unseen roots, knotted and branching truths, swallowing up present meanings in a hidden organization. The truth about the past, having been suppressed under a condensed, compacted form, now unfolds as an entire underground sequence of involutions and windings. It is because the novel is formally structured around the opacity, concealments, and self-divisions confronting subjectivity that its problematic intersects with the misrecognitions specific to capital.

In locating an aesthetic and narrative dimension in capital itself, in its perpetual misrecognition as self-valorizing value, I am departing from previous scholarship at the intersection of Victorian literature and political economy. That scholarship has seen the Victorian novel as engaged in constructing the aesthetic dimension by its very difference and removal from the economic and financial.[24] The ideological effectivity of the novel, on this telling, is to carve out for subjectivity a discrete realm apart from the ongoing catastrophe of social being. What I am claiming is revealed by the Victorian novel, by contrast, is that capital is *made out of* subjectivity: capitalist appropriation consists of nothing but the materialized misrecognition of labor's subjective aspect as it posits itself in production. Subjectivity, I am claiming, is not only constrained and warped by capital. It also takes place, and posits itself, in and through its mediations within capital. It is a process going on inside of capital. And capital, in turn, is predicated upon the entanglements of subjectivity. It appropriates the very subjectivity that it objectifies and usurps.

The question then is how novelistic form gets caught in—and reveals—the plot hole structured by capital. How does plot in the Victorian novel become knotted around the opaque inner processes of capital? How is the void left by capital's erasures translated into novelistic form, and how is it that Victorian novels drag the involutions of capital's inner mechanisms into their plot structure and, in particular, their recognition scenes?

The short answer is that Victorian recognition scenes position capital as a site of misrecognition, in which an ellipsis in one plot (the real social process of capital accumulation) interferes and intersects with another plot (the blind spots and illusions of novelistic subjectivity). There is a mix-up between the hidden parts of the self and the hidden production of capital—as we saw in *Great Expectations*.

The long answer involves the dialectical and self-annulling aspect of capital's misrecognitions. They are like those finger traps that get tighter the more that you pull to disengage what is caught. As we have seen, capital obscures the work of subjectivity in the production of value. It projects a pseudo-subject (capital as value in motion) deprived of any determinants, and represses the self-mediating dimension of labor's positing activity. But in bringing the misrecognitions of capital into plot structure, novels end up repeating and further entrenching the effects of fetishism and reification. Every step made by the novel to extricate subjectivity from its mediation by capital only grants those misrecognitions a deeper hold. Attempts to evade or call back the dislocation of subjectivity within capital only bind it further, because capital's appropriation is precisely appropriation of the involutions of subjectivity.

Capital's plot hole, the deleted temporality of capital's formation, is a determining absence for novelistic form. This plot hole functions as a dialectical engine driving the novel's development. The internal dislocations repressed in capital call forth the richness of the novel's plotting of subjectivity. The novel is thus not deformed by capital, but formed by it. For during its sojourn in the representational snares of the value-form, subjectivity is not just danced through so many trials and ruses to emerge unscathed. The constitutive diremption of subjectivity—its finding and losing itself—becomes inseparable from its appropriation and alienation inside capital. What we know as the temporal processes of the novel—duration, delay, cyclical repetition, digression, and retrospection—accrue to fictional interiority in their displacement (subtraction) from the inner motions of capital.

The recognition scene appears, at first sight, to be a very trivial thing. Nothing could be more hackneyed and overdone than this timeworn device. Its "unpredictable" revelations are predictability itself. Although recognition scenes can claim a distinguished lineage going back to ancient Greek tragedy, they have long since ceased to be reputable. Already in Aristotle's *Poetics* we find the concern that recognition scenes could be inartistically manufactured devices, producing a cheap dramatic effect.[25] Yet the recognition scene is something more than a gimmick.[26] My focus in defining this literary form is to distill the dialectic of *misrecognition* within recognition scenes, which has been neglected by previous criticism, and which will have important consequences when we turn to the narrative form of capital.

Aristotle's discussion in the *Poetics* of the plot function of recognition scenes (*anagnorisis*) is invaluable—in any event, inescapable—in delimiting and differentiating recognition scenes from a technical standpoint.[27] Aristotle issues a number of prescriptions for how recognition scenes should work in the dramatic plot. They "ought to be . . . rooted in the very structure of the plot."[28] They should mark "a change from ignorance to knowledge."[29] They should be "accompanied by a reversal" of the situation.[30] He stipulates that the best form of *anagnorisis* "is that which springs from the events themselves."[31] The inferior forms, on the other hand, are recognition by signs and tokens, by unmotivated contrivance, by memory, by a process of reasoning, and by the turn of incidents.[32] In all this, however, Aristotle does not offer anything like a sophisticated account of the subjective dimension. He names only two cognitive outcomes of *anagnorisis*: the recognition of persons, that is, finding out that person X is really (or also) person Y, and the recognition whether someone has done something or not.[33] When Jocasta in the *Oedipus Tyrannus* prays that Oedipus not learn who he is, for Aristotle this only means learning whose son he is, and his crimes of parricide, incest, and regicide. There is nothing in the *Poetics* to account for Oedipus's discoveries as productive of something like self-knowledge.

In his study of recognition scenes, Terence Cave reckons that the many "variants" and "permutations" that have accrued since Aristotle preclude any comprehensive definition of his central term.[34] Cave settles for "an elaborate para-definition, a pluralistic configuration" of the diverse commentaries on and practices of *anagnorisis* (its "patterns and contours") over the centuries.[35] This is a very catholic (not to say arbitrary and baggy) notion of recognition scenes, encompassing virtually any hermeneutical, psychological, or ethical self-discovery. This is something of a critical bait and switch; the more gentrified reconceptualization takes us very far from what Cave first advertises as the "scandal" of recognition.[36] A similarly expansive definition is also found in the work of Northrop Frye, who billows out the definition of *anagnorisis* to the greatest extent, so as to encompass "not simply the knowledge by the hero of what has happened to him . . . but the recognition of the determined shape of the life he has created for himself."[37] Consequently, for Frye there is ultimately just one plot: "the loss and regaining of identity."[38] This is true, but in the same sense that all colors become one color when you combine them: brown. Formal specificity has been abandoned altogether. Yet we should not lose sight of recognition scenes being precisely scenes—as in, "Stop making a scene!" There is something unheard of, even catastrophic, about recognition scenes. They should leave a mark.

Recognition scenes also need to be distinguished from the topic of recognition as acknowledgment in philosophical ethics. The latter term is closely associated with Hegel, who designates an important role in the socially mediated achievement of self-consciousness to the dimension of reciprocal acknowledgment, or mutual recognition.[39] But the German word Hegel uses for recognition as acknowledgment is *Erkennung*, or *Anerkennung*. Indeed, German has a different word, *Wiedererkennung*, to translate *anagnorisis*, recognition as a scene of retrospective discovery.[40] Furthermore, in his own dramatic theory, Hegel has next to nothing to say about recognition scenes, even in his discussions of Greek tragedy. When Hegel discusses Oedipus in the *Phenomenology*, he focuses not on the moment of discovery, but on the destructive recoil of what is unmastered, irrational, and opaque enforcing its rule over the vain certainty of knowledge.[41] As Cave puts it, "*anagnorisis* [does] not arise in the categories Hegel prefers."[42] More to the point, recognition scenes do not necessarily involve "the other" who is at issue in the theme of reciprocal acknowledgment. We can see this clearly in Paul Ricoeur's study, *The Course of Recognition*. Ricoeur interprets recognition in terms of empathy, as the acknowledgment of vulnerability and mutual dependence. It is telling that, when Ricoeur discusses the Oedipus plays, he concentrates not on the scene of unsettling discovery in the *Oedipus Tyrannus*, but on the endurance and acknowledgment of suffering in the *Oedipus at Colonus*.[43]

Aristotle's account in the *Poetics* is too narrow. It leaves out subjectivity. But the expanded sense of recognition (Cave, Frye, Ricoeur) threatens to be too broad. It leaves out plot. My strategy in what follows is to return to Aristotle's own preferred model of *anagnorisis*, the *Oedipus Tyrannus* of Sophocles.[44] (The other prominent example of *anagnorisis* for Aristotle is the recognition of Odysseus by his scar in the *Odyssey*—also the subject of a famous analysis by Erich Auerbach.[45]) It is imperative that we read the *Oedipus Tyrannus* unburdened by the accumulated interpretive framework inherited from Aristotle on down.

There is more to the question of (in Jocasta's words) Oedipus's "knowledge of who [he is]" than Aristotle accounts for.[46] It is not just a matter of finding out the facts about who his parents are and what sins he has committed. As Bernard Williams puts it, the action of the play is about Oedipus overturning his "own picture of his life."[47] Moment by moment, he has to unmake and make anew his definition of himself, how he understands his own shifting involvement in the unfolding catastrophe. The recognition scene does not only disclose Oedipus's fate, but hands over to him the ruins of his prior self-definition.

Furthermore, the revelations that come crashing down on Oedipus do not just fall into a void. They arrive by wrenching apart an already existing account, consisting of the explanations and self-definitions that are operative at the start of the play, and which become increasingly ragged and shaky as we proceed. The point of the recognition scene is not only to bring to light something hidden, unseen, but to scrutinize and discard, item by item, the first-pass version of events—what Peter Brooks calls the "official" plot.[48] This initial coherence constellates a version of events that falls into place for Oedipus as a kind of working picture. It blocks out the truth at strategic points, yet it also organizes and includes much of the real story. Over the course of the plot, this coherence is revealed to be full of gaps, contradictions, missed assignments, and short circuits.[49] As Karl Reinhardt puts it in his reading of the play, a "half-demolished world of illusion stands within the half-truth like an overhanging building of which part has collapsed."[50]

The official plot comprises a misrecognition. But this misrecognition is at the very least a placeholder account; it functions to cover over (to screen, in Freud's terminology) the narrative holes left by repression, leaving a neat organization instead of a glaring blank or question mark.[51] The official plot has to minimally hang together; the seams are not allowed to show. The screen or counternarrative is not all wrong. It is durable and can hold out until the end of the story, precisely because it has purchase on some elements of the real relationships. Within every misrecognition there are some glimmers of the truth set into a false arrangement. At the same time, the repressed secret organization cannot be entirely excluded.

Oedipus's true origins and his crimes are not only repressed by an official plot, but are also displaced from Oedipus onto other agents and fates. These two moments of misrecognition (repression and displacement) do not occur sequentially onstage, but as it were underneath the dramatic situation. First, the unbearable truth about Oedipus's origins and deeds is disguised by the screen of a counternarrative (the official plot), which presents an innocent Oedipus, who is not a native son of Thebes, but the son of the king of Corinth. The true story is repressed so long as this alibi holds out. But the plague that Oedipus is summoned to investigate requires that the cause of the pollution in Thebes also be displaced onto an unknown culprit, who is to be stalked down and outcast.[52] This accursed "unknown" is the uncanny bearer of the concealed part of Oedipus's fate.[53] His own unseen involvements thus confront Oedipus at the start of the play as the activity of a foreign agency. Yet in making imprecations against this miasmatic other, Oedipus has only "called curses on [him]self in ignorance."[54] He is not "a stranger to the deed," but the very murderer sought after.[55]

There are, then, two defining aspects in the plot of the *Oedipus Tyrannus* not included in Aristotle's discussion. First, recognition scenes are moments of discovery where subjectivity finds itself dislocated in the past; the history that is illuminated does not concern just any new information, but pertains to the hidden ways that subjectivity had posited itself, the ways its meaningful agency has been overlooked. Second, recognition scenes do not just assert a bare identity by tacking on unmotivated revelations; they unravel and revise a first-pass version of events. They always overturn a prior misrecognition: specifically, the overturning, by new revelations, of the subject's place in a past that is now found to be ongoing.

We met these last features previously in *Great Expectations*. The wrong picture of his life that Pip has is not just erroneous; the terms of his mistake are, profoundly, the very terms of his selfhood. "You made your own snares," Miss Havisham tells him (341). His entire conception of himself is built around his persistent mistake about Miss Havisham making his fortune, which screens out the real connection of his fortune to the help given to the convict in the long-ago churchyard. Not only does he have to come to terms with how things really stand, he also has to pry himself apart from the illusory terms of his misprision.

The most important scene in the novel, for seeing Pip laid bare to himself, is his last interview with Miss Havisham—the scene that ends with her catching fire. Nothing can be done against the hard truth concerning the source of his expectations, yet Pip has still to grieve and painfully wrench himself away from the shame of his wrong being. In this scene, Pip gives up on the loss occasioned by the recognition scene, the wrecked "dream," the "wild fancy" of his delirious hopes (130). He now pulls away from the deforming mediations he has long clung to. He forgives her: "There have been sore mistakes; and my life has been a blind and thankless one; and I want forgiveness and direction far too much, to be bitter with you" (377). No reproach is possible here, because those early illusions are no longer regretted. Pip meaningfully defines his own life in coming to terms with the way he got in wrong in the first place. After she catches on fire, Miss Havisham, charred like so much kindling, can stand for the hated, deteriorated remnant of what Pip had taken as his own fate, now the object of mercy. His self henceforth is modeled on this precious moment of ruin, a ruin previously staved off—suspended in its very denial—in the monumental timeless spectacle of the bridecake and the halted clocks. The point is that the degradations of origins, the aches of temporality, the blind harms radiating across the story, cannot be retreated from.

Marx dissects the commodity-form into its component misrecognitions of subjectivity, its repressions and displacements. In the commodity, "social relations . . . do not appear as direct social relations between persons in their work, but rather as material relations between persons and social relations between things."[56] The first misrecognition is the inversion of the social relations of production "between persons" into the "material relations" of commodity exchange, namely, the wage-form interposing between capital and labor-power. This is what Marx identifies as reification. Reification represses the subjective dimension of the labor process, which posits value as socially necessary labor time, under the thing-like objectivity of the commodity. "The mysterious character of the commodity-form consists therefore simply in the fact that the commodity reflects the social characteristics of men's own labor as *objective characteristics of the products of labor* themselves, as the socio-natural properties of these things."[57] The second misrecognition is the apparent autonomy of value, its spurious subjectivity, once detached from its determination in production, which leads a gregarious existence in commodity exchange, the "social relations between things."[58] This is what Marx identifies as the fetishism of the commodity. Fetishism displaces the repressed sociality of production relations onto the products of labor themselves. The commodity "reflects the social relation of the producers to the sum total of labor as *a social relation between objects*, a relation which exists apart from and outside the producers."[59]

When Marx observes, "the whole mystery of the form of value lies hidden in this simple form," I understand that mystery in terms of plot.[60] Marx's narrative exposition of fetishism and reification repeats the plotting of misrecognition found in literary *anagnorisis*. Specifically, the plotting of recognition scenes and the misrecognitions inherent in capital have in common the repression and displacement of subjectivity. In both cases, meaning (tragic responsibility in one case, value as social measure in the other) is constituted behind the backs of its unconscious bearers. Subjectivity's involvements are concealed, submerged, and disavowed. What then counts as meaningful or valuable presents itself instead as unfamiliar and alien, totally untethered from one's prior actions. In both cases, subjectivity can no longer discern its own purposes or history in the version of itself that it now confronts. Whatever meanings subjects posit in their blind activity, they do "without being aware of it."[61]

Reification and fetishism have not been adequately distinguished by commentators.[62] The term "reification" originates in Marx's writings, but has taken on a life of its own.[63] The Frankfurt School interpretation of reification in terms of rationalization, instrumental reason, and identity thinking has been particularly influential.[64] Where reification has shed any lingering Marxist reference, it most often just means something like ossified, hypostasized, or static.[65] In Marx's deployment of the term, however, reification never means anything like abstract conceptual rigidification. For Marx, reification refers to the way production relations in capitalism are mediated by the purchase and sale of a particular commodity, labor-power—in the form of wages. Exploitation and class domination are no longer discernible, neither in this commodity exchange nor in the capitalist's use of what he or she has purchased. Capital does not seem to be valorized by "living" labor, but to accrue from the interaction carried on between mere industrial components.

The indispensable theorist of reification after Marx is Lukács, who placed the concept at the center of historical materialism. In the central essay of *History and Class Consciousness*, Lukács puts forward an unequaled account of how subjectivity is mediated by the forms of capitalist production. In what follows, I am drawing on his insight that the operative categories of bourgeois society are unconsciously mediated by a misrecognized subjectivity at work in commodity production.[66] Subjectivity therefore has to be relocated in the collective social relations of production that constitute (posit) value. Because this role of subjectivity is repressed under the reified form of the commodity it produces, its value-constituting aspect is then fetishistically misapprehended as the "social" being of the commodity itself.[67]

Marx's theory of fetishism has also been widely misinterpreted. In the influential work of Frankfurt School theorists, for instance, fetishism means the absence of subjectivity, which has been drained from its objects.[68] However, fetishism for Marx has the exact opposite meaning.[69] It refers to how value is possessed of a bogus subjectivity and social life, how capital seems to elaborate itself as an autonomous agent. Fetishism is the displacement of labor's social productivity onto capital's relation to itself. It is this uncanny return of the repressed social genesis of value, which is now transposed onto commodities and capital as their own spontaneous pseudo-sociality.[70] Fetishism has also been confused with Marx's theory of ideology.[71]

Reification and fetishism are not just instances of mystification or false consciousness. They are not illusions, in the sense that the sinking of Alonso's ship in *The Tempest*, or the apparition of Macbeth's dagger, are illusions. Neither are they simply like the deletions of censorship, in which secret moments of capital are redacted from the official account. Marx specifies that these misrecognitions are *not* "a pure subjective illusion which conceals the deceit and the interests of the exploiting classes"; rather, the fantastic ascription of social form to things "arises out of the actual [capital-labor] relationship itself."[72] The very categories of capital's perpetuation thus unfold as repressions, and uncanny transpositions, of time and agency. Value, deprived of its subjective origin, is a misprision written into things themselves.

I read reification and fetishism as misrecognitions, in a formal narrative sense, in which the self-representing space of subjectivity is utterly overwritten by the forms of capital's apparent self-generation. The key point is that these misrecognitions are *internal* to the form of capitalist production. The result is to vacate from the outward plot of capitalist production the very subjectivity that capital appropriates as value and surplus-value.

My entire argument hinges on how subjectivity is misrecognized in its appropriation in capitalist production. Let us take a closer look. The subjective aspect of production consists of the temporalities, capacities, and conditions of labor as it engages in what Marx calls positing [*setzen*]. Marx takes this term from German philosophical idealism.[73] In the *Grundrisse* (more so than in *Capital*), Marx demonstrates how the positing activity of labor in the production process—the social temporality of value—is subsumed by capital and extinguished in the value-form. The actual agent of valorization is "living labor." The internal moments of production consist of labor's value-constituting activity. As subjectivity positing value, labor is an act of reflexive divestment [*Entäusserung*].[74] However, a grievous "inversion" of subjectivity takes place in capitalist production. Reification "extinguishes every trace" of the social conditions of production under the commodity-form of labor's product.[75] There is no way to discriminate the contributions of living and dead labor in the final heap of produced commodities, which capital entirely possesses. No sooner does value-positing labor blossom than it withers and is subsumed into "dead labor." What had been positing subjectivity a moment before has already become so nestled in the bosom of the original capital as to be indistinguishable from it, impenetrably veiled in the self-equivalence of the commodity-form. Its own activity confronts it, not as its product, but as capital, which labor no longer recognizes as having made itself.[76] Thus, labor "posits itself objectively, but . . . as the being . . . of capital," while "the possibilities resting in living labor's own womb exist outside it as . . . *realities alien* to it."[77] The sociality of labor, its collective aspect, is misrecognized "as something *alien, objective, ready-made*, existing without [workers'] intervention, and frequently even hostile to them."[78] The temporality of labor consequently disappears into the standing facticity of capital. In concise terms: "past labor always disguises itself as capital."[79] The subjectivity of labor positing itself in production is therefore repressed.

In fetishism, the subjectivity that first disappeared into capital as thing now shows up as displaced, as if its self-positing belonged to capital as subject. In the production process, labor "posits itself as insubstantial . . . posits its own reality not as a being for it, but merely as a being for others."[80] Its activity is necessarily misrecognized as the *"alien subjectivity* (of capital)."[81] We are dealing with a return of the repressed. The sociality of value is transposed onto the produced things themselves, which more or less convincingly impersonate subjectivity. The commodity now "stands on its head, and evolves out of its wooden brain grotesque ideas."[82] Furthermore, the temporality of labor in constituting value, its socially signifying activity, is usurped by capital. Value appears to originate not from labor but from capital itself. The value-forming activity of labor, and the temporality of production seem, by "a *displacement*, a *transposition*[,] . . . [a] *transubstantiation*," to belong to capital instead.[83] Capital now steps forward as pseudo-agent, transferring the creative capacities of labor to itself, swelling in its self-elaboration, a demiurge making the world over in its own image. In a dramatic "twisting and inversion," past labor in the agential guise of capital "assume[s] an ever more colossal independence," swelling into a "monstrous objective power which social labor itself erected opposite itself."[84] Whatever is done by labor seems instead to be the autonomous self-realization of capital.[85] Capital, in an uncanny reversal, becomes "the *personification and representative*" of the repressed positing activity of labor in production.[86] While it thereby replicates the founding moves of subjectivity, capital attains only a pseudo-subjectivity, like the body snatchers of science fiction. As an animated thing, capital is taken to be innocent of internal contradictions and temporality—the very stuff of subjectivity. It strides forth as an "automatic subject," a grotesque impersonation of a self-reflexive social being, having appropriated labor's subjectivity as its own.[87]

The past itself is rewritten by the form of capital. Now the origin and prehistory of value in labor's activity "appear as moments of the motion of capital itself, so that it has itself—regardless of how they may arise historically—pre-posited them as its own moments."[88] It is as though the social constitution of value, first obscured by the commodity-form, becomes "up for grabs," and this subjectivity of value positing can then be arrogated by its material products as if it were their own innate nature.[89]

Because the positing activity in capitalist production is structured according to value, aiming at accumulated value and surplus-value—not its own world of needs and capacities—living labor can be said to produce the very form of its own misrecognition. In piling up commodities, the productive activity of labor buries its own role in constituting value as a category of social meaning. Production therefore consists not only of labor's self-positing, but also its positing of itself as negated. Labor produces not only values and use-values, and ultimately capital; it also produces its own absence from those results. In this sense, the "hidden abode of production" is not a place tucked away somewhere, like Narnia hiding in the back of a wardrobe. It is wrong therefore to represent

Marx's critique as unmasking production relations as if submerged, veiled, or concealed under a false outer covering. Value's occlusions and usurpations are part and parcel of its form. What is concealed or repressed in capitalism cannot be brought to light outside of the value-form itself. This structured misrecognition of subjectivity is the plot hole of capital.

Misrecognitions tells a story about the rise and fall of critique within novelistic form. I read Victorian recognition scenes' immanent revision or undoing of misrecognition in the official plot as a mode of critique. The paradigm of critique for this study is Marx's critique of political economy. Critique in this sense is not a mode of thought that stands ready-made for application to whatever happens to wander into view. Rather, critique cannot be disentangled from the construction of its own object.[90]

Over the course of this book, I show how Victorian plots uncover the operations of capital within the heart of novelistic subjectivity. Recognition scenes are not just restoration and reunion, the sealing up of identities; rather, they always entail the revision and unraveling of a first-pass ordering, which is shown to be a misrecognition. They undo the claims of a prior or initial closure, tracing its dislocations and contradictions. Recognition scenes in the novel thus overlap with the illusions of agency and knowledge entailed by the capitalist form of value. Critique cannot evade or obviate those illusions; it can only show their inextricability.

What we see in Victorian recognition scenes is how critique occurs across the repeated failures, or straining, of novelistic form to take distance from capital. Capital is plotted only by a kind of staggering of the hermeneutic detours, bottlenecks, and doublings back through which subjectivity is both obscured and arrogated. Plotting the misrecognitions built into capital is thus an immanent critique of the novel's own categories. This does not mean a repairing of subjectivity, nor a reunion after a feinted divorce, but rather a lodging of subjectivity deeper within the jaws of its appropriation—and a laying bare of the scars that are left there. The Victorian novel thus effects a turning point in narrative form. The torsions of the Victorian novel transform recognition scenes so that subjectivity is for the first time rooted in its misrecognitions, held fast, and merged with them.

The history of the novel might then be seen as so many attempts at managing the divorce between subjectivity and its alienated basis. The strategies of managing that divorce, internal to novelistic form, may be said to both anticipate and to recapitulate the misrecognitions involved in capitalism. To be sure, not all misrecognition is owing to "the riddle of commodity-structure."[91] The misrecognitions of capital are not all-determining, reaching back into an invariant history. But from the outset, the novel is occupied with the hermeneutic problems posed by bourgeois categories and social forms. In the early history of the novel, there is no way to decide, for any given instance, whether its form is part and parcel of incipient reification and fetishism, or evidence of a sort of collaborative resistance to them. For the rule in the early history of the novel is that subjectivity not be resolved or converted back into any underlying, material process. Dissembling appearance and underlying identity are dualistic, not dialectical. From *Don Quixote* to the gothic novel, the enchanted or illusory version of events and identities is held asunder from the disenchanted, true version that comes home at last. The contradictions of subjectivity's formation are dissolved. Subjectivity is thus displaced from its material involvements, and steps forth as something unmarked. But this enforced separation of subjectivity from constitutive misrecognition is also the outcome of reification and fetishism. Novelistic form, in the course of protecting and enriching subjectivity, inadvertently reproduces capital's bad representation of subjectivity.

In Goethe's poem "The Sorcerer's Apprentice," the animating spirits that are conjured into gnarled wood and tattered rags, stirring these mute things into life, are at last exorcised. The mischievous objects recede into the corner, rude implements once more. Pre-Victorian novels attempt just such an exorcism: to release social facts from an enchanted or illusory causality. At the end of their plots, the fetishized entities stalking lifelike through bourgeois life, under the spell of capital's abstractions—the "ghost-walking" of "mere things"—are ultimately dispelled.[92] Recognition scenes in these earlier works are assigned the task of sorting out impostures of subjectivity from the real thing.

The paradigm for novelistic recognition scenes before the Victorian period is established by Henry Fielding's *Tom Jones* and the gothic novels of Ann Radcliffe. In these works, subjectivity is exposed to misrecognition only to be ultimately recovered untouched. The plot is one long detour in which the heroes tarry in a danger zone of misrecognition. Has Tom Jones slept with his mother? Are Emily St. Aubert and Ellena Rosalba spawned from murder and adultery? Of course not. The recognition scenes arrive at the eleventh hour to save subjectivity from the clutches of misrecognition. At long last, subjectivity is restored intact.

In *Tom Jones*, the discovery that Tom is nephew and heir to the benevolent Squire Allworthy is effectively a giant minus sign set against the preceding story, wiping out all its misrecognitions as arbitrary and external errors. Everything prior to this overturning and restitution—many comic slipups, near misses, accidental run-ins, and mistakes of identity, motive, and status—consists of other characters somehow getting Tom wrong. But these mistaken and arbitrary assessments never invade or mediate Tom's perspective on himself. And so the recognition scene does not revise or overturn the bearings of his subjectivity; rather, it confirms them point by point.

For most of the duration of Radcliffe's novels, the origins and destiny of her heroines seem to be at stake in the gothic phenomena of creaking, eerie chambers and spectral whispers. Yet however much the spooky appearances portend contamination and ruin to her heroines, the breathlessly anticipated discoveries eventually redound instead to their innocence and nonimplication. The apprehensions and conjectures of the plot gin up a specious mystery where there is none. The frightful image behind the black veil in *The Mysteries of Udolpho* has nothing to do with the actual story; the mistake (disclosed hundreds of pages later) is in thinking that was relevant at all. Not only is gothic subjectivity not mediated by its misrecognition, the hermeneutic ruse of there being any such mediation is itself the false appearance to be cleared away.

The recognition scenes in Fielding and Radcliffe thus return a verdict of complete innocence. Subjectivity is harried by a long detour, perhaps, but is none the worse for wear. The moment of misrecognition was only a kind of bad dream, not part of the self. The outcome is that subjectivity in the plot is rescued not only from bad mediation, but from any mediation at all. Yet subjectivity is fatally hollowed out when its deviations are thus deemed unreal, when misrecognition is only a passing, weightless illusion.

The shift we find in the Victorian novel is that the detours of subjectivity, its "bad" mediations, are plotted according to their "twisting and inversion" as the inner moments of capital. The plotting of subjectivity in its very misrecognition and appropriation is what drives capital; the structure of capital is then formally grasped as subjectivity's own itinerary of misprision and inversion—capital as the work of subjectivity barred from the historical subject's meaning and agency. The absent interiority of capital, its plot hole, then, can only take narrative form in the dislocations and inversions of plot, along the *via negativa* of subjectivity. Subjectivity is newly burdened with the displacements and repressions of capital as form, which migrate to the interior of the novelistic subject.

Insofar as novelistic form is organized around the distance taken by subjectivity from its constitutive moment, there is no clean way to evade or undo the dislocations of subjectivity operated within capital. Any attempt to spare subjectivity from reification and fetishism only further collaborates with the mystification of capital. If critique goes so far as to detach subjectivity from its imbrication in capital, it only rehearses the very misrecognitions it would undo. This impasse only ratchets up the novel's organizing problematic.

For example, one version of critique on display in Victorian recognition scenes postulates that capital is a mere facade with nothing going on behind. It is as if we peer into capital's "hidden abode of production" and find an empty works. The misrecognition is to think there was anything substantial backing capital in the first place. Capital accumulation is not really possible; it is only a sham or fraud. This is a rudimentary form of critique, in which capitalism is denounced as illusory. The problem here is that the temporality and social relations constitutive of value are elided all the same. To hollow out capital in this way only recapitulates the occlusion of its real formation. If one whisks away the very subjectivity that capital appropriates, capital is deprived of its interior determinations: the vicissitudes, retrospection, obstacles, and reversals of subjectivity. At the same time, subjectivity's own inner itinerary and formation within capital is thereby canceled. It becomes indistinguishable from the diminished pseudo-subjectivity, or personification, that animates the fetishistic representative of value.

Thus, novelistic form, in the course of protecting and enriching subjectivity, inadvertently colludes with capital's bad representation of subjectivity. For the misrecognitions of capital are not external masks or veils draped over subjectivity, but are composed of the displacements and occlusions in the subject's self-positing. Capital arrogates the subjectivity that lies behind its constitution, as if it were its own innate nature. (Subjectivity, having first been repressed, is now dislocated, up for grabs.) The social temporality that constitutes capital—but does not appear there—instead takes shape in plot in negative form, as plot's transpositions, partitions, truncations, and ellipses. The concealment of capital's origins by its outward result in the commodity-form is translated into the snags, evasions, and dead ends of plotting. In these terms, the plot hole of capital is more like a warren of ramifying egresses than a gaping pit. What is repressed in capitalist production—the misdirection and disguised ramifications that constitute value and surplus-value—has its uncanny return in the shape of plot.

However, the repetition of capital's misrecognitions in and as plot is also the basis for the novel to move through the misrecognitions, to unravel them according to its own problematic. In a more dialectical version of critique, Victorian recognition scenes deploy the plot hole not as a bare vacancy, but as a determinate negation. Capital has no interiority because the constitutive moments of subjectivity within capital have been occulted by its reified and fetishized stand-ins. What is misrecognized in capital's innermost processes is projected as the complete absence of those processes in the value-form. This kind of recognition scene fills in the plot hole, by recovering the detours of subjectivity that are elided and misrecognized by capital. What is revealed is how subjectivity comes about through its very misrecognition and concealment within capital. The dialectical point is that subjectivity is only missing from capital insofar as subjectivity posits itself in a decentered or barred form. Capital's appropriation and mediation of subjectivity devolves upon misrepresentations thereof, animating the hollowed-out things of the commodity world. Capital, in its finished and autonomous appearance, therefore suppresses the very history that would allow subjectivity to locate itself, to decode its meaning in the social hieroglyphic.

A dividing line between these two modes of critique cannot be cleanly drawn. As we will see in the following chapters, novels frequently try to have it both ways. The plotting of Victorian novels operates by a counterpoint of compromises and revisions of formal structure across distinct moments or levels of plot. In the novels by Charles Dickens, Anthony Trollope, and Henry James that I examine, the plotting of recognition scenes does not ultimately allow subjectivity to make a clean exit from the inner operations of capital. Both Dickens and Trollope in some moments figure capitalist accumulation as an empty facade, while at other moments they dialecticize this emptiness. As Hegel puts it, there is nothing to be seen in such an inner emptiness unless subjectivity itself is to go there: "as much in order that we may thereby see, as that there may be something behind there which can be seen."[93]

Subjectivity does not come out unscathed from its retrospective exposure. By contrast with the seamless appearance of capital, subjectivity is defined in these novels by processes of negotiation, error, insertion, assertion, and affronting. What we find in these recognition scenes is that the inner windings of capital are so mapped onto the terrain of the narrative self that no sorting of subjectivity from its misrecognized other into neat piles is possible. The outcome of their critique of capital is not to extricate subjectivity from its entanglements with capital, but instead to plot out the concealed determinations of subjectivity within the interior processes of capital. The splitting, abbreviating, and errancy of subjectivity—the repressed texture and material of its formation within the interior processes of capital—are displaced onto plot structure. Capital here remains opaque, a mausoleum whose empty tombs are still inaccessible. Yet its winding passages and dead ends are mapped by the dislocations of the Victorian plot.

Dickens, Trollope, and James use recognition scenes to reveal the troublingly unmoored autonomy of subjectivity when it is arrogated by capitalist value. They make a distinction between the spurious agency of capital, on one hand, and the forms of meaningful subjectivity that can be clutched at in the endings of their novels—those forms that endure only at the cost of some destitution or self-exile. When capital is stripped of its grandiose misrepresentations and counterfeit agency, subjectivity itself emerges chastened, subtracted from the pseudo-sociality of capital. James in particular goes furthest in marking the inextricability of subjectivity from capital, even while developing novelistic interiority to its highest (or deepest) point of refinement. The narrative critique of capital by recognition scenes can therefore be said to climax with James. The last chapter relates the fall of critique in novelistic plot. At the end of the Victorian period, Arthur Conan Doyle's Sherlock Holmes books revert to an uncritical separation of subjectivity from its misrecognized involvements. The detective novel thus paves the way for the fragmented and abstracted subjectivity of modernist literature. Modernist fiction dispenses with recognition scenes as old-fashioned relics of the Victorian past, but in doing so no longer yokes subjectivity to its material contradictions and dislocations—its plotting—in the vast articulation of capital.

Prior to that dissolution, the dialectical result of the Victorian novel is that its inward turn comes from its deepening involvement with the spurious subjectivity of the interloper, capital. Novelistic interiority is nothing but the unconscious of historical processes whose own material interiority is repressed and usurped in capital. There is thus no fork in the history of the novel where one path leads to subjective issues and another path leads to some set of concrete facts comprising capitalism. The very critique of capitalist misrecognition ends up pursuing capital into the category of the subject.

CHAPTER 1

Financial Crisis and the Partitions of Subjectivity in *Little Dorrit*

Perhaps no novelist is so closely identified with recognition scenes as Charles Dickens. When critics throw around the adjective "Dickensian" to describe a plot, it is a byword for unconvincing coincidences and implausible revelations. Dickens's plots tend to climax by transforming a jumble of arbitrary appearances into a network of secret relationships, elaborately overturning established identities and excavating buried links to the past. This plot machinery is all-encompassing. None of the dispersed narrative flotsam that has once been pulled into the whirlpool of mystery stays lost. Nothing remains unincorporated or unilluminated.[1]

This totalizing plot structure is inseparable from Dickens's social criticism, which frames problems of legality (institutions) and illegality (criminal violence) alike in terms of secrecy and repression. The terms of his social criticism call forth plots of exposure as the complementary response. The mysteries that hang over his novels—the familiar series of illegitimate children, suppressed wills, murder, disguises, blackmail—are initially set out in an atmosphere of shadows and clandestine menace. However, these enigmas veil, all the better to be unveiled; they are not impenetrable forever. They are only so many feints, spurs to ultimate disclosure, transparency, and scrutiny.[2] The meeting point of Dickens's all-encompassing plot machinery and his social criticism is that both abhor secrecy. There are so many recognition scenes in his novels partly because Dickens understands social ills as requiring exposure—sunlight is the best disinfectant. The systemic critique is frequently made in terms of the recovery of a personal past.[3] This topography of retrospective coherence further extends from a critique of repressive institutions into a subjective hermeneutics. The conclusion of a Dickens novel thus effects a sort of Haussmannization of the story. A byzantine warren of walled-off, poorly ventilated no-thoroughfares is leveled and paved over by a well-lit boulevard linking far-flung narrative elements.

At first glance, *Little Dorrit* would appear to follow this standard model of Dickensian plotting, in which climactic recognition scenes bring to light secrets hidden by grotesque villains and bad institutional actors. *Little Dorrit* poses capitalist accumulation itself, in the person of the financier Mr. Merdle, as the answer to a long-running mystery. Mr. Merdle's speculations and vast capital projects are subjected to a shocking discovery, where they are unmasked as so much fraudulence and bankruptcy. When Mr. Merdle commits suicide to escape the revelation that he is penniless, London quickly discovers that all his astounding investments and his spectacular enterprises were based on criminal deception. Capitalist accumulation turns out to be a mere con game. The great financier takes everyone's money and erects a glittering appearance of supposed investments and projects, but he really is a charlatan with nothing to back up his speculative profits. His financial empire is a kind of Potemkin capitalism. On this telling, capital is the simplest kind of misrecognition: a fake mistaken for the real thing.

However, this critique of financial capital (what Dickens calls speculation) runs into a formal contradiction once it is plotted in terms of discovery and exposure, as a recognition scene. In *Little Dorrit*, it would appear that capital's dark places are to be excavated and its machinations laid bare. But—this is the contradiction—it turns out that there is nothing in Mr. Merdle's fraud and forgery to uncover as the inner secret of capital. There is no secret; the secret is just the emptiness and unreality of speculative profits. Behind the dubious allure of investment schemes, Dickens sees nothing but a hollow shell.[4] The recognition scene finds nothing to expose, no past to reconstruct. Although the financial plot of *Little Dorrit* is initially set up as if to culminate in a spectacular revision and linking of scrambled narrative elements, the actual recognition scene pursuant to Mr. Merdle's suicide is altogether rudimentary and stunted. It consists only in a cramped and arbitrary nomination reducing the mechanics of a financial crash to unelaborated "Forgery and Robbery."[5]

In *Little Dorrit*, then, Dickens thereby denies to financial capital the kind of complex, temporalized formation that his heroes recover in the recognition scenes of his other novels. In the early *Oliver Twist*, our orphaned hero improbably ends up being related to both the kindly Maylie family and the blackguard

Monks, while Dickens's last completed novel, *Our Mutual Friend*, resurrects John Harmon, whose corpse (it seemed) had been dragged out of the Thames in the first chapter. But in *Little Dorrit*, the plotting of capital leaves no secret to excavate, no convoluted history to recapitulate. The revelations about Mr. Merdle do not reveal speculative capital to have any origins apart from dissimulation and lies. The recognition scene involving Mr. Merdle remains abortive and abstract. As we will see, the financial misrecognitions in this part of the novel are held quite apart from the misrecognitions of subjectivity housed elsewhere.

This plot hole concerning Mr. Merdle's "secret," which stands in for the secret of capital, is a result of Dickens's conception of financial capital as empty and hollow. He depicts speculation as a form of fraud. The speculative financier merely shuffles around the real money deposited by investors, promising profits that never seem to materialize.[6] (Speculative gains or pseudo-gains are therefore to be distinguished from earnings arising from the practical ingenuity and individual perseverance we find in entrepreneurial engineers like Daniel Doyce.) In other words, Dickens understands capitalist finance as a deceptive facade. There is nothing real going on behind the false front of speculation. No internal process of capital's self-valorization underlies speculative profits. As a result, there can be no retrospective illumination of capitalist accumulation as a misrecognition in our sense: an inversion of agency and an appropriation of temporality.

Dickens plots Mr. Merdle's speculations leading up to an inevitable crash as a nominal mystery. The revelation of his bankruptcy has the ruined investors sifting through the ruins of his empire, asking where their money disappeared to. But the novel's financial mystery is sealed off. It is not solved, but left abbreviated and abstract. *Little Dorrit* thus underdetermines capitalist crisis. It is telling that Dickens labels the pervasive speculation that produces the crash as an "epidemic" (571). Just as the authorities at Marseilles quarantine the travelers from the plague in chapter 2, Dickens effectively quarantines the outbreak of capitalist speculation from the other major revelations that conclude the novel.[7] A contrast can also be made here between the Merdle "epidemic" and the spread of smallpox in *Bleak House*. In that novel, the progress of the disease can be reconstructed and mapped as an outcome of subterranean contacts and latencies, by tracing backward the movements of the infected streetsweeper Jo. But no such explanatory framework is granted to capital in *Little Dorrit*.

Dickens isolates the Merdle crash and its (absent) determinations from the sweeping recovery of subjectivity that draws the novel's other plots in its wake. In doing so, he obstructs the spectacular revelations of the novel's family romance plot from migrating into the financial plot. Because Dickens constructs crisis as devoid of retrospective explanations or recognition-like involutions, he has to stop any leakage from one plot to another.[8] The finance plot is not, in the end, recovered into subjectivity or moral redemption by the novel's movement to closure.[9]

On one hand, then, the very plotting of *Little Dorrit*'s critique of speculation works to absolve capital of any inner repressions and contradictions. The Merdle recognition scene evacuates the structural misrecognitions of capitalist accumulation—namely, how the temporal and subjective determinants of value-production are subsumed under the commodity-form of the surplus product. The origins of capitalist crisis cannot therefore be traced back to the repression of subjectivity within production, but remain opaque. Crisis remains outside the plot framework that Dickens employs to examine other social forms in terms of subjectivity. The critique of capitalism in *Little Dorrit* is thus kept separate from the criticism elsewhere in the novel of repressive institutions and imprisoning postures of denial. Capitalism is not taken to be hiding anything, and so it cannot be exposed by a recognition scene in Dickens's wonted fashion. He confines the underdetermined causality of valorization and its vicissitudes to a discrete zone, to a truncated recognition scene whose faint gestures of discovery do not intersect with the revelatory pyrotechnics of the novel's other plots. The recognition scene concerning Mr. Merdle's bankruptcy does not expose any inner process of repression and appropriation going on behind the facade of speculation. So, while *Little Dorrit* certainly mounts a critique of financial capital as a certain misrecognition, a false idol, this critique simultaneously exonerates capital.

On the other hand, while *Little Dorrit* does subtract subjectivity from the operations of capital, it is not a clean exit. The novel registers the costs to subjectivity of being pried away from the determining involvements of capital, in order that subjectivity might not (retrospectively) fill in for capital's missing internal mediations. Subjectivity manages to get free of the wreck of capitalist speculation without its own temporality (retrospective determination) being implicated in the Merdle deception. But subjectivity bears the scars of this escape. The recognition scenes in earlier novels like *Tom Jones* or *The Mysteries of Udolpho* restored subjectivity intact, albeit impoverished of mediations, after the trials of alienations that turned out to be merely apparent. In *Little Dorrit*, however, the recovery of origins and buried meanings takes a high subjective toll. To pull subjectivity out of its contaminating involvements with capitalism here involves a reduction, a denial, a loss of access to the whole truth about one's past and formation. In order to prevent Arthur Clennam's family secrets from being recuperated as part of capital's backward glance, Dickens prevents him from ever learning the whole truth whose repression smothered his childhood. Subjectivity and its temporality are ultimately cordoned off from capital's unmediated inside, its "plot hole," but the self is diminished and obstructed in this process.

In the rest of this chapter, I specify the formal points of contrast in the plotting of capitalist crisis as a truncated recognition scene versus the intricate plotting of *Little Dorrit*'s family romance. I first examine how Dickens yokes together a particular temporal model of subjectivity with his criticisms of *Litle Dorrit*'s nonfinancial (especially bureaucratic and carceral) institutions and social forms. I then analyze the family romance plot, as it builds up to the recognition scene where Rigaud blackmails Mrs. Clennam over the long-hidden codicil to Gilbert Clennam's will. This sequence of suppressed connections, false identities, and concealed evidence, plus the dizzying manner in which it is all brought together, make for Dickens's most elaborate recognition scene.[10] The next section weighs the formal features of this scene against the revelations about Mr. Merdle's bankruptcy and suicide, which I take as a recognition scene cut short or abbreviated. In the latter plot, Dickens plots crisis as a mystery, but only a skeletal one—leaving out any of capital's internal misrecognitions.

In the final section, I discuss the novel's ending, when Amy Dorrit has Arthur burn the codicil of the will, of which she is the beneficiary, unread. I read this act as part of a rescue operation to save subjectivity from entanglement with capital, so that capital consequently does not encompass any temporal process or social relation. By this act, Dickens severs any conversion of subjective involvements (especially of tabulated moral debits brought to light) between one plot and another. The point for Dickens is not to equate Arthur's imprisonment for debts incurred in Merdle's financial speculations, on one hand, with his family's past wrongs, on the other hand. In this way, Dickens preserves subjectivity at the end of the novel, divorced from implication in the inner vacancy of capital. The cost to subjectivity, however, is that Arthur remains to a degree shut out from his past and his own formation, since Little Dorrit suppresses the fateful harms that brought her and Arthur together.

From his first appearance, *Little Dorrit*'s daydreaming protagonist already seems to have been defeated by the world. Returning to England after twenty years abroad, Arthur Clennam encounters the forlorn setting of his upbringing with weary eyes and finds that he has "no will" to face it, unaltered and stagnant as it may be (20). How does this world confront him?

> It always affected his imagination as wrathful, mysterious, and sad; and his imagination was sufficiently impressible to see the whole neighborhood under some dark tinge of its sad shadow. As he went along, upon a

dreary night, the dim streets by which he went, seemed all depositories of oppressive secrets. The deserted counting-houses, with their secrets of books and papers locked up in chests and safes; the banking-houses, with their secrets of strong rooms and wells, the keys of which were in a very few secret pockets and a very few secret breasts; the secrets of all the dispersed grinders in the vast mill, among whom there were doubtless plunderers, forgers, and trust-betrayers of many sorts, whom the light of any day that dawned might reveal; he could have fancied that these things, in hiding, imparted a heaviness to the air. The shadow thickening and thickening as church-vaults, where the people who had hoarded and secreted in iron coffers were in turn similarly hoarded, not yet at rest from doing harm; and then of the secrets of the river, as it rolled its turbid tide between two frowning wildernesses of secrets . . . (542)

The drama of the entire novel might be thought of as Arthur Clennam's struggle to keep his head above these shadowy depths of secrecy and enclosure, while the plot drags him through a "turbid tide" of concealment. Upon his return, Arthur begins to suspect that William Dorrit's imprisonment for debt might somehow be traceable to the family firm, Clennam & Co. This rising current of suspicion ends up, after hundreds of pages, encompassing all manner of "plunderers, forgers, and trust-betrayers"—nor is it lacking in the "iron coffers" and "papers locked up in chests" anticipated here. Along the way, numerous petty fictions, shameful pretenses, and outright deceptions enjoin Arthur to turn a blind eye to this ambient proliferation of "oppressive secrets."

In his reverie, Arthur anticipates all of these images as locking him *out*, as secrets kept from him. They are a projection of the exclusion he has already felt from his own mother on returning home. But the course of the novel works to lock him *in*, to bring him to the heart of all these secrets by imprisoning him in the Marshalsea, so that the "dark tinge of . . . shadow" here is later localized in the more definite image of the "shadow of the [prison] wall" (735). In short, this early vision of a terrifying night world confronts Arthur as a padlocked door marked "Do Not Enter." But the story ultimately places him on the other side, in the midst of these opaque secrets. He is to be plunged into a sort of ragged crypt where his fortune, the true story of his birth, and his life's love unfold. Like many of Dickens's heroes, the meaning of "who I am" for Arthur has been organized in advance and without his consultation. These unconscious determinations turn out to have mediated his subjectivity elsewhere, without his knowing anything about it. The truth about his past lies behind all of these imposing doors and closed shutters. Though it may be that he can never close this distance entirely.

But what if the truth about oneself could be locked away, not only stowed in "chests and safes," but within one's own consciousness? If Arthur's story shows an ignorance of one's identity owing to external conspiracies hiding the truth from him, then Mr. Dorrit's story is that of the collapse of a partition set up within the self. With the acute rigor that shame induces, Mr. Dorrit divides his shabby gentility from knowledge of the reality of the debtors' prison he is confined in: "While he spoke, he was opening and shutting his hands like valves; so conscious all the time of that touch of shame, that he shrunk before his own knowledge of his meaning" (226). Knowledge here is not a mystery kept locked up by others, but rather something kept at an (internal) distance by oneself, skirted around or obscured under highly evolved modes of pretense. Reading Mr. Dorrit, one is forever glimpsing the unspoken words that are being set aside, just as, in a photographic negative, empty spaces take on an uncanny substantiality. It would appear, then, that these internal locks are ultimately no more effective at holding their secret contents than the "iron coffers" confronting Arthur. Mr. Dorrit's painfully self-conscious loquacity is overdetermined, urged onward by "two undercurrents, side by side, pervading all his discourse and all his manner" (642). His suppression and avoidance—even within himself—of his Marshalsea past and of his daughter's sacrifices and devotion anticipate a psychological formation later described by Freud: "the strange state of mind in which one knows and does not know a thing at the same time."[11]

In *Little Dorrit*, this not wanting to know is symbolized by the novel's prison motif, which is plainly a vehicle for Dickens's criticism of social and psychological coercion, narrowness, and distorting solipsism.[12] The Marshalsea is not only a place of physical confinement, like Newgate in *Barnaby Rudge* or the Bastille in *A Tale of Two Cities*. The prison here is also a cognitive structure of secrecy and suppression—in other words, of the partitioning of subjectivity. Whenever in *Little Dorrit* we hear that some place is "like the Marshalsea," we are prepared to hear next of some odious collective deception and consoling fraud. Mr. Dorrit, thoroughly tainted by the prison atmosphere, is also the character most strenuously avoiding knowledge. In his character as the "Father of the Marshalsea," he is "an illustration of the axiom that there are no such stone-blind men as those who will not see" (280). He erects an absolute barrier of denial and condescension between his life in the first half of the novel, "Poverty," and in the second half, "Riches." Mrs. Clennam also frames her self-imposed seclusion and ignorance as an imprisonment. She is by her own hand "shut up from the knowledge of some things that [she] may prefer to avoid knowing" (184). In refusing to make amends for past wrongs, but also for refusing to hear about it or be reminded (as her dying husband intended her to be), she pleads her confinement to her rooms as though it were a penitential suffering: "Look at me, in prison, and in bonds here" (50).

In prosecuting his case against the debtors' prison and the other bad English institutions in *Little Dorrit*—the obstructing bureaucracy and the hard Calvinist theology—Dickens crosses and recrosses a notional boundary between a damning exposé of how entrenched institutions fail to work and an epistemological indictment of how they hide the truth and perpetuate a disabling cognitive opacity. Once the objects of social criticism are framed this way, as instances of unsustainable self-repression, they begin to participate in a curiously self-annulling trajectory. What Dickens criticizes, he also shows to be doomed, internally compromised by a flawed structure. The Circumlocution Office, possessed of a kind of anti-omnipotence, is magically circumvented by the inheritance that descends upon Mr. Dorrit. Like Rumpelstiltskin, the nefarious agents of Circumlocution are reduced to stamping frustration: "When the fairy had appeared and [Dorrit] wanted to pay [the Circumlocution Office] off, Egad we had got into such an exemplary state of checking and counter-checking, signing and counter-signing, that it was six months before we knew how to take the money" (565). Later, the chilling Clennam house implodes and is left a "heap of ruin" (794), like those Gothic structures in the film versions of *Frankenstein, The Fall of the House of Usher,* and *Rebecca,* which collapse in flames while the end credits roll. The Marshalsea has vanished before the book has even started: "it is gone now, and the world is none the worse without it" (56). In the preface, Dickens goes to see if any traces of the prison remain, and finds "the outer front courtyard . . . metamorphosed into a butter shop" (xvii). To apply Marx's consoling expression to the self-repressing institutions in *Little Dorrit*: they have to be annihilated; they are annihilated.[13]

The inner retreat from knowledge ("not wanting to know") is likewise destined to fail. When Mr. Dorrit has a stroke, he relapses into his past character as the "Father of the Marshalsea," which he has been vigilantly suppressing. In the same vein, once her long-ago falsifications are thrust upon her, Mrs. Clennam becomes frantic and loses all power of speech soon after. For the utmost internal distancing involves a dynamic interplay of returns. The hard knowledge that one would be "shut up from" finds some irresistible channel of expression. Just as the quintessential prison-escape films, John Sturges's *The Great Escape* and Jean Renoir's *La Grande illusion,* tell of human spirits so resilient that no prison bars can hold them in, so the lesson of the prison motif in *Little Dorrit* is that there is no prison yet built strong enough to keep knowledge of the past out.

The (attempted) partitioning of subjectivity—literalized in the prison motif, and carried over to the suppressions of Mrs. Clennam's religion and the

Circumlocution Office—furnishes the novel with its systemic criticism of opaque and mystery-engendering social forms. We have just seen how the return of the repressed is built into those institutions and psychological postures, as their inevitable term of expiration. For Dickens, it is just a feature of reality that every wall built to keep out knowledge also contains, somewhere, a lurking crack that will bring down the structure. This aspect of Dickens's social criticism even allows it to detach from the plotting of mystery and the narrative recovery of secrets; it comes to describe any self-dividing style of subjectivity that somewhere blocks out large swaths of reality from view. Reality has a very slight hold on the minds of *Little Dorrit*'s population. Nearly every character and every milieu has some loophole that lets obvious falsities slip through unchecked. This condition infects even the most likable characters: Flora Casby in her "mermaid condition," where she lapses into giddy romantic blabbering "as if she really believed it" (286), or Pet Meagles, who "conceals all of [Gowan's] faults . . . even from herself" after she marries him (552). Dickens's attack on divided consciousness is thereby extended beyond objective social mysteries (debts whose origins are buried in red tape, concealed wills, or the erasure of class origins), encompassing a widespread subjective distortion.

The official position of *Little Dorrit* thus far could not be clearer. Dickens is *against* concealment, mystery, and repression—whether that of the self-imprisoning characters, or those institutions judged by the yardstick of bad faith. For this reason, the novel's paradigm of a damaging act is Mr. Dorrit's effort to "obliterate" all recollection or suggestion of the Marshalsea (478). And then Dickens is *for* the will-to-knowledge that brings secrets to light, as when Arthur Clennam, who dogs the Circumlocution Office with his refrain of "I want to know" (113), determines to get to the bottom of the injustices that confront him, or when Mr. Pancks tracks down the entangled inheritance that frees Mr. Dorrit from prison, or whenever Little Dorrit proves incapable of dissimulation, of denying the past as she is instructed. To be sure, when we come to the recognition scene of the family romance plot, which unsettles so many long-ago harms from their quiet repose, those revelations do not come about because of benevolent truth-seeking. They are instead the results of blackmail by the villain, Rigaud. He is not interested in bringing the truth to light; he is only interested in others' secrets so as to grind out money and advantage from them. Likewise, Mrs. Clennam, even while confessing to Little Dorrit the harm she has done her, begs her to stay silent about it. Even more troubling is the scene where this entirely good character, Little Dorrit, burns the evidence that occasioned the blackmail. I will return to this moment at the end of the chapter, since interpreting it requires a detour through the novel's plotting of capital.

Even confining ourselves to the instances of concealment and self-division outlined above, it is not the case, as George Orwell influentially asserts, that "Dickens's criticism of society is almost exclusively moral."[14] *Little Dorrit* has a definite systemic criticism, but it is one rigged up on the basis of an anti-repressive psychologization of social structures. Repression is not a moral category. It is a cognitive and narrative one. Counterintuitively, perhaps, "repression" is an indication of full knowledge—what is repressed is at the same time fully preserved.[15] To be very schematic: what is repressed leads to mystery, what is mysterious can be brought to light, and what can be brought to light is posited in advance so as to emerge in the concluding recognition scene. In the family romance plot, this repressed content is the truth about Arthur's origins: the truth we first encounter from the outside, when Arthur confronts his past as something locked up in a preexisting mystery. The vantage point we immediately adopt—of Arthur's inquiry into his own absence of will—and from which we encounter the novel's "depositories of gloomy secrets" as external enigmas (542), is finally the point on which our gaze is fixed in the conclusion.[16] What is produced out of the Dickensian mystery plot is always this same truth that was initially put there. The point is to exhibit a restored subjective coherence as the antidote to what has been criticized as mystery all through the plot's windings. To quote the film *The Red Shoes*: "Not even the best magician in the world can produce a rabbit out of a hat if there is not already a rabbit in the hat."[17]

At the same time, however, this concluding knowledge is also knowledge of that subject's symbolic impossibility, of his or her "emptiness." It is a mark of Dickens's human courage that his subjects of ethical knowledge, in pursuing the truth of how their world is organized, recover not an ideological plenitude or substantiality but their own historical dissolution. So we have, most literally, Esther Summerson's effacement by disease; Pip's illusions about Miss Havisham's designs for him crumbling in the daylight of truth; and John Harmon's resolution never again to "come to life." In *Little Dorrit*, Arthur's only payout from the recognition scene is to have his supposed personal history dismantled.

So far, I have been considering the Dickensian plot as a narrative strategy in the service of social criticism, encompassing its mandate to totalization, to exposure of what is repressed, and to route all this through the organization of subjectivity. I now want to consider the specific mechanisms of the recognition scene where Rigaud, Affery, and Mrs. Clennam reassemble the long-form account of Arthur's birth and Gilbert Clennam's will. The scene pulls together questions that have been left hanging for hundreds of pages: Affery's dreams, the cause of the noises heard in the Clennam house, the meaning of the cryptic "Do Not Forget," and Rigaud's apparent recognition of Flintwinch while meeting him for the first time. These questions, like furniture coverings, at once hide the contours of the full knowledge of which they are aspects, while reserving the space of the final disposition of revelations. I proceed now to a closer look at the temporal structure of *Little Dorrit*'s (fairly contorted) recognition scene.

☙

Dickens keeps his mysteries before the reader rather like the performance of a chess prodigy who is playing a dozen games at once—making only one move at a time, but with the endgame of each contest already clearly envisioned. Flashes of mystery appear from the beginning, only to be left in suspension for hundreds of pages. So, the first doubt overhanging Arthur Clennam's return is whether Clennam & Co. "had unhappily wronged any one, and made no reparation" (48). From the very beginning of these suspicions, and after having met Little Dorrit in his mother's room, Arthur begins to connect her, and subsequently the Dorrit family, with these nagging doubts about his mother:

> What if his mother had an old reason she well knew for softening to this poor girl! What if the prisoner now sleeping quietly—Heaven grant it!—by the light of the great Day of judgment should trace back his fall to her. What if any act of hers and of his father's, should have even remotely brought the grey heads of those two brothers so low!
>
> A swift thought shot into his mind. In that long imprisonment here, and in her own long confinement to her room, did his mother find a balance to be struck? I admit that I was accessory to that man's captivity. I have suffered for it in kind. He has decayed in his prison; I in mine. I have paid the penalty. (89)

As with the characteristic tics, epithets, or catchphrases that accompany Dickens's minor characters every time they come on, Arthur's doubts recur periodically but, after their first full statement, do not develop further. Once he has seen the Dorrit family in the Marshalsea, he wonders if William Dorrit's debt could be traced back to his own parents; the very next time the suspicions recur, they are already "old doubts" (274). The thread is at one time picked up by Pancks, at another time put down again after a deceptive exculpation of Mrs. Clennam. The mystery has thus been set in motion, but a peculiar sort of recurrent motion—more an iterative leitmotif than a suspenseful complication.

Several of the novel's mysteries are continually resurfacing in this way—for example, the noises in the Clennam house, and the inscription "D.N.F." on Mr. Clennam's watch. Others are left strikingly unelaborated: the appearance of Mr. Flintwinch's doppelgänger with an iron box in Affery's dream, or Miss

Wade's nighttime meeting with Rigaud. These mysterious occurrences are set before us, but then left untouched until the conclusion takes up all of the strands once again for a final ordering.

The recognition scene that settles all of these questions, retroactively aligning all pertinent information and producing a coherent image of the past, is found in the chapter "Closing In" (part II, chapter 30). By contrast to what we will see in the case of Mr. Merdle's secrets (which he has bottled up inside himself until he is almost ill), the cumulative facts about Clennam & Co. now put in play have not been previously known by any one person. Instead of belonging to a privileged keeper, the secret is assembled collaboratively. Rigaud has only the partial knowledge of the lost will he obtained from Flintwinch's twin brother in Belgium. Affery has only the fragmentary and delirious data of her "dreams" (this is what she calls her observations so as to render them less threatening). Flintwinch and Mrs. Clennam do not know the afterlife of the incriminating information, as it passes from Flintwinch to his brother to Rigaud to Miss Wade. And Arthur (not present) has only his suspicions and confused observations upon his return. Hence the need for the somewhat implausible piecing together of the whole story by Rigaud, Flintwinch, Affery, and Mrs. Clennam in her room, with interruptions and corrections divided between all the characters.

This four-way retrospection takes up a dozen pages of the novel and cannot be conveniently reproduced here. The main outline of the revelations is as follows: Mrs. Clennam, after she married Arthur's father, discovers that he has a love child with another woman, a singer. This affair was to have been quashed by his marriage, which is mandated by a domineering uncle, Gilbert Clennam. When Mrs. Clennam finds out, she adopts Arthur as her own, and secrets his mother away under the protection of Flintwinch's twin brother Ephraim. However, on his deathbed, Gilbert Clennam relents toward this fallen woman, leaving her one thousand guineas, and also "a thousand guineas to the youngest daughter her patron might have at fifty, or (if he had none) brother's youngest daughter, on her coming of age" (779). This patron is Frederick Dorrit, the brother is William Dorrit, and the would-be recipient of this benefaction is of course Little Dorrit. But Mrs. Clennam suppresses this will, and refuses to make any reparations except the smallest step of hiring out Little Dorrit for needlework.

Rigaud is blackmailing Mrs. Clennam with this information, which he has come into possession of in acquiring the iron box (containing the suppressed will) from Ephraim in Antwerp, Flintwinch having removed the box thither from the Clennam house in order to have something to hold over Mrs. Clennam's head. But the fate of this iron box (which, recall, Affery has "dreamed") is more curious still. Rigaud has left it in safekeeping with Miss Wade, by whom he has been employed to spy on Mr. and Mrs. Gowan in Italy—Henry Gowan being Miss Wade's former lover. The end point of all this is that when the tempestuous orphan Tattycoram (née Harriet Beadle) breaks from Miss Wade and returns to the Meagleses, she brings back this iron box with her.

I want to isolate several formal aspects of this recognition scene:

1. The discovery works to *retroactively organize* its material. Everything falls into its place, or else is excluded from the new dispensation of meaning as so many false leads.
2. The truth moves under the surface, is *immanent even in its misrecognition and latency.* The truth, even if unregarded or suppressed, is not simply dormant and powerless.[18]
3. There is a *built-in delay* of meaning since the hermeneutic ironies are not available on a first pass. Seemingly innocent pieces of life turn out to wiggle and spin with implications beyond themselves.
4. There is a principle of *narrative economy.* The recognition scene does not merely send us from pillar to post, substituting new questions, or else parachute unheard-of narrative reinforcements to plug plot holes. The discoveries are pertinent; they deal predominantly with what has already been placed on the table set before us.

Now to take these points in turn:

1. The new revelations act like a sifting device. Some details leap into connection with one another, while others are shown to be meaningless or outright red herrings. Arthur's original suspicion that the firm of Clennam & Co. is responsible for William Dorrit's debt is mistaken. As it turns out, the specifications of the suppressed will crazily zigzag from Frederick Dorrit (Arthur's mother's musical patron) to Little Dorrit somehow without actually touching William Dorrit. However, the coincidental aspects of Mrs. Clennam's relation to Little Dorrit (always suspicious) now forge an ominous chain of significance. When, early in the novel, Arthur hears that Little Dorrit has been employed to do needlework for Mrs. Clennam, he traces this link and finds it to be a fortuitous connection that came about through several intermediaries—Mr. Plornish, Mr. Pancks, and Mr. Casby. He accepts the explanation that Little Dorrit found the work through the mere chance of her name being passed along (86, 140). But the recognition scene brings to light that Mrs. Clennam had wished to make small reparation (for her private conscience at least) by hiring the very girl

she has injured (without Little Dorrit knowing it) through blocking her from an inheritance. The longer explanatory circuit and the element of chance in connecting these characters are now seen to belong to the purposeful dissembling of Mrs. Clennam's motives and covering her tracks. Thus, some earlier material that had been cued for the reader, to be taken up later, falls outside the eventual explanation, while other material (not cued, seemingly returned to the pile as spent) is reconfigured and cemented as part of the full disclosure.

2. What is revealed was there all along, but as a silent determinant; its effects precede its announcement and recognition. How does it happen that Miss Wade—seemingly a couple of plots removed—serves as the depository for the documents that Rigaud has acquired from Flintwinch's brother, and is using to blackmail Mrs. Clennam? When Miss Wade first takes Tattycoram away from the Meagleses, encouraging the younger woman in her rebelliousness, this appears to be motivated by the bitter magnetism of Miss Wade, Tattycoram's own headstrong nature, and the deep condescension she feels in her position as Pet Meagles's maid. The reader does not press further. But what cannot be suspected at the moment of Tattycoram's running away is that Miss Wade has any personal hostility toward the Meagleses (whom she has innocently "just" met on their travels, apparently as much by coincidence as their meeting Arthur Clennam). In truth, Miss Wade is burning with hatred of Pet Meagles, the wife of Henry Gowan. We learn in Miss Wade's own "History of a Self-Tormentor" that Gowan has painfully spurned Miss Wade. She is not in Marseilles at all by chance, but because she is following—tracking—her rival. This is how she comes to bargain for information with Rigaud. And it is for this same motive of revenge that she exercises her dark influence over Tattycoram. We see all of this puzzling sequence unfold long before we understand its causes. What comes to be known has not been all along inert or dormant—indeed, the past is bitterly consuming Miss Wade at every moment—but instead has been active and determining, well prior to its being pronounced and incorporated in the recognition scene.

3. The various screens and feints set up along the way point to the secret at the conclusion, but also to a belatedness of interpretation at every moment. After Arthur's return and his first meeting with Mrs. Clennam, she chastises Flintwinch for being "needlessly significant" to Arthur—but this significance has necessarily been passed over unremarked by the reader (180). We now have to turn back quite a few

chapters, and to read Flintwinch's instructions to Arthur—that "he mustn't lay offences at his father's door"—as screening some further knowledge left unmentioned (51). If Arthur were to pull at this strand, Mrs. Clennam implies, the whole fabric of secrets might unravel. By the end of the novel, we do know how to read this admonition. Flintwinch meant: Arthur must not lay offenses at his *father's* door—but at his supposed mother's. But even as Dickens signals this surplus meaning, by showing Mrs. Clennam's paranoia that too much had been implied, he prevents the characters from saying the secret out loud, where the reader could overhear. When Flintwinch begins to say to Mrs. Clennam something "about yourself, who are—," Dickens has her interrupt: "Hold there, Flintwinch" She tells him he "may go a word too far" (181). So we are alerted to a structure of suppressed knowledge, but at the same time we see that the secret might pop out at a stray word. Language is no sealed tomb, but a porous catacomb of uncertain openings. Mrs. Clennam's paranoia is, of course, matched by Arthur's.

To be sure, scholarly criticism of Dickens has been charged with its own paranoia.[19] But paranoia on the reader's part is not an optional stance that one can take up or not. As in the example above, the reader of *Little Dorrit* is made to feel after the fact that she has been mistaken in reading some exchange of dialogue as "innocent." Any moment could be "needlessly significant." Better to keep up, over the novel's 826 pages, an unflagging suspicion. Still, Dickens ensures that we will always be too late. When Arthur, after his first interview with Mrs. Clennam, asks Affery, "what girl was that in my mother's room just now?" we are told of Little Dorrit that "*She's* nothing" (39, 40). That seems unlikely, given the title of the novel, but since this line of questioning is the very first mention of Little Dorrit, we have already, and unavoidably, missed her first appearance. The reader is continually hailed into an interpretive project that is just as continually made to come up short. There is no possibility to "wait and see." To be in the novel as a reader is to be hustled into premature error in this way.

4. The accumulated revelations refer to and explain what is already there to be tied up. The explanations are resolutions, according to the principle of narrative economy and causal parsimony. The disclosures do not just brand a new, arbitrary identity on the forehead of textual objects, as in the cheap (because "unearned") betrayals of bad thrillers. That kind of pseudo-explanation merely proliferates entities, pointing to a further series of terms in need of explanation. For instance, when we learn that Mrs. Clennam is not Arthur's birth mother, although this overturns

the basic way we have slotted her into the story, she now makes more human sense than before. Dickens does not unveil an unglimpsed "true" dimension of her character (and thus more backstory) behind the known and "false" one. Her hardness to Arthur, her self-condemning religion, and her weak gestures of recompense toward Little Dorrit are more convincing when we know all. Her character resembles a pile of compensations and countermeasures, apologetic buttresses jutting out from an overburdened structure, which is then mined anew, calling forth new cantilevers of remorse. This outermost and most recent line of defenses is what we first encounter in meeting her.

This same circularity also holds for Dickens's social criticism. The subjective teleology of the mystery procedure guarantees (but we will shortly see the exception) that there is no "outside" left, no resisting garrison that has not bent its knee to the rule of closure. Exposure is built into the mystery's initial coordinates such that its itinerary aims, if indirectly, only at itself. That there is a mystery plot and illuminating recognition scene in place promises that all secrets, all the concealed past, will be ultimately knowable. Whatever belongs to the domain of a belatedly coherent subject will, in the fullness of time, be reconciled to her uncovered past. Given Dickens's social prescription of a responsibility to revise one's self-knowledge, his recognition scenes are confined to the domain of the knowing subject's return to self and the closed dynamics of repression and exposure.

The financial plot in *Little Dorrit* runs parallel to the story of Clennam & Co. and the Dorrit family for several hundred pages. As with the criticism of institutions made in the family romance plot, Dickens casts his criticism of Mr. Merdle's speculation in terms of repression and teleological knowledge, as yet another mystery. The mystery concerning the great financier is announced in book I, chapter XXI, "Mr. Merdle's Complaint."[20] Mr. Merdle suffers a "deep-seated recondite complaint" that is not apparently physiological; he "suppose[s] himself unwell without reason" (253). The cause of this mysterious illness, it will turn out, is that Mr. Merdle's speculations are more or less fraudulent shells, strung along by forgery and the ruination of new and ever-larger investments. After having drawn in the principals of Mr. Dorrit, Arthur Clennam, Daniel Doyce, and Mr. Pancks, and "numbers of men in every profession and trade [who] would be blighted by his insolvency," Mr. Merdle's schemes finally catch up to him (710). Before he can be published as a bankrupt, he commits a gory suicide.

Dickens describes the fallout from this act in a dialogical manner, as if overheard in the midst of an escalating panic, or as if narrated by *fama* herself:

> As the whispers became louder, which they did from that time every minute, they became more threatening. He had sprung from nothing, by no natural growth or process that any one could account for; . . . he had been taken up by all sorts of people, in quite an unaccountable manner; he had never had any money of his own, his ventures had been utterly reckless, and his expenditure had been most enormous . . . The late Mr. Merdle's complaint had been, simply, Forgery and Robbery . . . [He] was simply the greatest Forger and the greatest Thief that ever cheated the gallows. (709–10)

This debriefing raises more questions than it answers. I will confess that, having read and taught this novel quite a few times, I have no clear idea of what Mr. Merdle actually did. Dickens does not provide the retrospective narrative glue that would fill in the gaps between what we knew already about Mr. Merdle and this startling turn of events. Instead, he only elevates those same unknowns to the status of explanations. The unknown source of Mr. Merdle's wealth remains an unspecified "nothing." His astonishing rise is negatively accounted for by no "process that any one could account for." The extensive reach of his holdings and connections likewise remains "unaccountable." We are informed that his crime has been "simply, Forgery and Robbery," and that he is—again "simply"—"the greatest Forger and the greatest Thief." But what exactly did Merdle forge? Bank notes, receipts, contracts, or what? Was he engaged in illegal activities all along, or only belatedly, perhaps in order to cover some unforeseen loss in a reactive chain? How were the massive projects that he had been entrusted with kept from too-close scrutiny this whole time? And not only the final catastrophe is left unspecific. The most basic details of Merdle's investments are missing from the start: "Nobody knew with the least precision what Mr. Merdle's business was, except that it was to coin money" (394).

Compared with the prolonged rehearsal of secrets that Dickens sets up around Mrs. Clennam, the revelations about Mr. Merdle are starkly denuded of interpretive reversals and retrospective sequencing. Indeed, the former recognition scene is so cumbersome that, in some editions, it is summarized in a clarifying appendix. The explanation here—"Simply, Forgery and Robbery"—does not require an appendix. Whereas every line of dialogue between Mrs. Clennam and Arthur can be reinterpreted in the light of the discovery that he is not her son, or every chance appearance of Miss Wade reinterpreted and differently stressed in the light of her obsession with Henry Gowan and hatred of Pet

Meagles, all of the passages dealing with Mr. Merdle read the same backward as forward.

Dickens does not illuminate the verso of the financial mystery he has been weaving. He just slaps a new label on its empty placeholders. To put this in biblical terms, it as though Dickens had said, like God to Abram, "Neither shall thy name any more be called 'mysterious complaint,' but thy name shall be 'unspecified crimes.'" This nominal swap is hermeneutically inert. One cannot flip back to earlier sections of the book and then revise or amplify the scenes where Mr. Merdle's unease and illness first appear. In those scenes, *something* seems to be wrong with him, but the reader armed with the real explanation can only make a one-to-one substitution, supplying Mr. Merdle's bad conscience over his unspecified fraud where there had been unspecified bad feeling. It is the interpretive equivalent of stamping "GUILTY" in red ink on a mug shot. It does not tell you much.

Dickens initially frames the exposure of Mr. Merdle as if anticipating a full-fledged recognition scene. The attending physician who reads his suicide note marvels at the hermeneutic interconnectedness and revealed depths of the case: "He could not sufficiently give utterance to his regret that he had not himself found a clue to this. The smallest clue, he said, would have made him master of the case, and what a case it would have been to have got to the bottom of!" (707). But the reader never sees this note, and we never become masters of the case, even after the fact.

The account we are left with lacks all the features of recognition scenes we identified above in the Clennam and Rigaud blackmail plot. The workings of finance capital do not admit of the same exhibition of full knowledge found in the other plot. By contrast:

1. The discovery of Mr. Merdle's fraudulence and bankruptcy does not sift or rearrange details into new links, or discard some hints as false leads, because no other textual matter is drawn into the wake of the revelation. Whatever tempered skepticism one had about Mr. Merdle's schemes is now validated, but no more than that.
2. There is no sense that Mr. Merdle's perfidy could have been detected in advance, located in silent determinants that escaped an innocent first reading but that now peek out from behind their latency. Dickens has not, so to speak, stocked the earlier scenes with "the smallest clue."
3. There are no "needlessly significant" textual reverberations. The effect of Mr. Merdle's suicide is only to put an enormous negative sign next to the immensity and prominence of his wealth.

4. There is no pertinent explanation that ties up the enigmas concerning
   that wealth. For instance, Dickens has earlier described Mr. Merdle
   almost as the site of the state-capital nexus: "he was so much wanted by
   the men in the City and the rest of those places, and was such a doosed
   extraordinary phenomenon in Buying and Banking and that, that
   Mr. Sparkler doubted if the monetary system of the country would be
   able to spare him" (500). But we do not finally know if his appropriations
   and losses were accrued as a capitalist, as a lender, as an investor, or what.

Whereas, in the family romance plot, the secret contents of an iron box are
at long last recovered into an exhaustive transparency, the collapse of Mr. Merdle's financial empire does not bring submerged and determining aspects of the
past into light. The retrospective chain of hidden causes that Dickens so elaborately forges around the Gilbert Clennam will—and that is extended to the social criticism of the prison, unforgiving Christianity, the bureaucracy, and forms
of willed unknowing—is not employed to plot the financial crisis. The mystery
of Mr. Merdle's speculations is not subjected to retrospective exposure or un-
veiling, but is sequestered from the ultimate recovery of identities available in
the novel's other plot. *Little Dorrit* thereby renders the origins of crisis opaque
by isolating the financial plot in a discrete narrative space where the gestures of
a recognition scene occur only as abbreviated or inoperative. The scaffolding
of a recognition scene remains, but only as a bare, unenclosed framework.

Dickens, like Marx, does not represent capitalism as a sphere "where everything takes place on the surface and in full view of everyone."[21] However, in
imputing to Mr. Merdle concealments and furtive machinations that are never
relayed, *Little Dorrit* only manages to indict its representative capitalist with a
criminal project whose mystery is merely formal, a secret without a content.
Instead of unmasking crisis as a real misrecognition of the subjective processes
internal to capitalist accumulation, Dickens presents capital's inner workings as
empty and abstract. He does not endow capital with the internal, detour-like
ramifications of appropriated subjectivity. Indeed, Dickens does not see any
contradictions internal to the production of surplus-value. Neither does he as-
sociate the inner categories of capital with the formal mediations of value and
agency. When it comes time to unveil the hidden causes of Mr. Merdle's collapse, the usual machinery of Dickens's social criticism can find no inner gears
to expose.

Dickens critiques capitalist speculation as "fetishism" in the anthropological
sense.[22] Mr. Merdle's enterprises are exposed as objects of false belief. His projects are said to be "model structures of straw" (711). He has drawn investors

after him like "human bees [swarming] to the beating of any old tin kettle" (738). Yet he is endowed with the demiurgic powers reserved for pagan idols:

> The famous name of Merdle became, every day, more famous in the land . . . Nobody had the smallest reason for supposing the clay of which this object of worship was made, to be other than the commonest clay, with as clogged a wick smoldering inside of it as ever kept an image of humanity from tumbling to pieces. All people knew (or thought they knew) that he had made himself immensely rich; and, for that reason alone, prostrated themselves before him, more degradedly and less excusably than the darkest savage creeps out of his hole in the ground to propitiate, in some log or reptile, the Deity of his benighted soul. (556)

There is a crucial difference between Dickens's critique of capital as fetishistic, and Marx's. Both authors mean to update the anthropological sense of primitive fetishism for bourgeois society by showing how value deceptively appears to emanate from some "misty realm" of belief.[23] But for Dickens, there is nothing finally to uncover behind capital's deification. Its extravagant manifestations depend solely on contagious belief in and prostration to a false idol. The deluded investors do not perceive that within the false idol, there is only "the commonest clay." Once its exterior fraudulence has been dispelled, there is no inner machinery to be examined and dismantled. Marx, by contrast, understands commodity fetishism as a misrecognition of structures of social productivity: value is represented as if it belonged to autonomous figures as their own proper agency. Thus, value is erroneously projected as something not socially constituted but innate to commodities. For Marx, "fetishism" does not mean that there is nothing behind value (as it does for Dickens), but that value has usurped the social agency by which it is constituted, as its own doing.

By plotting capitalist crisis as a mystery, ending in an explosive set of revelations—even if those revelations are abstract and frustrate the requirements of a recognition scene—Dickens depicts speculative capital as a species of misrecognition. Ultimately, though, the plotting refuses any subjective content to capital accumulation. Dickens (here well within the horizons of bourgeois thought more generally) does not see capital as a process of appropriation, in which the subjective activity of living labor erects the very edifice of dead labor that will obscure it. In effect, Dickens departs from his usual method of plotting, precisely so as not to endow capital with an extended, ramifying course of subjectivity that could then be read back into Merdle's projects and wealth. We have seen that Dickens's social criticism is premised elsewhere on the full recovery of self-coherence (in the light of an excavated personal history) concealed under forms of institutional and moral opacity. In that vein, the family romance plot reveals the truth of the Clennam family to be "locked up" in a roiling, unstable enclosure of repressed determinations. But this dialectic of retrospective subjectivity, the collision with meaning and forms of agency that have been mediated in misrecognition, vanishes when we come to the Merdle plot. The consequence is that capitalist crisis is also underdetermined and causally vacated.

At this point, one may ask why we should insist that Dickens, in criticizing Mr. Merdle as a fraud, or even as a case of speculation run wild, is saying anything at all about financial crashes or crises of capitalism. If Dickens is content to identify "Forgery and Robbery" as the causes of the widespread insolvency that follows from Mr. Merdle's bankruptcy, why should we tendentiously correct that account to read instead "Reification and Contradiction"?

To meet this objection, we should first note that "Forgery" shows up only on one page, after Mr. Merdle has committed suicide and is found to be bankrupt. As Mary Poovey points out, the reference to forgery is vague and abstract, briefly glossing over any specific details of his crimes.[24] It is not at all obvious what Mr. Merdle is supposed to have forged, in his capacity as a capitalist and investor. After all, it is perfectly possible to lose vast sums of other people's money without committing any such crime. If we look at the originals for the Merdle episode Dickens explicitly references in the novel's preface, some are spectacular financial crimes: "a certain Irish bank" (a reference to the Tipperary Bank and the suicide of John Sadleir after a prodigious bout of embezzlement) and "the public examination of late Directors of a Royal British Bank." But Dickens also includes "the Railroad-share epoch" (xvii). This was not an isolated felony, but a period of speculation culminating in the crash (extending to agriculture and banking) of 1847. The railroad shares were a speculative bubble and cannot be easily peeled apart from the boom-and-bust cycle of that era's economy.

In fact, the target of Dickens's critique of Mr. Merdle's speculations is blurry. On one hand, Dickens wants to reduce the profits conjured by speculation to feats of criminal prestidigitation, so that the revelation of forgery tells us what speculation really meant, all along. On the other hand, Dickens suspects that by reducing speculation to specific acts of financial malfeasance, like embezzlement or forgery, he is letting the noncriminal varieties of investor mania off the hook. The problem, he wants to say, is inherent in speculation itself, whatever its outcome. This requires making a conceptual difference between risky "ventures" and solid "investments" (580). When Mr. Pancks, regardless of having lost his money to Mr. Merdle, still insists that "it ought to have been a good investment," since "the figures [his calculated projections of return] are not to be disputed," the narrator inserts this correction: "Mr. Pancks still clung to that word [investment] and never said speculation" (765). By this rhetoric, the gross illegality and fraud of which Mr. Merdle is guilty disappears under the very different criticism of Mr. Pancks's profit "calculations" and the doubtful security of investment "schemes" (582).

The categories of forgery, speculation, and legitimate capital investments in *Little Dorrit* run together along a spectrum, shifting but never quite decidable as one or the other. In the immediate aftermath of Mr. Merdle's suicide, Arthur Clennam can hardly say whether his own role is "fault—or crime" (713). But this shuttling between different terms, and our inability to pin down the object of Dickens's critique, is itself the phenomenal structure of capitalist crisis. The very form of crises is self-dissembling. As Fredric Jameson puts it, "events like financial crises . . . are not self-explanatory" because their "very nature as 'events' in the first place is not secured in advance"; crises only "come into visible existence as temporal phenomena" retroactively, as explanatory constructions.[25] Capitalist crisis is not, to use the language of phenomenology, directly "given" for social experience. It only shows up as something other than itself, for instance as criminal misallocation, or as localized panic. Illegality, profit, and contingency are thus linked together in a desperate chain—a high-stakes game of musical chairs. Marx writes, "In every stock-jobbing swindle everyone knows that some time or other the crash must come, but everyone hopes that it may fall on the head of his neighbor, after he himself has caught the shower of gold and placed it in secure hands. *Après moi le déluge!* is the watchword of every capitalist and every capitalist nation."[26] Whatever swindle happens to be exposed is simply the straw that broke the camel's back, not the entire weight of systemic causes.

The contingency and undecidability of the immediate cause of a crisis are themselves its essential determinations.[27] It is only the positivist naivete of bourgeois economics that expects a crisis to show up as itself, like the Red Death in Edgar Allan Poe's tale. Whereas it is in the untimely and inconvenient nature of crises to arrive not only uninvited, but under a false name. The ultimate causes of crises are inapparent because they arise from contradictions within production that are concealed by reification. Specifically, the antagonistic class dimension of surplus-value, which disappears into the commodity-form of the product of labor, carries over, misrecognized and obscured, into the sphere of surplus-value realization. Having been suppressed at one level, these contradictions cannot be dispelled or forced to reassume their true shape when they reappear in the "noisy sphere" of circulation.[28]

The elusive phenomenology of crises stems from reification.[29] For the limits to capitalist production are built into and concealed by the commodity-mediated form of valorization.[30] The reproduction of capital is constricted and

rendered ever more volatile by its "conflict with the specific *conditions* of production."[31] Capital cannot keep moving without expanding. Each new cycle of
production has to repeat the ongoing subordination of living labor to the swelling powers of constant capital. Capital in its prodigious motion appears to
bourgeois political economy as a self-moving thing, a fetish. The dynamic of
expanded reproduction thus manifests not as inner contradiction but as so
many hypostases of capital communing with itself. But in crisis this imperative
to growth is halted by a bottleneck, situated back in capital's earlier metamor-
phoses. No matter how diligently the capitalist has exploited his workers, the
mass of produced commodities is not yet surplus-value so long as it is encased
in use-values. This surplus-value has to be *realized* by purchase, under conditions of the (relative) decline of workers' buying power. If the produced
surplus-value has not been realized, turned back into money, then it cannot be
converted into capital and invested into new (expanded) means of production.
This contradiction in the dimension of social production is "reified" insofar as
the antagonistic social element (class exploitation) vanishes under its capitalist
expression, the magnitude of its value output. In crisis those antagonisms ex-
plode into view.

Crises of accumulation thus reap, in the obstructed realization of surplus-
value, what reification has sown, in misrecognizing the surplus-labor accumulated under the commodity-form as primordially belonging to capital as its own
being. In a crisis, value becomes socially revisable and capable of devaluation,
even destruction.[32] As the specifically social character of value (its representation
of necessary labor time) moves to the fore, the delay between the purchase of
means of production and the sale of the products assumes a tragic aspect. In
other words, a crisis visits the denial of value's inner formation upon capital, by
interrupting (Banquo-like) the outer process of its circulation. The misrecognitions taking place in production—how labor's subjective, value-constituting activity disappears under the alien masses of produced commodities—leave no trace
in the finished capital, except as a "return of the repressed" during crises.

When Dickens reveals the "secret" of Mr. Merdle's insolvency, the inner
contents of his profit-making are seen to be truncated and empty. Reification
has done its work. Dickens, in unmasking capitalist speculation as fraudulent or
even "fictitious," reproduces the exact misrecognitions effected by reification
by obscuring under a minimal narrative output how exploitation takes place
within and through commodity-determined labor. Ironically, by presenting
surplus-value as chimerical or criminal, Dickens provides capital with an alibi. He presents capital as unfettered from the contradictions of production.[33]
But capital itself would like nothing better than to be disencumbered that
way! As Marx observes, "all [capitalist] nations . . . are periodically seized by

fits of giddiness in which they try to accomplish the money-making without the mediation of the production process."[34]

For Dickens, nothing like crisis can be discerned with respect to Mr. Merdle's enterprises, because capital's inner contents have been whisked away from the plot, as if there were no more reality back there than a "clogged . . . wick." Capital is thereby deprived of any internal moments: no causation, no temporality, no internal connection, no processes of complication. Consequently, the Merdle mystery has no precipitating cause, no connection or clue between the shocking outcome and the lead-up, no specifics of any document forged, no accomplices, and no light shed on Mr. Merdle (who remains altogether a cryptic and distracted character). The outcome, the "reaping the whirlwind" of his ruination, allows no hold for a recognition scene to sequence the successive stages of contradiction (711). Dickens does not see capital as a series of *mediating* misrecognitions, the most prominent of which occur through the appropriation of labor's agency and temporality in the production process. For this reason, capital does not have the form of self-occluding subjectivity that is the vehicle of Dickens's social critique in the family romance plot. Dickens thereby exculpates capital of the very operations of obfuscation and alienation that he indicts so vividly in other institutions—even while he condemns capital as an empty facade.

The retrospective reconstruction we find in recognition scenes is therefore no longer available when it comes to the phenomenology of financial crises, since Dickens sees crises as instances of non-immanence and experiential vacancy. The anarchy of capitalist production appears to be separated from subjectivity by an unbridgeable epistemological remove. Capitalist crisis comes to resemble "crisis" in the Kierkegaardian sense: an infinite divide between the unprotected catastrophe of Being and our own miserable categories of understanding. Instead of crisis being a result of identifiable tendencies, traceable backward in time, that is, a topic of a recognition scene, it is instead an impasse for plot. Crisis in *Little Dorrit* is more a tear in the fabric of economic reality than an occurrence in itself. Dickens thereby precludes crisis from being stitched onto a project of retrospective subjective coherence.

So far I have been arguing that the revelations around Mr. Merdle's bankruptcy and criminal fraud do not attain the expected dimensions of a recognition scene on display in the novel's other plot. The Merdle plot sits outside of the totalizing circuit of social transparency and moral coherence demanded by Dickensian closure. It cannot be knit into the retrospection of teleological subjectivity. Why? Because Dickens throws out the "baby" of production with the "bathwater" of profit. In emptying capitalist accumulation of the misrecognitions inherent in the production of surplus-value, he also excludes the involutions and disloca-tions of subjectivity from the past moments of capital. For Dickens, *nothing is repressed* in the inner movement of capital. His whole critique is that nothing is going on "inside" capital. Capital does not appear to him as a social relation, but instead as an automatic activity purporting to possess the "occult ability" to summon profits from out of thin air.[35] Because no rabbit is put into the hat of finance capital, no rabbit can be later pulled out by the plot. When it comes to capital, Dickens forfeits the key technique of his gothicized social criticism: un-veiling a chamber of long-repressed secrets. Although we still find such criticism in *Little Dorrit*, it is brought to bear only on villainous aristocratic figures like Rigaud, and on grasping old skinflints like Mrs. Clennam—not on the structures of modern capitalism.[36]

The foregoing analysis of the narrative dimension of capital can help us to make sense of certain crucial interpretive problems in *Little Dorrit*'s ending. Why does Little Dorrit burn the codicil to Gilbert Clennam's will, of which she is the legatee? And why does she agree to Mrs. Clennam's request to de-lay revealing her secret to Arthur?

> The secret was safe now! She could keep her own part of it from him; he should never know of her loss; in time to come, he should know all that was of import to himself [who his birth mother was]; but he should never know what concerned her, only. That was all passed, all forgiven, all forgotten. (812)

Readers often assume that Little Dorrit is renouncing the inheritance of one thousand guineas, which Mrs. Clennam promises to restore to her, in order to gain Arthur's love.[37] She knows that Arthur regards her own personal fortune (later to be lost in the Merdle collapse) as an obstacle to their marriage, vowing that he must "never touch it, never!" (760). This new inheritance would be a further impediment. But surely there are no assets remaining from Clennam & Co. to inherit. Mrs. Clennam has already told Rigaud that she has "not the pre-sent means of raising the sum [two thousand pounds] you have demanded. I have not prospered" (784). That is before the Clennam house itself collapses into a heap of rubble. After that, we learn that Flintwinch thought to have been crushed in its fall, is alive and has been "converting securities into as much money as could be got" (795). He then absconds to the continent with whatever could be realized of the firm's holdings. Besides this, Mrs. Clennam is struck dumb and insensate by the collapse of her house. She could hardly execute the restitution she had earlier proposed.

So Little Dorrit could not possibly be renouncing the inheritance of any empirical funds that would continue to stand between her and Arthur. What then? It is simply begging the question to answer that keeping Mrs. Clennam's secrets after her death is by itself testimony of Little Dorrit's unprofaned goodness.[38] Secrets in Dickens do not work that way. Neither does it go without saying why burning and suppressing the past should amount to "all" being "forgiven."

The burning of the will makes sense only when we put it in relation to the Merdle plot and its moral consequences for Arthur. Having disallowed capital any inner narrative content, Dickens is careful in the ending of *Little Dorrit* to avoid filling in the empty mystery of the Merdle plot with any of the subjective contents (moral, erotic, familial, etc.) that have been dislodged by the family romance recognition scene. He is concerned not to recover the Merdle plot as available (even indirectly) for a spectacular moral redemption. The danger is that the empty space behind the facade of speculation would then become populated with subjective meaning, and yoked to a significant personal history. The Merdle plot would in that case siphon off the moral coherence of the family romance as its own interior content. So, when Little Dorrit burns the sole proof of the guilty contents of the family romance, her action ironically preserves the pristine interiority of capital, where Dickens does not permit subjectivity to trespass. This act bars any influx of subjective "filling" into the emptiness of financial phenomena.

Because there is no full-fledged retrospective coherence affixed to the Merdle plot, it lies wide open to being cathected with excess or unattached narrative impulses from elsewhere in the novel. The emptier the explanation for the financial crash, the more it is available to being made equivalent to, or invested with, unclaimed deposits of guilt. In the wake of Mr. Merdle's suicide, Arthur immediately transfers his long-standing retrospective guilt over to this new pretext. He interprets his own role in the crash as a kind of answer to his earlier concern that Clennam & Co. had been involved in William Dorrit's imprisonment for debt. He now has something to really feel bad about. As Elaine Hadley reads Arthur's character, his problem is that he claims "too much" accountability, because he is "haunted by guilt he cannot attach to his own intention."[39] But in drawing undue resentment upon himself, Arthur is only grasping at yet another misplaced culpability to validate his floating sense of familial guilt.[40]

In allowing himself to be arrested for debt for losses accrued in Mr. Merdle's enterprises and jailed in the Marshalsea, against the advice of his friends, Arthur draws the public ire and a "storm of animosity" upon himself (716). Once in prison, he languishes in weary oblivion, guiltily reproaching himself. Yet his self-punishment, what he figures in terms of "atonement," is out of all proportion to his responsibility for the losses of countless others in his same position (715). In his moral ledger, he balances his limited involvement in the Merdle crisis against all of his felt accountability for a failed life and his ineffective responsiveness to what is broken in the world around him. Arthur would reduce the relations of neglect and malice that he has all along suspected to be lurking in his past—relations that, as we have seen, turn out to be inordinately convoluted—to the emptiness of the financial implosion.

The very possibility of regarding guilt as convertible and transferable first originates in the family romance plot. Mrs. Clennam's rigid moral bookkeeping tallies up guilt and reparation as measurable quantities, "always balancing her bargain with the Majesty of heaven, posting up the entries to her credit, strictly keeping her set-off" (50). Pointedly, in coping with his lost capital, Arthur urges the same contentious term, "reparation," that he had used in charging Mrs. Clennam with having wronged William Dorrit somewhere (714). In that earlier scene, she had exploded at him for demanding an account for what the firm had built up "with wear and tear, and toil and self-denial," as if it were all "so much plunder; and asks to whom they shall be given up, as reparation and restitution!" (50).

This mechanism of moral equivalence opens a potential channel for the flow of bad conscience overcharged in the family romance plot into the hitherto vacant interior of the Merdle plot. Until now, Dickens has been as vigilant in separating out the moments of repression and retrospection from the Merdle plot as Jacob is in dividing the ringstraked, speckled, and spotted animals from Laban's flocks. Once moral debits are taken to be quantifiable and convertible, they become so much mobile "filling" to be set against past transgressions. Arthur objectifies his unspecified culpability for his own damaged life by transferring this guilt over to the Merdle plot, so as to stand in for the exaggerated responsibility he takes for the miscarriage of speculation. He now takes the sham solidity of Mr. Merdle's projects, which have caught "fire and were turned to smoke," to be an emblem of his own inner waste (711). This transfer of subjective contents from Arthur's beleaguered conscience into the space of fallout from the Merdle crash spells trouble for the project of holding apart the (empty) plot of capital from the (totalizing) plot of family romance.

When Little Dorrit burns the document that is the last proof of the extensive wrongs disclosed by the family romance, she obstructs exactly this equivalence of moral debits, and puts a halt to their leakage from one plot to another. Arthur's response to the Merdle crash, by positing the empty contents of the fraudulent financial erections as the null measure of his own empty life, threatens to flood capital with a transferred subjectivity, lending capital the involutions of his past as its own. Arthur's guilt about his involvement in speculation threatens to pull the existential entanglements of his familial guilt over to the Merdle plot as a moral counterweight, infusing capital with subjectivity borrowed through a back channel. By burning the will—the only evidence of the Clennam family's transgressions and the harm done to herself—Little Dorrit prevents the extensive revelations of the family romance from entering into this commerce with the Merdle plot. She thereby severs any equivalence between the losses incurred in Mr. Merdle's speculations and the "shadow of the wall [that] was dark upon" Arthur in the debtor's prison.

In other words, the moral subjectivity imagined by the ending is not a higher level of response that suspends and cancels the ills of capital. Dickens is not (*pace* Orwell) making a moral critique of capitalism, that is, he does not propose moral reparation as a solution or cure to the ills of capitalism. Instead, the strands of subjectivity recovered in the conclusions represent a change of topic, a non sequitur that simply drops the issue of capitalist crisis without resolving it. Once Arthur's debts are settled by the deus ex machina of Mr. Doyce's return from abroad, that is the last we hear of Arthur's outsize guilt for the crash. Having paid off Arthur's debts, Mr. Doyce instructs him, "not a word more from you about the past" (823).

In reinforcing the separation between the comprehensive illumination in the family romance plot and the truncated solution found in the financial plot, Dickens extricates subjectivity from mediating the "inside" of capitalist accumulation. However, the ending also decisively registers the high moral price of maintaining subjectivity as cordoned off from involvement with capital. After all the contrasting choreography of *Little Dorrit*'s recognition scenes, the subjectivity that is left over is internally blocked, without full access to its origins. In preventing the contents of Arthur's past from being recuperated as capital's own retrospection, Dickens also keeps Arthur from interpreting his life in full view of the facts about his past. The contradictory strategy that Dickens adopts in his narrative critique of capital—plotting capital as a mystery but denying it any inner contents to be retrieved by a culminating recognition scene—here returns to undermine his closural rendition of subjectivity. In order not to steer subjectivity into the dead end of capital, Dickens ordains that Arthur cannot derive a meaningful orientation of his life from the authority of his own past. He never learns the whole truth about the motivations, repressions, prejudices, and restitutions that make up his family's history and so forcefully smothered his own childhood. He cannot supply, from out of his own experience, a complete account of the warrants for the values at which he has now arrived. In other words, Arthur's subjectivity is maimed in the course of being dragged out from the jaws of capital. What is new here is that the novel's hero crawls out of the plot hole of capital worse for the wear.

In the last accounting, then, the conditions for meaning in Arthur's life remain partially subterranean. The proof (the destroyed codicil to the will) and the complicated determinations of those disclosures are lost to him. He has only the active humanity of Little Dorrit—the structuring "vanishing-point" of his life's new orientation—with which to go forward (733). But Little Dorrit is a vanishing-point in another sense because her concentration of the moral import of the plot is itself evanescent.[41] Arthur is never to know "what concerned her, only." Her experience is barred from being any kind of resource—if it is not altogether repressed, on the model of her father's own not-knowing. I can see what Dickens is getting at. As if to dissolve the grip that resentment has had over other characters in the novel, when Little Dorrit learns about her own position in the harmful repressions of the past, she immediately disavows any blame or consciousness of harm. Forgiving is thus simultaneous with forgetting. But I think Dickens is wrong in this. The basic, tragic fact is the harm that people do blindly, in their misprision and their defense against painful self-knowledge. Reconciliation or forgiveness consist of this determination of the past as past, rather than as ongoing rift or oblivion. The damage has to be mourned and narrated, not just forgotten or snuffed out.

Because Dickens sees capital accumulation as only a trap for misplaced faith and empty idolization, rather than as a deforming mediation of subjectivity occurring in production, the novel's ending illuminates the past only for so long as it takes to tell a dream before its vanishing. The truth is then smothered, exhaled like a dying breath under the collapsing rubble, or burned. In any event, its whisperings are soon to be inaudible under the incessant, heedless "uproar" of the streets in the book's last line (826).

CHAPTER 2

Interest-Bearing Capital and the Displacement of Affect in *The Last Chronicle of Barset*

Thou comest in such a questionable shape
That I will speak to thee

—Shakespeare, *Hamlet*

Anthony Trollope seems like he does not belong at all in a book about plot. He writes in *An Autobiography* that plot is "the most insignificant part of a tale," necessary only as a "vehicle of some sort" for the exhibition of his characters and their feelings and concerns. He disapproves of fictions that exert all their ingenuity on elaborate plotting, comparing them to a "vehicle without the passengers, a story of mystery in which the agents never spring to life."[1] He contrasts his own method with Wilkie Collins's sensation novels, which feel like they are "all plot." Trollope grumbles about Collins: "I can never lose the taste of the construction."[2] In *Barchester Towers*, he even halts his own narrative in order to deprecate the recognition scenes of gothic fiction:

> When we have once learnt what was that picture before which was hung Mrs. Radcliffe's solemn curtain, we feel no further interest about either the frame or the veil. They are to us merely a receptacle for old bones, an inappropriate coffin, which we would wish to have decently buried out of sight.[3]

The danger of too much plot is that the narrative scaffolding will cease to be a support and become instead an obstruction, getting in the way of the moral legibility Trollope claims as the purpose of his fiction.[4] In his autobiography, he is continually remarking how far his novels succeed despite their thin or faulty plotting.[5] He seems amused to have gotten away with something, admitting that "I have never troubled myself much about the construction of plots."[6]

But Trollope's novels are not so absolutely devoid of plot, mystery, suspense, or recognition scenes as he sometimes makes out. His crabby and self-serving contrast with Collins notwithstanding, Trollope is not above writing a jewel-theft novel of his own, *The Eustace Diamonds*. (To be sure, there is no pretense of keeping up anything like the mystery of *The Moonstone*. The titular diamonds, thought to have been stolen, are out of sight of the reader for only about two pages, before we learn that only the jewel case has disappeared; Lizzie Eustace, although she keeps silent about this fact, slept with the diamond necklace safely under her pillow.) There is a more sustained mystery, over a disputed will, in *Orley Farm*. But Trollope, unable to conceal crucial matters from the reader, gives away the solution halfway through, when Lady Mason confesses to forgery. Although he still judges the plot of *Orley Farm* to be "probably the best I ever made," Trollope concedes "it has the fault of declaring itself . . . too early."[7]

The plot of *The Last Chronicle of Barset* is a different matter.[8] *The Last Chronicle* is, as the title suggests, the final volume of the six Barsetshire books (preceded by *The Warden, Barchester Towers, Doctor Thorne, Framley Parsonage*, and *The Small House at Allington*) that Trollope wrote from 1855 to 1867, and that are loosely centered around the clergy of the fictitious cathedral town of Barchester. It centers on an accusation against Reverend Crawley, the poor curate of Hogglestock, of stealing a bank check for twenty pounds. Trollope lays out the circumstances of the mystery right away; the first chapter is titled, in his characteristic manner, "How Did He Get It?" (The unsuccessful stage adaptation of the novel was *Did He Steal It?*) But for once Trollope keeps up the mystery, delaying the explanatory recognition scene for about eight hundred pages.

There is no critical consensus concerning the aesthetic status of this protracted mystery. Does the plot bear any significance, or is it only a complicated technical exercise? Does the recognition scene that resolves the mystery of the check also elucidate or mediate Crawley's subjectivity? How much attention should we pay to the features of Victorian checks and credit instruments that Trollope so minutely specifies? These questions are answered in one fashion by Northrop Frye. He regards the plot of *The Last Chronicle* as "a conventional, mechanical, or even . . . absurd contrivance."[9] The hulking narrative apparatus in this book is particularly superfluous, since the "twist" of the intricate recognition scene does not bring to light any hidden truth.[10] Frye supposes that Trollope is engaged in a "kind of parody of a detective novel . . . The point of the parody is that Crawley's character is clearly and fully set forth, and if you imagine him capable of stealing money you are simply not attending to the story."[11] To remain in suspense over, or to anticipate, the solution of the mystery is just to be a bad reader. Since Frye finds it impossible to suspect Crawley, it follows that he pays no attention to the financial details of the case, observing (not quite accurately) only that "some money has been stolen."[12] A completely different set of answers is given by Mary Poovey. She sees Trollope's "disjunctive" plotting as inseparable from the novel's ideas about value, money, and gender because the disassembled chronology of the story "install[s] belatedness at the heart of significance."[13] The technique of staggered retrospection, in turn, disrupts and problematizes Crawley's subjectivity. His psychology is "distended," turned inside out, and distributed like so many crumbs across the windings of the plot.[14] Poovey further argues that the entire "problematic of representation" in the novel depends on the appropriation of the differential properties of the specific financial instruments involved (check, bill of exchange, bank note).[15]

As divergent as these two sets of answers are, neither accounts for the basic misrecognition that organizes *The Last Chronicle*'s plot. In stressing either the continuity or the discontinuity underlying the ultimate discovery of Crawley's innocence, Frye and Poovey overlook the way the "official" story—the communal acceptance of Crawley's evident guilt—plausibly hangs together for most of the book. When Crawley cannot account for how he came into possession of the check, everyone eventually takes it as settled that he did take it from Mr. Soames's pocketbook. The issue shifts to whether he can be pardoned for doing so, owing to various mitigating circumstances. In other words, the novel is not a whodunit. It is an "and-so-what?" What is striking about the end of the novel is that Crawley's proved innocence does not undo or cancel the procedural dilemmas raised by his presumed guilt. Frye is mistaken that Crawley's subjectivity is so secure; Poovey is mistaken that it is belatedly secured by the financial instrument.

My contention in this chapter is that the solution of the mystery is not meant to resolve the "and-so-what?" plot, for the reason that the structuring misrecognition is not confined to the narrow one of whether Crawley stole the check. There is a further misrecognition, in which the Barsetshire community loses its grip on the coherence of its legal and ecclesiastical norms. The incoherence that comes to shroud the social and institutional forms in the Barsetshire plot is itself misrecognized as originating there. When the recognition scene resolves the local issue of the check, its temporality pertains not to the resolution of Crawley's subjectivity, but to the plot hole of capital—specifically what Trollope sees as the superficiality of interest-bearing capital in the financial London subplot. The havoc wreaked on subjectivity—the dysfunction of social responsiveness in moral and institutional life—in the Crawley plot thus really belongs to the alien workings of finance.

After a brief plot summary, the next section of the chapter examines the pervasive anxiety that descends on Barsetshire like a mysterious fog. From the first novel in the Barsetshire series, *The Warden*, Trollope's concern has been the same: to anatomize English institutional practices and conventionalized social forms (especially marriage), diagnosing the forms of self-reflexivity available under the pressures of money and hierarchy therein. Trollope is especially interested in moments when entrenched justifications, definitions, and rules come into conflict with moral conscientiousness, so as to bring their background commitments into explicitness.[16] In *The Last Chronicle*, however, once Crawley is suspected of theft, the unreflective inhabiting of peculiarly English norms around the case is pulled (if I may invoke Yeats) into a "widening gyre" of weakened social meanings. No one seems to know quite how anything works. The commitments to institutional minutiae defended so bitterly in the earlier Barsetshire novels now come to seem arbitrary and indecipherable, "lacking all conviction."

This anxiety, which cripples the authority of the norms explored in the earlier novels, does not arise from the patterns of provincial life that it undermines. It is an interloper. (Here I am following Freud's early description of anxiety as an affective response severed from its original context, unmoored from its corresponding object.[17]) The failing grip of these norms and their fractured coherence stem instead from the phenomenology of capital, how Trollope assesses finance capital as social experience. The next section of the chapter therefore turns to Trollope's conservative view of interest-bearing capital. Trollope intends a contrast between finance capital as a fraudulent, insecure, and corrupting form of accumulation, on one hand, and landed wealth, which is genuine and honorable, on the other hand.[18] Finance capital is ungrounded and specious, while landed wealth rests on an unquestionably solid basis. This is fetishistic in precisely Marx's sense.

I then turn to the mechanics of *The Last Chronicle*'s recognition scene. Here the discovery of Crawley's innocence, which turns on the most delicate technicality, is grossly mismatched to the communal anxiety sown by the supposition of his guilt. The solution turns out not to mediate or involve Crawley's subjectivity because the right explanation has just been sitting there all along, not complicated or developed. The recognition scene is pushed forward, after the mystery has stalled out for hundreds of pages, by a somewhat arbitrary anticlimax that disregards the enormous social machinery that has been worrying the question. It has all been a case of breaking a butterfly on a wheel. The plotting therefore does not "fit" the plot. Crawley himself does not consider the solution to be relevant to his subjective outcome. It would seem rather that the static narrative form of the recognition scene belongs to the plotless and superficial form of finance capital.

For Trollope sees capital as shallow, lacking any depths to uncover, and absent temporal detours or density of social mediations. Trollope does not make his conservative critique of financial capital directly, but only transferentially, in effigy. Thus, the check mystery is not the bearer of its own meanings, but carries over an alien social significance from the finance plot into the benign ecclesiastical setting of Barsetshire, where it becomes unrecognizable. The risks, coercions, and magical thinking that are draped over "City money" as its wonted accoutrements are experienced in their displacement as unwelcome and debilitating.

In the last section of the chapter, I consider the resolution of Crawley's moral fate, his self-determined ending, apart from the resolution of the check mystery. His subjectivity is not ultimately reduced to the consequences of the evidence that clears him. Unlike the heroes of *Tom Jones* or *The Mysteries of Udolpho*, Crawley is not restored intact by the recognition scene, as if none of this had ever happened. It is as if he picks up his chips before the roulette wheel is done spinning so that his subjectivity is not gambled on the recognition scene. For Trollope, because the plot hole of capital is not a site of social and temporal mediations, its forms are not determinative for Crawley's subjectivity at last. He commits his fate to time and endured social mediations—not to the absent mediations of displaced plot.

Because *The Last Chronicle* not only concludes the Barsetshire novels, but in doing so gathers the preceding books into a series for the first time, the plot of Mr. Crawley and the stolen check is only the most central among many narrative strands. Trollope is busy elsewhere, reviving characters from the other volumes (such as Dr. Grantly, Lily Dale, Lady Lufton, the Thornes), or killing them off (in the case of Mrs. Proudie and Mr. Harding). Just as, whenever one is reading *War and Peace*, it is necessary to scribble out the diminutive forms of Russian names on a back page, so the web of cousins and Barsetshire's fictional geography will have the reader of *The Last Chronicle* taking pencil in hand to make little maps and family trees—who are the Dunstables again?—for private reference. In the plot summary that follows, however, all of that can be safely left out. The exposition of the check mystery is complicated enough.[19]

The Reverend Josiah Crawley will be known to readers of *Framley Parsonage* as the impressively learned but impoverished and disgruntled perpetual curate of Hogglestock. "The crime laid to his charge was the theft of a check for twenty pounds, which he was said to have stolen out of a pocket-book left or dropped in his house" (4). The check, "for twenty pounds drawn by Lord Lufton on his bankers in London . . . had been lost early in the spring, by Mr. Soames, Lord Lufton's man of business in Barsetshire, together with a pocket-book in which it had been folded. This pocket-book Soames had believed himself to have left at Mr. Crawley's house" on the occasion of remitting "a rentcharge to Mr. Crawley on behalf of Lord Lufton, amounting to twenty pound four shillings" (9). This payment had been made by Mr. Soames "personally to Mr. Crawley. Of so much there was no doubt. But he had paid it by a check drawn by himself on his own bankers at Barchester, and that check had been cashed in the ordinary way on the next morning. On returning to his own house in Barchester he had missed his pocket-book, and had written to Mr. Crawley to make inquiry . . . No pocket-book had been found . . . All this had happened in March" (9). In October, facing down considerable debt to the tradesmen of Silverbridge, Mrs. Crawley "paid the butcher twenty pounds in four five-pound notes" (9). Then, in November, inquiry is made over the lost check, which is then "traced back through the Barchester bank [where it had been cashed] to Mr. Crawley's hands" (9). And these are "the identical notes" used to pay the butcher (10). This is everything we learn directly of the trajectory of the check until chapter 70.

In the first few chapters, there are a few exculpatory conjectures, none of which ultimately hold. "When inquiry was made, Mr. Crawley stated that the check had been paid to him by Mr. Soames, on behalf of the rentcharge due to him by Lord Lufton" (10). But no—"the error of this statement was at once made manifest. There was the check, signed by Mr. Soames himself, for the exact amount,—twenty pounds four shillings," as distinct from the lost check for only twenty pounds (10). A different explanation is offered when Mrs. Crawley suggests that the check had been "part of a present given by Dean Arabin to her husband in April last . . . Mrs. Arabin had told her [Mrs. Crawley] that money had been given,—and at last taken. Indeed, so much had been very apparent, as bills had been paid [after the Crawleys had received this gift] to the amount of at least fifty pounds . . . [Mrs. Crawley] had felt no doubt that the money [for the butcher's bill] had been given by the dean" (10–11). But again no—this account is contradicted by Dean Arabin himself. Arabin, who is abroad with his wife, writes upon inquiry that "on the 17th of March he had given to Mr. Crawley a sum of fifty pounds, and that the payment had been made with five Bank of England notes of ten pounds each, which had been handed by him to his friend in the library at the deanery" (12). A third explanation is that Crawley "often knows not what he says . . . There are times when in his misery he knows not what he says,—when he forgets everything," and so cannot be held responsible for his actions or his memory (11). Because the other explanations are quickly refuted, this woolgathering explanation is the only one left standing, and is left to ferment and perpetuate itself for several hundred pages. Although he is thought to be guilty—insofar as he had "undoubtedly appropriated the check through temporary obliquity of judgment"—people can say that and still be "unanimous in . . . acquittal of Mr. Crawley" (101). The crime is mitigated by "various excuses" (478): the obvious desperation and the certainty of being caught suggest he was not in his right mind . . . he had not tried to conceal anything . . . besides that he was so poor . . . besides that he was so dedicated and hard-working a clergyman. The Barsetshire community mostly accepts, or does not explicitly reject, some such shifting and inconsistent, but apologetic, account of what happened.

After the community and Crawley himself evidently reconcile themselves to saying that he took the check without knowing what he was doing—and every character has their own version of this understanding, although none has any privileged information to base it on—the introduction of clues and theories about the case comes to a standstill for several hundred pages.[20] At this point the plot becomes more like a *procedural* than a *mystery*. On the legal front (the criminal charge against Crawley), the focus shifts to issues of bail and the timing of the next assizes. On the ecclesiastical front (how far the Church will discipline him), focus shifts to the formation of commissions, and whether Crawley will give up his pulpit at Hogglestock to an underling sent by the Proudies, or whether it will be necessary to proceed against him in an ecclesiastical court. As we will see, this procedural resembles something of a "clash by night" since the maneuvers of the contending parties are hardly legible even to themselves except as "confused alarms," and it is ultimately inconclusive. (In the event, Crawley resigns his curacy, and remains obstinate against taking it up again even when the opportunity presents itself after Mrs. Proudie's death.) Having brought the plot up to this point, we can now have a closer look at this pervasive illegibility and its origins.

The Last Chronicle drops the reader into a morass of doubt. Its first sentence, "I can never bring myself to believe it" (1)—spoken by the attorney's daughter, Mary Walker, who cannot fathom that a man should be a clergyman and yet be accused of stealing—sets the prevailing tone of uncertainty and irreconcilable cognitive demands. The case against Crawley is like a slippery, cobbled footpath, not affording any firm step of condemnation or vindication. The basic facts require at least three tedious, fine distinctions—between a check drawn on Lord Lufton himself and a check paid by Mr. Soames *on behalf* of Lord Lufton; between a check for twenty pounds and one for twenty pounds four shillings; and between two Barchester banks, the one where Mr. Crawley has the check cashed emphatically not being, "as will be understood, the bank on which the check was drawn" (9). And Mr. Crawley himself hardly helps clarify matters: "In all that he said he was terribly confused, contradictory, unintelligible" (13).

He is not alone in his confusion and explanatory stumbling. Hardly *any* character in *The Last Chronicle* seems to understand how English institutions work. They appear not to have read the fine print in the instruction manual. When Mark Robarts, the vicar of Framley who sits on the Clerical Commission assembled for Mr. Crawley's case, discusses the issue of bail with Mrs. Crawley, he tells her, "I don't understand much about it, and I daresay you do not either" (79). Anne Prettyman, the schoolteacher, considers that "They have found [Crawley] guilty; they have indeed. They have convicted him,—or whatever it is . . . I don't understand it altogether; but he's to be tried again at the assizes" (84). But her sister points out the mistake here: "'Committed him,' said Miss Prettyman, correcting her sister with scorn. 'They have not convicted him. Had they convicted him, there could be no question of bail'" (85). Later, when the assizes are to be held at the same time as the ecclesiastical inquiry, there is some undefined concern whether this amounts to a kind of double jeopardy, and "that a double prosecution for the same offence was a course of action opposed to the feelings and traditions of the country. Miss Anne Prettyman went so far as to say that it was unconstitutional, and Mary Walker declared that no human being except Mrs. Proudie would ever have been guilty of such cruelty" (573).

This uncertainty about procedure and powers extends even to those who themselves wield institutional authority. When Bishop Proudie considers how far his jurisdiction extends, Trollope remarks, "Now, episcopal authority admits of being stretched or contracted according to the bishop who uses it. It is not always easy for a bishop himself to know what he may do, and what he may not do" (106). The fine points of this are totally disregarded by Mrs. Proudie, who urges her husband to disregard the bounds of his office and nearly to clap handcuffs on Mr. Crawley himself, referring to the curate as "a convicted thief." She is corrected by her husband—Crawley is only accused, not convicted—but she repeats, "'A convicted thief,' . . . and she vociferated the words in such a tone that the bishop resolved he would for the future let the word convicted pass without notice. After all, she was only using the phrase in a peculiar sense given to it by herself" (105).

So far, the breakdown in terminology and protocol is confined to the Crawley case itself as it moves through official channels. Trollope is well aware that English institutions can be byzantine. (And as a secular American reader, I might share some of Anne Prettyman's confusion. Please do not ask me the difference between a vicar, a curate, a prebendary, an archdeacon, and a canon.) Trollope elsewhere describes the nonintuitive hodgepodge of irregular statuses and rules in English law as being learned by those "who are brought up among it . . . as children [learn] a language," whereas "strangers who begin the study in advanced life, seldom make themselves perfect in it."[21] The residents of Barsetshire have somehow lost this knack, and are operating as if they were "strangers" to their own form of official life. But the anxiety in *The Last Chronicle* is not confined only to the difficulty of making out and inhabiting the vocabulary of power, its sequences and limitations. Anxiety is like a pall that spreads over the most unlikely reaches of provincial interaction. (Though not every zone in the novel is paralyzed with anxiety. The bureaucratic world, also in London, continues to operate as a system of legible gestures, maneuvers, tactics, and protocols.[22])

When Henry Grantly goes to Allington to persevere in his declarations to Mr. Crawley's daughter Grace, the setting is already known to readers from *The Small House at Allington*. For us, then, Allington is familiarity itself, a thoroughly imagined "real country" (891). But Grantly quickly becomes disoriented among the placid but monotonous country lanes and brooks.

> He was careful not to go out of Allington by the road he had entered it, as he had no wish to encounter Grace and her friend on their return into the village; so he crossed a little brook which runs at the bottom of the hill on which the chief street of Allington is built, and turned into a field-path to the left as soon as he had got beyond the houses. Not knowing the geography of the place he did not understand that by taking that path he was making his way back to the squire's house; but it was so; and after sauntering on for about a mile and crossing back again over the stream, of which he took no notice, he found himself leaning across a gate, and looking into a paddock on the other side of which was the high wall of a gentleman's garden. To avoid this he went on a little further and found himself on a farm road, and before he could retrace his steps so as not to be seen, he met a gentleman whom he presumed to be the owner of the house. It was the squire surveying his home farm, as was his daily custom; but Major Grantly had not perceived that the house must of necessity be Allington House, having been aware that he had passed the entrance to the place, as he entered the village on the other side. "I'm afraid I'm intruding," he said, lifting his hat. "I came up the path yonder, not knowing that it would lead me so close to a gentleman's house."
>
> "There is a right of way through the fields on to the Guestwick road," said the squire, "and therefore you are not trespassing in any sense; but we are not particular about such things down here, and you would be very welcome if there were no right of way. If you are a stranger, perhaps you would like to see the outside of the old house. People think it picturesque."

Then Major Grantly became aware that this must be the squire, and he was annoyed with himself for his own awkwardness in having thus come upon the house. He would have wished to keep himself altogether unseen if it had been possible,—and especially unseen by this old gentleman, to whom, now that he had met him, he was almost bound to introduce himself. But he was not absolutely bound to do so, and he determined that he would still keep his peace. Even if the squire should afterwards hear of his having been there, what would it matter? But to proclaim himself at the present moment would be disagreeable to him. He permitted the squire, however, to lead him to the front of the house, and in a few moments was standing on the terrace hearing an account of the architecture of the mansion. . . .

Then he followed the squire down to the churchyard, and was shown the church as well as the view of the house, and the vicarage, and a view over to Allington woods from the vicarage gate, of which the squire was very fond, and in this way he was taken back on to the Guestwick side of the village, and even down on the road by which he had entered it, without in the least knowing where he was. He looked at his watch, and saw that it was past two. "I'm very much obliged to you, sir," he said again taking off his hat to the squire, "and if I shall not be intruding I'll make my way back to the village."

"What village?"

"To Allington," said Grantly.

"This is Allington," said the squire. (287–89)

It is as if Allington, that most legible of places, suddenly belonged to the landscape of Kafka's *The Castle*, or as if Grantly had started out on the Méséglise way only to find himself unaccountably on the Guermantes way.

I am calling all of this "anxiety" partly in an everyday sense, especially in the case of Mr. Crawley, who is so distraught that he feels himself losing contact with his sanity, plunged into all-consuming worry. But it is anxiety in a more technical sense, too, since we do not know the origin for this pervasive uncertainty and inability to say what anyone is doing, or why, or to put the right names to things. As Martin Heidegger reminds us, anxiety arises from something "completely indefinite . . . Anxiety 'does not know'" what it is anxious about. The world itself, the structure of concern and assignment belonging to us, comes before us as somehow obstinate and intrusive.[23] In *The Last Chronicle*, the stability of self-orientation and definition seem to be sapped from within. But the protracted, self-annulling form of the novel's recognition scene allows us to trace back the widespread anxious affect that paralyzes Mr. Crawley, Bishop Proudie, Henry Grantly, and others to the *social form* of financial capital it has been displaced from.

I am using "displacement" here in a sense borrowed from psychoanalysis, specifically the section on affect in *The Interpretation of Dreams*. In dreams, says Freud, it frequently happens that "the ideational material has undergone displacement and substitutions, whereas the affects have remained unaltered."[24] Consequently, "the ideational material, which has been changed by dream-distortion, [is] no longer compatible with the affect." But dream interpretation can "put the right material back into its [original] position."[25] In Freud's example, when a woman dreams that "she saw three lions in a desert, one of which was laughing; but she was not afraid of them," the frightening image is at odds with the neutral affective response.[26] Analysis reveals the lions to be only substitutions for some nonthreatening acquaintances. The affect belonging to the latent dream-thoughts, of *not being threatened*, has therefore been preserved (displaced) in the dream, even though it does not match the threatening manifest content. As Freud puts it, "So this lion was like the lion in *A Midsummer Night's Dream* that concealed the figure of Snug the joiner; and the same is true of all dream-lions of which the dreamer is not afraid."[27] And "the same is true," too, of the anxiety (disorientation, crisis of norms) that incompatibly adheres to the familiar Barsetshire setting. Anxiety here "appears in connection with subject-matter"—such as finding one's way around Allington's country lanes—"which seems to provide no occasion for any such expression."[28] We now have to trace this affect back to where it belongs.

Just as, when a museum has loaned out some objet d'art to another institution for exhibition, one finds only an apologetic card in its place, so the anxiety in *The Last Chronicle* is in one place, only because it is missing in the other. This anxious structure of feeling is displaced from the situation to which it is originally a response. The "latent" source of this anxiety is the phenomenology of interest-bearing capital. When Allington, the quaintest place in existence, becomes a maze dominated by disguise and avoidance, this is the *same* anxiety that has become detached from the financial sphere. I am tracing this interloping affect back to the tautological and superficial self-representation of capital in the form of interest. That is to say, the problem is not located in the "real" of Victorian finance or political economy.[29] Neither are the shaky norms being undermined in the Barsetshire plot attributable to cultural patterns of untruth, irony, or desire ushered in by a dominant bourgeois ideology.[30] The disruptions to moral coherence in this novel are emitted from the financial sphere, as also in Trollope's *The Way We Live Now*, but (owing to their displacement) without any longer being identifiable in directly moral terms. The target is not the bad behavior of the tarnished London set; rather, it is the tautological and unnarratable form of financial capital itself.[31]

❦

Interest-bearing capital is capital at its most static and self-enclosed. The interest rate is a form of magical thinking, quantifying an apparently unmediated yet self-expanding relationship of money to itself. Unlike the drama of speculation depicted in *The Way We Live Now*, the automatic return of interest is unusable as a plot. It allows no grip for the authority of social responsiveness, which is Trollope's primary concern. There is no social space relative to interest from which to countenance its arbitrariness or supply subjective differentiation to its workings. It is as if Trollope, who from one end of his work to the other is mining the difference between implicit and explicit commitments, can only address the deficiencies of interest when translated into his preferred arena.

By moving the opacity of interest to the Crawley plot where it can only be misrecognized, Trollope effectively defamiliarizes finance capital. Its atemporality and blankness manifest as an uncanny disturbance within provincial mores. Torn away from its natural environment, the cognition that is "at home" in finance capital just feels unaccountably wrong. Trollope's strategy here is a more prosaic version of the estrangement effect Jonathan Swift employs in *Gulliver's Travels*. Swift has Gulliver explain English jurisprudence to the Houyhnhnms. Detached from Gulliver's lifeworld and related as a piece of ethnographic description to a master race of horses, the venerable and unquestioned traditions in English law sound like detestable unreason. Just so, the gaps in causality and the automatic, inscrutable character of interest-bearing capital that belong to the giddy rush of the money market as its natural element are felt as unease, low-grade panic, and dissonance only when imported into Barsetshire—where they cannot be directly interpreted or resolved.

Trollope's procedure in *The Last Chronicle* therefore stands in contrast to *The Way We Live Now*, where a recognition scene directly unmasks the financier Augustus Melmotte as a criminal charlatan, exposing the false center of a gigantic web of credit. When Melmotte takes cyanide to evade the consequences of his frauds, it is brought home to readers that the way we live now is by colossal self-deception, misplaced trust, suspended principles, and collectively mediated (but erroneous) belief. All of these modes of social credit rest on Melmotte's adept running of his confidence game, so long as he can keep it up. When he is toppled, the social performance is discovered to have been without substantial basis. The topos of financial speculation itself concentrates and heightens the moral corrosiveness of modern life lived as an insincere, inauthentic performance. In *The Way We Live Now*, Trollope levels this charge at speculative capital in propria persona, not by a displaced logic.

In *The Last Chronicle*, financial capital is also seen to be a wrong basis for social norms and accountability. But here that basis is hidden, unconscious. The Proudies, the Robartses, the Dales, all of our friends—none of them understand their own commitments as having anything to do with financial capital. The anxiety blurring their accustomed form of life is displaced from the superficial, empty, and arbitrary workings of interest-bearing capital. This blanket of obscurity is not precisely locatable but ambient, like the waste fallen over the land in the Grail legend. Consequently, no recognition scene or dosage of cyanide can directly expose its hollow basis, this sudden loss of the community's grip on its norms.

The mystery over the stolen check carries over to the ecclesiastical realm what is without content, arbitrary, and causally stalled in the financial sphere, under the affective haze of anxiety. Just as, in biblical source criticism, scholars frequently posit some lost original text as the underlying basis of the documents that have come down to us, so the anxiety belonging to the novel's financial dealings has to be posited as once located there, but now missing. Consequently, the novel's financial subplot does not itself manifest this anxiety. Because the affect pertaining to finance has been distributed elsewhere, where we would expect to find anxiety—amid the, as it were, hands-on dealings with fluctuating interest and risky rates of return—we find instead lucidity and brisk comprehension.

The financial subplot is only very tangentially connected to the mystery of Mr. Crawley and the stolen check. We first meet the social set of Dobbs Broughton, Mrs. Van Siever, and Mr. Musselboro through John Eames (introduced in *The Small House at Allington*). Eames is dispatched about halfway through the novel on an embassy to Florence to ask Mrs. Arabin about the money given to Crawley, but otherwise they are entirely separate plots. Besides Eames, Trollope brings into this plot a further character from *Small House*, Eames's rival Adolphus Crosbie, who is involved in a debt with the firm of Broughton and Musselboro. The plot climaxes in Broughton committing suicide, owing to excessive drinking and to being pushed out of the firm by the silent partner, Mrs. Van Siever, who intends Musselboro to take over the business and marry her daughter. The financial dealings in question are stock trading on account, buying and renewing bills (debts), and borrowing at low rates to lend at exorbitant ones. Their earnings are frankly regarded by Broughton and Musselboro as "dirty money" (375).

Now, readers of *The Last Chronicle* may object, contrary to what I am asserting, that there is actually a great deal of anxiety hovering over this plot. First, there is considerable difficulty for certain characters, not initiated in the secrets of finance, in discovering how precisely money functions in the City. When Crosbie goes to renew his bill at Broughton and Musselboro's offices, he feels sitting there that he does "not quite understand the manner in which the affairs of the establishment were worked" (441). The exact disposition of his obligations escapes him once they become matters of financialized debt: "Though he knew a good deal of affairs in general, he did not quite know what would happen to him if his bill should be dishonored . . . He did not know what his creditors would immediately have the power of doing" (447). And Mrs. Dobbs Broughton is equally mystified when it comes to her husband's affairs: "She had never understood much about the City, being satisfied with an assurance that had come to her in early days from her friends, that there was a mine of wealth in Hook Court" (534). Second, there is a recurrent discussion of "risk," "uncertainty," "speculation," "chancy" money, and an impending "smash." We hear that "City money is always very chancy," that for "City people . . . risk is every thing," since "they are always living in the crater of a volcano" (259, 399). These concerns would seem to be borne out by the catastrophic fate of Dobbs Broughton.

As to the first point, whatever the discomfort and ignorance of Crosbie and Mrs. Broughton, it stops at the door of the inner office. Once the threshold of business is crossed, everything unfolds in the precise language of "the three per cents," the tightness of the "money-market," how "the best commercial bills going can't be done for under nine," and so on (375, 441, 438). Broughton is "very candid" in telling Crosbie how he proposes to take advantage of Crosbie's present need for funds (439). When the silent partner Mrs. Van Siever comes to Broughton and Musselboro's offices, she is in no doubt as to how things work there, however much Crosbie may be. When Musselboro, declining to remit the payment due her, condescendingly informs Mrs. Van Siever of the workings of credit, she is not at all cowed or put off.

> "And as to not cashing up, you must remember, Mrs. Van Siever, that ten per cent. won't come in quite as regularly as four or five. When you go for high interest, there must be hitches here and there. There must, indeed, Mrs. Van Siever."
>
> "I know all about it." (381)

Trollope apparently concurs that this correlation of higher interest and higher risk is as calculable and rational as Mrs. Van Siever considers it. Risk is to that degree orderly and manageable. Outside of the office, characters who are excluded from this professional knowledge scratch their heads. But Mrs. Van Siever's "I know all about it'" stands above the entryway to the City like a Dantean inscription. Inside, everything proceeds like clockwork.

As to the second point, it is easy to forget, with so much else to keep track of in the novel, that all of the talk about dangerous and uncertain financial risk cited above comes from only one character, the far from trustworthy Madalina Demolines. These remarks belong to the delineation of her character, rather than representing a neutral judgment. They are not Trollope's view, and possibly not even her own view. The idea that City people are living on a volcano of risk is only giving voice to Miss Demolines's vendetta against her erstwhile friend, Mrs. Dobbs Broughton (née Maria Clutterbuck). They are the jabs of a spurned rival. Other characters do not share this anxiety about risk. John Eames, by far the more level-headed character, is apt to answer Miss Demolines's gossip with anodyne remarks such as, "Life is always uncertain, Miss Demolines," or, "I think that's the same with all money" (259). We have already seen that Mrs. Van Siever, however predatory and treacherous she may be, does not see risk as risky, but rather as predictable and already built into the calculation of expected returns.

When the small-time financier Dobbs Broughton suffers a precipitous fall, "is ruined," and commits suicide (644), the reader may expect the novel to take up the criticism of speculation, panic, and fraud introduced by the suicides of Mr. Merdle in *Little Dorrit* and Mr. Melmotte in *The Way We Live Now*. In other words, one anticipates that similar anxiety will now grip the novel's financial zone. This does not happen. Broughton's ruin is instead chalked up to his personal failings—"rather through the effects of drink than because of his losses"—and his having "fallen lately altogether into the hands of Musselboro, who . . . was backed by the money of Mrs. Van Siever" (714). When it comes to judgments of financial involvements in *The Last Chronicle*, Trollope applies a moral standard rather than a systemic one. If debt is seen to be risky, that is because it is corrupting and contagious. Broughton is ruined not because of an anxious stock market, but because he has morally (in a favorite phrase of Trollope's) "touched pitch." We find the same moralizing about debt in *Framley Parsonage*, concerning Mr. Sowerby, but without any recourse to finance or speculation. In *The Last Chronicle*, then, risk is not represented as a systemic dimension of interest-bearing capital or the outright usury practiced therein. There is no sense of risk in the modern economic sense, as a reflex of market instability.

The interest rate (the profit on money loaned out as capital) is only one of several very specific rates of return tabulated in the novel. When Archdeacon Grantly is lecturing his son about the importance of owning land, he remarks, "It is astonishing how land has risen in value . . . and yet rents are not so very much higher. They who buy land now can't have above two-and-a-half for their money" (623). Meanwhile, Dobbs Broughton "rais[es] money on his own credit at four or five per cent., and lend[s] it on his own judgment at eight or nine"—on commission (439). The owner of the firm, Mrs. Van Siever, "draw[s] close upon two thousand a year for less than eighteen thousand pounds" of principal, more than an 11 percent return (377). The most concise formulation of all is Mr. Butterwell's statement of the going interest rate to Crosbie: "Money's about seven now" (453).

If we disregard the ideological value Trollope attaches to landed wealth, rent (profit on land) is manifestly a worse application of capital than interest (profit on money), by several percentage points. But whereas rent has an obvious source in agricultural labor, interest appears to return its 7 percent like clock-work on its own, as if money has this rate built into it somehow. When someone says, "Money's about seven now," what we are hearing is not just the quote of the going interest rate, but also the voice of capital in its most abstracted form.

In chapter 24 of volume 3 of *Capital*, Marx analyzes the *apparent* workings of interest, as distinct from its arcane inner determinations by the rate of profit and the composition of capital. He is not decoding interest's social hieroglyphic here. Marx is describing interest in a phenomenological manner, as the "super-ficial and fetishized form" in which "capital presents itself."[32] This is why his analysis lines up with Trollope's presentation. Trollope is also talking about how interest spontaneously appears to work. Neither Marx nor Trollope is un-veiling any esoteric underlying structure.

In interest-bearing capital, all traces of capital "as the product of a social *rela-tion*" vanish. Interest-bearing capital is "money that produces more money, self-valorizing value, without the process that mediates the two extremes." The process-character of capital—the dialectic between capital and labor, and the staggered moments of its realization—"is obliterated in . . . the form of interest-bearing capital." While other forms of capital at least exhibit the social move-ment of capital insofar as they present profit as arising from circulation, in interest-bearing capital, the return on capital appears as having no need of inter-mediary: interest is "a ratio between the principal as a given value, and itself as self-valorizing value, as a principal that has produced a surplus-value."[33]

In Marx's famous discussion of commodity fetishism in chapter 1 of volume 1 of *Capital*, value that is socially constituted appears as an innate property of commodities in their own social character. Here in volume 3, he shows how this fetishism extends to the apparent capacity of capital to throw off surplus-value. Interest-bearing capital manifests "as a mysterious and self-creating source of interest, of [capital's] own increase . . . The result of the overall reproduction process appears as a property devolving on a thing in itself." Interest appears as an "automatic fetish . . . elaborated into its pure form, self-valorizing value, money breeding money, [which] in this form . . . no longer bears any marks of its origin. The social relation is consummated in the relationship of a thing, money, to itself." Because interest seems totally unrelated to the application of capital as capital (the necessity to purchase means of production, etc.), the "capital fetish is now complete," and we are dealing with "the misrepresentation and objectification of the relations of production, in its highest power . . . the capital mystification in the most flagrant form."[34]

The vital piece Trollope's conservative criticism of finance capital is that, as Marx puts it, "the source of profit is no longer recognizable," and the "distinctions" of capital's components "are obliterated."[35] Trollope's conservative ideology contrasts this empty form (associated with "City money") with the grounding of values in land and established hierarchies (associated with Barsetshire). He wants to differentiate forms of surplus-value as forms of personal self-definition and social relationship. For instance, because the 2.5 percent return on land is underwhelming, Archdeacon Grantly makes the case for landed wealth to his son in broadly ideological terms: landed wealth "is the only thing that can't fly away"; "land gives so much more than the rent," such as "position and influence and political power, to say nothing of the game"; and so on (623–24). But capital as "Money" consists only of a tautological relationship to itself (M-M′). When one has stated the rate of interest, a "meaningless abbreviation," there is nothing more to be said about it.[36] The return of interest lacks the texture of specification, social positionality, justification, implicit and explicit commitments, and meandering analytical discrimination that is the stuff of Trollope's fiction. Because interest is a self-identical, mirroring relationship, no other appeal, reference, or external nomination is available to thicken it experientially. Interest presents itself in the same terms that Satan claims for himself in *Paradise Lost*: "self-begot, self-raised."[37]

Trollope's negative view of interest-bearing capital aligns with Marx's up to a point. (It is not meaningful but only a "fun fact" that *The Last Chronicle* was published the same year as the first volume of *Capital*.) Both Marx and Trollope see interest as superficial and tautological, a form that leaves out the most important content. They part ways when it comes to specifying that content. For Marx, the conversion of capital into "this particular commodity," money, reifies the enormous cycle of reproduction (production, class struggle, the market, crises, the worldwide project of Victorian imperialism).[38] Trollope, however, sees nothing of this material itinerary of capital, and does not critique interest in terms of repression or concealed content. For Trollope, anxiety around interest stems not from what is repressed in the material genesis of capital but from what is missing in the dimension of social responsiveness.

Since interest is a relation of money to itself, one does not inhabit interest-bearing capital as a form of life. One can only stand in inert proximity to it. This contrasts with landed wealth, which posits a tangle of titles, rights, obligations, histories, and ideologies, along with the mode of income. Interest-bearing capital, which shows up only under the curtailed aspect of a tautology, leaves out the exhaustive parsing of social forms—their codes, their habitus, their flexibility—which is paramount for Trollope. There is no room for compromise, disappointment, settling, woundedness, or concessions. There are no rules, dispositions, social adjustments, or different sides to take up when it comes to the interest rate. However we comport ourselves toward interest will be as incoherent and unintelligible as any other approach. Nor could any such comportment vis-à-vis interest be integrated into the rest of what we know about ourselves and the history of our social and self-relations. One has to rest content with being in thrall to an arbitrary, capricious power. For interest reduces the ceaseless outflanking determination of value by capital's real interactions to a tautological explanation: the rate varies because of variations in the rate. But love is not love which alters when it alteration finds, and the volatility of the market is destined to be swallowed up in the tautology of the interest formula, since money just "is" whatever the rate says.[39]

The point here is to consider the phenomenology of this form of capital in plot terms:

1. Interest as a form of income or profit is "the superficial form of the return, separated off from the mediating circuit."[40] Interest-bearing capital does not appear as having gone on a long journey through many divested forms of purchase and consumption. The increase on the principal never has to leave home; it just shows up in the bank account without exertion. For Trollope, this means that the tautology of "Money" resides in isolation from those social practices and norms that contextualize and justify forms of value, relating only to itself. In Money, there is no subjectivity-like narrative detour through otherness.

2. The interest rate itself ("Money is about seven now") is a kind of magical incantation, not open to view, but dependent on the arcane and inscrutable divinations of a caste of speculative priests and usurers. The rate is determined from somewhere outside the self-relation of Money, supplied more or less arbitrarily, as if by an oracle.

3. Interest is static, plotless. Watching interest accrue is like watching paint dry. Whereas the money-form of capital (disposable for investment) makes up only "an evanescent moment . . . of mere transition" within a dialectical process, in the case of interest capital is kept in an unchanging state, trapped in "continuing existence as money."[41] For Trollope, the indistinctness of interest as a social form means there is no conflict, nothing like the acrimonious wars of position that

structure time elsewhere in his novels. Interest is boring—because it allows no foothold for contrary alignments, the parsing of social motives, or the momentary advantages of tactical struggle.

4. Interest appears to be a self-contained fount of profit, not derived from the toil and materiality of production and the market, but rather spawning from its own greenhouse fecundity. Its outcome appears self-generated, having nothing to do with industry, labor, exploitation, the vicissitudes of realization, and so on. Interest is "a form in which the source of profit is no longer recognizable, and in which the result of the capitalist production process—separate from the process itself—obtains an autonomous existence."[42]

If we understand (with some help from Marx) interest-bearing capital as narrative form, as a particularly isolated, arbitrary, static, and self-referential "plot," we are set up to trace the anxiety of the main Barsetshire story back to the London financial setting because the temporal structure of the check mystery (itself isolated, arbitrary, static, and self-referential) rehearses the phenomenology of the interest rate. The inordinately prolonged ramifications concerning the (mislaid or stolen) check repeat the superficiality of interest-bearing capital and its absence of internal subjective mediation and difference.

When we last left the progress of the check mystery, the inquiry into the stolen check had settled into a consensus among the community that Crawley probably did take it, but under so much duress that he did not know what he was doing. After Crawley's initial error in asserting the check to have been paid to him by Mr. Soames, the only explanation he feebly offers is that "he still believed that the money had come to him from the dean" (13). Although Dean Arabin refutes this explanation, Crawley persists in saying that the check had somehow been included with Arabin's gift. No new account is put forward after that, and so the case does not advance toward resolution for several hundred pages. Then, when John Eames seeks out Mrs. Arabin in Florence, she drops the following bombshell: "I gave him the check, you know" (757). This is the novel's recognition scene.

What had happened is that Mrs. Arabin received the stolen check as part of a rent payment for a property, The Dragon of Wantly (an inn), and slipped it into the envelope her husband gave to Reverend Crawley, as if it were so much cash.

The history of the gift of the check was very simple. It has been told how Mr. Crawley in his distress had called upon his old friend at the deanery

asking for pecuniary assistance . . . Previously to Mr. Crawley's arrival at
the deanery this matter had been discussed between the dean and his
wife, and it had been agreed between them that a sum of fifty pounds
should be given. It should be given by Mrs. Arabin [i.e., it is her money],
but it was thought that the gift would come with more comfort to the
recipient from the hands of his old friend . . . At last it was agreed that
the notes should be put into an envelope, which envelope the dean should
have ready with him. But when the moment came the dean did not have
the envelope ready . . . And then Mrs. Arabin explained to John Eames
that even she had not had it ready, and had been forced to go to her own
desk to fetch it. Then, at the last moment, with the desire of increasing
the good to be done to people who were so terribly in want, she put the
check for twenty-pounds, which was in her possession as money of her
own, along with the notes, and in this way the check had been given by
the dean to Mr. Crawley. (758–59)

This sudden unraveling nullifies the tumult and conjecture that has built up
around the supposed theft of the check for hundreds of pages. The solution is
the most banal one imaginable: just as Crawley maintained, the check was simply given to him. To be sure, some further complications are required in order
that the misrecognition take hold, such as how the check was stolen and why it
was not deposited by Mrs. Arabin. But the massive plot scaffolding that is built
up around the inciting incident is just that—scaffolding, utterly external to
Crawley's agonized reflections. The other pieces of the misrecognition do not
tell us anything about his self-accounting, for the good reason that he has nothing to revise. The recognition scene therefore does not illuminate a course of
subterranean mediations of subjectivity. The temporality of the reconstruction
now put forward recapitulates, in the dimension of plot, the fetishistic features
of the interest rate outlined above. When we come to the solution at long last,
we find that it has been cut off from development, catalyzed by arbitrary material, stalled out, and remains ultimately self-referential. Now to take these aspects in turn.

1. Just as the form of return on interest occurs as if there is no dialectic or
   detour, as if "separated off from the mediating circuit," so the discovery
   of Crawley's innocence shows that the real solution has been sitting in
   the same place, unmoved from its first enunciation. The true explanation
   is already present from the first pages, if Crawley's words were only read
   correctly.[43] This is what Crawley has maintained in some form all along.
   He does not depart from his insistence that "the check had been with" or

been "found . . . with" the dean's money (82, 326). The trouble for him is
that when the lawyer Mr. Walker inquires of Arabin, he curtly replies
that he had given Crawley fifty pounds in Bank of England notes. This is
taken as disproving Crawley's account.[44] But while Crawley is technically
accurate, his words are susceptible of a double meaning. This is a case
where the solution turns on a kind of pun—a feature which Viktor
Shklovsky points out in the construction of mystery stories.[45] In saying
that the money had *come to him* (indirectly) from Arabin, and that the
check was *with* (not part of) Arabin's gift, Crawley does literally indicate
what really happened, but through an impossibly subtle distinction that is
open to apparent refutation by Arabin's recollection. Misrecognition here
is rooted in an elaborate concatenation of meanings gone awry.

2. We saw above that the interest rate cannot be extrapolated from the
form itself but has to be imported from somewhere outside the
self-relation of "Money"—in other words, arbitrarily activated by
outside material. So too with the recognition scene in *The Last Chronicle*. Although Crawley is telling the truth, that the check was passed to
him on top of the bank notes from Arabin, he cannot account for how
a stolen check could have gotten mixed up in the dean's money. To
solve the puzzle, one needs to connect Mrs. Arabin to the Dragon of
Wantly, where the check was first lost.[46] Without such a connection,
neither reader nor characters can make any headway. But the missing
clue is available, outside the novel, in a minuscule detail in *The Warden*,
published twelve years earlier. The Dragon of Wantly appears in a very
brief listing of the property of Mrs. Arabin's first husband, John Bold.
That is the last we hear about who owns the inn for five books and
several thousand pages. Then, in *The Last Chronicle*, this long-forgotten
detail crops up as the crux of the entire protracted mystery. For
Mrs. Arabin "had taken the check as part of the rent due to her from
the landlord [Dan Stringer] of 'The Dragon of Wantly,' which inn was
her property, having been the property of her first husband" (759).
What had seemed in *The Warden* to be merely realist notation—and
there is so much of this in Trollope that one would hardly register any
specific enumeration of property—turns out to be a vital clue, several
books later. But the Dragon of Wantly and its disposition by John
Bold's will do not take on any new significance here. They are not
retrospectively enriched. The inn's appearance in *The Warden* was not a
clue pointing to its later decoding. To solve the mystery in *The Last
Chronicle*, we have only to recall, not to revise. The solution is dragged
in from the outside, an arbitrary point with no meaning in itself.

3. We also saw that interest itself is static—plotless, so to speak. In the Crawley plot, too, there has been no movement on the side of the mystery all along; it remains stationary after its initial statement up until the recognition scene. Even before it concludes, the check mystery has exhausted itself, has gone out with a whimper. What really happened is no longer a pressing question, and the parties involved have moved on. Trollope is parachuting a solution into a mystery that has not so much concluded as simply exhausted itself. It has been superseded as a concern. When Mrs. Arabin tells John Eames that she gave Mr. Crawley the disputed check, Trollope is not bestowing the final touch on a complex retrospective assembly of events. Eames's journey to Florence has as much to do with proving himself, with escaping his hobbledehoy-hood, as with a conviction of Crawley's innocence. There has been no continued accumulation of clues after the opening chapters.[47] Trollope has apparently dropped the mystery, as a child would neglect an old toy. Archdeacon Grantly, after much resistance to his son marrying Craw-ley's daughter Grace, decides that he will not regard the matter of the theft as a mystery or even a topic of concern: "Could he desire in his heart that Mr. Crawley should be found guilty? . . . If it might be possible he would have no wish on the subject whatsoever" (615). Crawley ceases even to defend himself, reckoning that "in accordance with all law and all reason he must be regarded as a thief" (662). He resolves to submit to Bishop Proudie without further protest, since the tide of public opinion has turned against him.

4. When we come to the consequences of the recognition scene, the fallout of Reverend Crawley being cleared of the theft is surprisingly self-contained. Just as interest-bearing capital appears to be discretely cordoned off from the actual production process, kept at a remove from the vicissitudes and contradictions of capital in its circuit of externaliza-tion and realization, so the recognition scene does not stitch together or accomplish a formal unity between disparate parts of the plot. Although the question about the check had allowed Trollope to bring in numerous other narrative strands (e.g., to redeploy Mark Robarts, the main character of *Framley Parsonage*), when the solution does arrive, the parties involved have already moved on. Crawley has already resigned his parish. Very little hinges on the unveiling of the real history of the check.

The novel's recognition scene, in its very stiltedness and minimal circuit, does unveil a concealed, secret origin lurking behind the check plot. But this disclosure is not the expected discovery of how the stolen rent check was passed along into Mr. Crawley's possession. For the novel's recognition scene terminates, but only minimally resolves, the mystery concerning the mislaid check. It is pointedly anticlimactic. Crawley is found innocent, but he declines to take his subjective bearings from the resolution of the check plot. His self-determination is not put on hold until his innocence has been unveiled, since he removes himself beforehand, withdrawing his subjectivity from this particular hermeneutic sequence.

The secret, the hidden origin, disclosed by the recognition scene is rather how the flimsy plotting inherent to interest-bearing capital is at the root of the anxiety besetting Barsetshire. The unmediated, arbitrary, static, and self-contained aspects of the recognition scene show the financial origin of the anxiety that has crossed over from the City subplot and attached itself to the check mystery. Anxiety by definition is intrusive and unplaceable. The anxious feeling of being deracinated and untethered has itself become uprooted and untethered from the social form of interest.

The recognition scene in *The Last Chronicle* is therefore not a case of pulling a rabbit out of a hat, supplying a lack defined in advance. It is instead a case of misdirection. We expect a rabbit (the confiscated check), but in our concentration on the hat, the real trick is that our watch and chain have been lifted meanwhile. For the overarching misrecognition in the novel concerns not the check but the anxiety displaced from financial interest. The misdirection does not depend on the content of what is in the hat (rabbit or dove or handkerchief) but on the form, the technique of the sleight of hand. Trollope's conservative critique of capital involves tracing back, via the plot mechanics, the anxiety belonging to its fetishistic presentation as a detached and mobile deformation of bourgeois norms. Contaminated with the arbitrariness of capital, the structures of accountability in legal and ecclesiastical life lose grip on their accustomed authority, so that institutional actors know not what they do.

Capital, to be sure, is not *only* the imposture of a set of (value-determined) material relations in the guise of (free, bourgeois) social relations. But with the odyssey of financial anxiety away from its homeland in *The Last Chronicle*, Trollope plots out that imposture. The very terms of social responsiveness, such as a tacit accord about how things work, get swept up unawares in the derivative structures of financial tautology. Although provincial characters like Mark Robarts, Anne Prettyman, Bishop Proudie, and Henry Grantly take their balked understanding as their own spontaneous responses, the affect of these scenes better matches the arbitrariness and emptiness of commitments and orientations available in a life premised on automatic returns. The recognition scene is an aha moment, not because it settles anything about Crawley, but because it points us to capital's plot hole as the hidden cause of this anxiety.

Trollope does not subject capital itself to an unmasking of its inner workings. The novel does not trespass into the "hidden abode of production," exposing the material basis of surplus-value mystified in the interest-form. Although Trollope laments interest-bearing capital as an ungrounded and unaccountable mode of value, he still grants that interest is as automatic as it appears to be. He imagines that the interest-form of capital, at least, really has nothing going on underneath its sham accumulation. The check plot of *The Last Chronicle* rests on a presumption about the indiscernible origins of money: "A man isn't bound to show where he got his money" (409). Currency is, as it were, anonymous, untraceable. The problem in Crawley's case is that "It is presumed that a man can account for the possession of a check" (409). On my reading, Trollope is in effect raising a question about the unaccountable profit of financial capital. The owner of interest-bearing capital also cannot show where he got his money. Trollope details the large-scale incoherence and arbitrariness that result. But he only deems this to be problematic from the point of view of normative social accounting, as a departure from "positive" forms of income (like inherited land) whose origins are out in the open. His critique does not go further to expose the origin of interest in the real movement of capital, that is, its application in commodity production. He therefore does not interrogate capital as concealing its constitutive social relations.

Trollope does not pose capital accumulation as a mystery in itself, as Charles Dickens had in *Little Dorrit* (even if Dickens declined to fill in that mystery). For Trollope does not see capital as *having* a secret. In an important respect, however, Trollope's conservative critique of capital is more penetrating and negative than that of Dickens, the liberal reformer. For Dickens, any confusion of subjectivity with capital is a sort of category error; the two registers are totally incompatible. But in *The Last Chronicle*, the basic structuring misrecognition is precisely that of mistaking capital's tautologies, the "plot hole" of accumulation, for subjectivity's own temporality. Unlike Dickens, for Trollope it is a real problem that capital could usurp the trappings of subjectivity and bleed over into the normative being of provincial life. But we also have to distinguish between Trollope and Marx. For the latter, "past labor always disguises itself as capital," that is, the value-form conceals the social origins of appropriation.[48] For Trollope, however, capital can only arrogate to itself an inoperative, stalled-out subjectivity, since the whole point is that it has none of its own.

❦

Critics have found the operations of subjectivity in Trollope to be peculiarly confined, as if his characters were somehow hermetically sealed up. Nathaniel

Hawthorne pictures their social space as quite literally bounded: "the novels of Anthony Trollope . . . [are] just as real as if some giant had hewn a great lump out of the earth and put it under a glass case, with all its inhabitants going about their daily business, and not suspecting that they were being made a show of."[49] Modern critics have updated and refined Hawthorne's fanciful image, but have retained the sense that Trollope's people are as if enclosed or intensely circumscribed.[50]

I am claiming something quite different about *The Last Chronicle.* Subjectivity in this novel is intersected and deformed by an anxiety coming from *outside*, from the experience of interest-bearing capital. As we have seen, there is a crisis in the authority of Barsetshire's norms, commitments, and practices, that is, a breakdown of what counts implicitly or explicitly in the giving and taking of public reasons. This breakdown affects the possibilities for characters to take themselves to be doing one thing and not another, how they know that, and why. All of this becomes considerably fraught. I have traced this displaced anxiety to the social unresponsiveness and the stunted temporality of finance capital in the novel.

Furthermore, Crawley's own subjectivity, how he comes to interpret his role in his own story—especially where past intent and comprehension cannot be grasped—is externally threatened by reification. I mean that his self-understanding is in danger of being reduced to the itinerary of the lost or stolen check. The stand-in for his subjectivity might be this inanimate thing, unable to speak itself. On that basis, whatever conclusion he would come to about his moral being would be decided for him by the brute evidence (a smoking gun) of how he came into possession of the check. Standing in place of a deliberative grappling with the lacunae of Crawley's self-accounting, retracing the convolutions of his inner life, there would simply be the bare positivity of the check, an economic instrument.

Since that evidence does ultimately vindicate him, however, what is the real harm of referring his own truth over to whatever facts emerge about the check? Just this, that the narrative structure of this exculpatory recognition scene is not modeled on the revisions and temporality of subjectivity but rather on the immaterial, deracinated time of finance. By the time Crawley is shown to be innocent, he has already declined to take his image of himself from the distorted mirror of the novel's "awful plot." When Crawley resigns his living at Hogglestock, he is spurning the novel's hermeneutic closure in advance. The revelations of the novel's recognition scene turn out to be irrelevant to Crawley's self-determined revisions of his character and history. The authority for his eventual self-understanding does not depend on, and is resolved outside of, the reconstruction made available by the recognition scene.

The turning point for Crawley is not the admission by Mrs. Arabin, but instead when he is struck by the words of the Hoggle End brickmaker Giles Hoggett: "It's dogged as does it" (666). Crawley translates this into his own terms, such that "doggedness simply meant self-abnegation" (667). Having been summoned by Dr. Tempest to a meeting where he would be called upon to accept that the verdict of the coming legal trial by jury would also settle the ecclesiastical question, Crawley now decides to go to Silverbridge a week early and resign on the spot. True to his character, Crawley is obstinate and peremptory even in his supposed self-abnegation. Tempest can hardly wrap his head around Crawley giving up the contest with the Proudies he has carried on, and stammers, "You mean in the event—in the event—." Crawley cuts in, "I mean, sir, to do this without reference to any event . . . I will not wait to be deprived by any court, by any bishop, or by any commission . . . I will deprive myself" (669). He goes on to say, "My decision has nothing to do with the jury's verdict," even though the jury would likely go easy on him, given his personal circumstances (670). As it turns out, he is cleared of the accusation before it ever comes to trial.

Nobody in the camp supporting Crawley can understand this. Dr. Tempest deems his resignation "an indulgence to your pride," and Mark Robarts says his resignation was "a little too much in a hurry" (672, 744). They wish to recruit him back into the perpetual struggle waged between the High and Low parties in the Church of England. Crawley has himself been a redoubtable pugilist in these battles. But now he is steadfast in holding back from the fray. Even his own daughter, Jane, laments that his successor in the Hogglestock pulpit, Mr. Thumble, is plainly incompetent. But Crawley will have none of it. He reprimands her, "Be critical of Euripides, if you must be critical" (753). This is an astonishing moment, because Thumble is only a toady and errand boy for Mrs. Proudie. Everyone in the novel condescends to him, and he is a magnet for humiliation. It is not easy even for a reader, myself, to let go of my contempt for Thumble, which had seemed to belong to the game being played. Crawley here is truly "dogged." If he can suppress his resentment and superiority toward Thumble, surely he can "endure anything that might be sent upon him, not only without outward grumbling, but also without grumbling inwardly" (667).

The important thing is that Crawley's submission and disengagement are accomplished on his own terms. As he has said earlier, "I cannot trust to any one,—in a matter of conscience" (211). So he does not entrust his conscience of guilt or innocence to the outcome of contests within the cathedral close—specifically, he does not change course after his party's supreme antagonist, Mrs. Proudie, dies. Nor does he leave it up to a jury to decide: "I care nothing now for the verdict" (671). When Crawley submits to Bishop Proudie, allowing Mr. Thumble to take the pulpit at Hogglestock, he is not conceding his guilt.

Indeed, once Crawley is known to be innocent of the theft, the assumption is that he will go back to the pulpit at Hogglestock—"as though nothing had happened," as Arabin puts it (841). But Crawley's "dogged" separation from the plot means he will not take direction from the changed circumstances. Crawley's response to Arabin is a masterpiece of captious quibbling. First, he could "hardly" resume his post "without the bishop's authority" (841). And then, "though it may certainly be in [Arabin's] power to nominate [him] again," it may be that this "patronage" belongs to Arabin "in rotation only" (841–42). In any event, Crawley "would [not] condescend to supplicate the bishop," but insists everything go through the most tortuous of proper channels (843). The usual mode of self-definition in Trollope is to "dig in." Character is elaborated primarily as a form of resistance. Crawley is doing something else here. He is marking an inner difference, not subject to verification by external proofs.

In other words, Crawley does not allow the plot to decide his moral fate. The original topic of how he came into possession of the check is left far behind. The self-abnegation he arrives at does not include any provision depending on the verdict at the assizes. Crawley is vindicated by the recognition scene only in an ironic sense. His ultimate non-identification with the mystery plot should be read as a rebuke to capital, as just such an illegitimate impersonation of subjectivity. Whereas Crawley withdraws from the hermeneutics of his own plot to settle his private interpretation and reconstruction of what he has done, no such revision is possible in the immediacy of finance. So, while Crawley accomplishes a profound subjective revision outside of the plot, interest itself is capable only of an anticlimactic, sham illumination. Crucially, for Crawley to be defined from outside of himself, by the plot outcome, would be to submit to the inert and tautological pseudo-subjectivity implied by capital. The recognition scene's unmediated and derivative structure and its substitution of spatial displacement for temporal illumination negatively confirm his resolution not to await that plot's outcome.

Given that the recognition scene demolishes nearly all of the attempts at explanation and justification occupying the provincial community, what remains usable after Crawley's nominal vindication within the plot? J. Hillis Miller argues that the community of Barsetshire survives *because* "Crawley did not steal the check."[51] In other words, the restoration at the end of the novel depends on the "blank spot" of Crawley's forgetfulness being filled in—everything previously jeopardized by his forgetfulness is thereby secured.[52] I am less optimistic (and I find Trollope less optimistic) that things can be cleared up, that subjectivity can be restored to a lost condition of "universal transparency."[53] My claim has been that the anxiety in the novel stems from a breakdown in the coherence of legal and ecclesiastical protocol—which are themselves shown to be obscure, mystifying, and contested. Since the mystery is resolved outside of those forums of institutional authority, it makes no sense to say that that authority and those norms are back on firm ground at the end of the book, even once Crawley's innocence is established. The threats to normativity are not decisively hurled back like the Huns at the Battle of Châlons. They are let off on a technicality. The recognition scene does not make the final determination on how Crawley grasps his moral position—but it does disclose how the normative criteria of the ecclesiastical and legal norms became as if possessed, bearers of an unconscious paralysis. Whatever is put back together on the grounds of Crawley's vindication in the mystery plot must remain suspect. Meanwhile, the workings of finance capital remain untouched by the exposure, in the recognition scene, of its (displaced) affective structure. Presumably capital is still emitting anxiety after the last page, totally unaffected by what is going on in Hogglestock. Its mystification is dispelled only in displaced form, in the Barsetshire plot. "City money," as a dubious (superficial) ground of value, is still unreformed—like a master villain whose associates have been nabbed but who remains at large.

We have to take what we can get. Crawley at least has been able to exit from the determination of his subjectivity by the static form of the plot derived from capital. Trollope is committed to subjectivity as an outcome of difficulty and resistance, as against the empty quantitative progress displayed in the interest-form of accumulation. Selfhood is for Trollope a repeated negotiation with the available but insufficient public reasons for what is at last nonnegotiable, absolute for that character. This articulation of subjectivity is not readymade, as an available and articulated position. Rather, it has to be evinced or improvised in more or less awkward, painful, and humiliating social gestures—like a sort of existential game of charades. Subjectivity for Trollope is not an inner essence removed from the fray; it is an unceasing friction. Trollope thereby differentiates the renunciation and "doggedness" of Crawley, his kicking against the pricks, from the truncated and static temporality of interest. For Trollope, capitalist finance, as a social form that reiterates itself without ever thickening or differently inflecting its social meanings, is in every sense a bad plot.

CHAPTER 3

The Fetishism of the Subject and Its Secret in *The Portrait of a Lady*

Henry James's fiction seems to be at a pretty safe distance from Marx's critique of capital. At least with the other Victorian authors I write about here—Charles Dickens, Anthony Trollope, and Arthur Conan Doyle—one can see how they cast capitalists as villains, or how they configure their mysteries from the opacity of capitalist finance. Whatever else might be said about the depictions of proletarian labor found in *Hard Times* or *The Valley of Fear*, or the skepticism toward financial speculation evinced in *The Way We Live Now*, those books directly show capitalism at work. Capital functions there not as an agent but as a narrative "agency," in Kenneth Burke's sense: it is openly *wielded*.[1]

But in James's fiction, the dramas and intrigues effected by capital go on, as it were, elsewhere. It is as if a screen has been erected in front of all the operations of accumulation, shielding them from view. The point about the monopolistic industrial concern owned by the Newsomes in *The Ambassadors* is that James considers it to be non-narratable. Not only does he not specify the article manufactured, but we have a story at all only because Chad Newsome has left all that behind in America. Of course there is a great deal of money at issue in James's novels, but it is money that was formerly capital, and is no longer. Gilbert Osmond and Isabel Archer, in *The Portrait of a Lady*, agree on only one thing, which is that her inheritance is to be spent (consumed), rather than set to work for further accumulation. Adam Verver, in *The Golden Bowl*, is buying museum pieces with his fortune, not further means of production. Before it can show up in the pages of James's fiction, capital has to withdraw from the realms of industry and finance, shedding its character as an element of production and reverting to a state of mere wealth.

Looking only at the content of his novels, then, James does not so much as represent capital. So what can he tell us about how capital works? Or how could he offer (as I believe he does) its most powerful novelistic critique? The answer is in the form of subjectivity that his fiction observes close-up. Jamesian subjectivity is built on a set of misrecognitions. His characters frequently take themselves to be autonomous and self-defined, possessed of an object-like finality. The misrecognitions are the deferrals, retreats, and obstructions by which such characters evade the indignities, crude usages, deprivations, and dependencies bound up in their origins. For instance, in the short stories "The Beast in the Jungle" and "The Jolly Corner," John Marcher and Spencer Brydon define themselves as exempt from the leaps and maimings of life—they are those who have *not* been ravaged by duration. They attempt to block out from view the history and materials from which their lives are made. Subjectivity in James is just this rending of itself from the conditions and contingencies of its own formation.

James's idea of a plot is the inevitable exposure of subjectivity's painfully suppressed unconscious determinations and its insertion in the degrading mediations of temporality. Hence, the importance for James of retrospective recognition scenes, where subjectivity is confronted with the history of its own involvements. Thus John Marcher confronts a blazing "illumination" laying bare "the sounded void of his life," so that the meaning of all that he had missed within life now "fell together, confessed, explained, overwhelmed."[2] And Spencer Brydon must see *himself*—not a "stranger . . . evil, odious, blatant, vulgar"—in the "grim" and "worn" specter that looms fantastically before him; he has to give up his conception of himself as standing for "the achieved, the enjoyed, the triumphant life."[3] These recognition scenes expose subjectivity as a self-separation: the subject, mistaken for an inborn autonomy, is only so constituted by dividing itself from the humiliating traces of temporality and life that produce it in the first place.

The Portrait of a Lady offers a kind of fable of how capitalist value effaces the role of subjectivity in its production, indeed how the divorce of value from its formation in the material life of capital occurs *through* subjectivity. When Isabel Archer comes into her half of Mr. Touchett's banking fortune, she is unaware of the strings being pulled backstage to arrange her "destiny." Her inheritance therefore appears to her as absolutely undetermined, not burdened by any trace of its origin in Ralph Touchett's intervention in his father's will. She interprets this money instead as an imperative to the future. It means the abstract potential to do, to act and move while remaining undefined. This also becomes her model of subjectivity. Like the value of the money bequeathed to her, her own purpose and fate are taken to be innate properties rather than effects of constraining social relations. Both value (the banking capital) and its corresponding model of subjectivity are thus divorced from the social process of their constitution. The recognition scenes at the climax of the novel bring home to Isabel how that value, and her own image of subjectivity derived from it, are deeply rooted in unseen manipulations. Subjectivity takes place within the formation of value, but the outcome of production covers up those origins, involvements, and dependencies.

What the plot reveals is how the unmarked, object-like form of Isabel's subjectivity is staged by the misrecognition of its underlying inversions and detours of agency, which are eliminated from view in the final output of her "self" and its "value." This is not just because the Jamesian subject is a kind of thing detached from its social and material origins, as many critics have noticed. Because Isabel does not perceive her tragic manipulation at the hands of Ralph Touchett, Gilbert Osmond, and Madame Merle—the concealed relations that establish her fortune—she innocently transfers the constituting dimension of those secret entanglements onto her inherited capital. The hidden operations behind "Isabel Archer" appear instead as an autonomy emanating from value itself. In other words, she mistakes her inherited capital as constituting (it is taken as freedom) rather than constituted (taken as manipulation).

Certainly, *The Portrait of a Lady* is not offering a critique of political economy. Nonetheless, across the book James plots the self-obscuring social process that lurks behind the fetishism of bourgeois appearances.[4] The novel's overriding concern is how bourgeois categories for representing the self are cut off from the social relations that yield those categories. In particular, the plot misrecognitions in *Portrait* construct (and the recognition scenes take apart) the fetishism of the subject, in the sense that Marx analyzes the fetishism of commodities in *Capital*.[5] I read the novel as making a sustained argument about what goes wrong when agency and value are read off from a finished possession—when subjectivity is understood as one material "appurtenance" among other "things," in Madame Merle's expression—rather than as temporally mediated by underlying, concealed social relations.[6] The plot carefully winds through the narrow defiles of misrecognition, leading both Isabel and the reader out of a fetishized conception of subjectivity.

By thus aligning the plotting of *The Portrait of a Lady* with Marx's critique of fetishism and reification, I am running afoul of the main body of Marxist scholarship on James. Marxist critics have been hostile to James on the grounds that he figures consciousness as protectively sealed off, organized as a spectacle entirely unto itself, blotting out anything outside of this self-reference.[7] If it were so, it was a grievous fault. But Isabel's tragedy is to be reified in the specifically Marxian sense: her subjectivity is itself the reified thing concealing the seething and crude relations that went into its formation but which have vanished in its immediacy. We are always hearing about what Isabel is metaphorically "worth," as if she were "some curious piece in an antiquary's collection," possessed of "incalculable value" (325, 349). The value thus ascribed to her will turn out to be, in Marx's formulation, "a relation between persons," but "a relation concealed beneath a material shell."[8] James even has his own version of this metaphor, in Madame Merle's remark that one's "shell" does not conceal but rather exhibits the fetishized self (207).

To be sure, it is a critical commonplace that Isabel is "reified" over the course of the novel, and even that she is complicit in her own objectification.[9] Jonathan Freedman identifies a "reifying vision" not only in Gilbert Osmond and Madame Merle, the villains, but also in Ralph Touchett, Isabel, and even James himself.[10] Ross Posnock also sees Isabel as complicit in her own reification; he blames this on her idealized, abstract conception of subjectivity.[11] "Reification" in these accounts refers to how Isabel exchanges an indeterminate, abstract freedom for the lacquered definiteness of being a rare acquired object among her husband's other fine things. But to pose Isabel's misfortune as a matter of her objectification comes with its own set of critical prescriptions and remedies. Reification is thus prepackaged along with its own supposed antidote: the recovery of "sympathy" and the acknowledgment of "otherness," which is to rejuvenate the passivity of enclosed subjectivity.[12] This recommendation of sympathy is surely edifying— but is that really what Isabel finds out about herself over the course of the book? What is left out of the picture is how reification proceeds through the intricate plotting of misrecognition, not by the exclusion of "otherness." As in Marx, reification means not just the conversion into objects, but the obscuring of relations under the form of objects. In the novel, Isabel is manipulated by concealed puppet strings. Her perspective, her subjectivity, is produced by others, but she takes it up as something self-given, an autonomy without any backstory.

My contention is that the novel, and especially its ending, cannot be understood without reference to its recognition scenes. But there has been a long-running critical rescue operation to save *The Portrait of a Lady* from the untidy confines of its Victorian context, especially from the awfulness of Victorian plots.[13] I want to drag it back into the muck. After all, its plot is fully as "awful"— lurid and contrived—as anything you will find in Victorian fiction. Ralph Touchett's design behind his father's will, making over half of his own fortune to Isabel without her knowing about his involvement, resuscitates one of the hoary tropes from *Bleak House*, *Felix Holt*, *Orley Farm*, and *The Woman in White*:

the forged or contested will, or its wrongful inheritance. The other secret in the novel, that Madame Merle is really Pansy Osmond's mother, while Mrs. Osmond's suspicious death in the Italian Alps (shades of *Udolpho!*) allowed the deception of a legitimate birth, is even more sensational.

Critics have deemed these revelations to be anticlimactic, mere confirmations arriving after the main event: untransmuted lumps of retrospection.[14] But if we want to see why Isabel goes back to Rome at the end of the book, there is no getting around them. For they are not only discoveries about what has been done *to* her. They pull back the curtain covering the social processes constitutive of her point of view. James identifies the problematic of the novel as "the business of placing" Isabel (8). The plot frames and determines her, however, by way of obstruction and blindness. The recognition scenes expose and dismantle the concealed social machinery and transactions determining the false immediacy of her "placement." The appalling disclosures resolve her privileged point of view into so many compounded blind spots. She is not "free." In the words of the Gospel, another has girded her and carried her whither she would not—and she took this for her freedom. What Isabel does at the end of the book makes sense only if we see it as a repetition of an earlier "placement"—a repetition and a revision of her "destined" perspective as misrecognized, covertly determined.

My reading focuses on three parts of the novel. First, I read James's 1908 preface to the New York Edition of *The Portrait of a Lady* as a disguised interpretation of the novel it introduces.[15] I set aside the way James styles the preface, partly as a recollection of writing the novel in Florence and Venice, partly as a justification of the morality of art in terms of "felt life" (7), partly as a post-Aristotelian account of character and plot, and partly as a renewed appreciation of James's own craft. Purportedly, the famous allegory of the "house of fiction" is about James's own artistic consciousness. But the imagery of observers "perched," each at a "pierced aperture," is (I am claiming) really a critical redescription of how Isabel is "placed" by the plot (7, 8). The house of fiction allegory thus announces, in disguised form, the apparatus of backstage scaffolding, pulleys, and backdrops that determine (but also vanish into) Isabel's fetishized subjectivity.

In the next section, I walk us through the sequence of insights, intimations, and regrets that Isabel arrives at on her own in the second part of the novel, in other words, how far she gets *without* the help of Merle and the Countess Gemini's extravagant confessions, so as to delineate what is then added by the novel's two successive recognition scenes. The novel itself does not provide an inventory of what Isabel keeps and what she discards from her picture of her life based on each of these episodes. Too many critics have tried to make sense of Isabel's resolutions at the very end of the book based on her shifting understanding prior to the recognition scenes, when she is substantially in the dark.[16] This is irresponsible. Whatever Isabel says *before* she finds out that her husband cheated in his first marriage and passed off another woman's child as his dead wife's is not very binding to her assessment of her marriage *after* finding this out. It just cannot be that what she has said beforehand still applies as if nothing had happened.

In the last part of the chapter, I reexamine, in light of the preceding recognition scenes, Isabel's decision to return to Rome on the last page of the book. I do not see Isabel as going back to Osmond, which is how most readers have seen the ending. Far from making any submission or renunciation, Isabel as I read her is going down into the "hidden abode" of unseen interference and stage-managing that produced her fetishized self-relation in the first place.[17] If she is at last "to wake from [the] long pernicious dream" of her misrecognitions and blindness, she can do so only by relocating her agency within the site where it was first forged, namely, the fallen world of "hideously unclean" materialist motives (508, 428). But she can take up a new relation toward the humiliation and wreckage of her own past, only from within those confines—not by retreating. Going ahead, nothing will count for her as taking up a different, unfetishized self-relation, other than locating her agency retrospectively within the ugly and maiming social relations that "made" her.

The allegory of "the house of fiction" in the preface to the New York Edition of *The Portrait of a Lady* stands as perhaps James's definitive statement on authorial consciousness.[18] By calling the house of fiction an allegory rather than a metaphor, I am already moving it away from aesthetic doctrine and into the realm of narrative as such. Notice that James introduces the house of fiction while describing how he came up with his protagonist, Isabel Archer, who is originally unhoused. She is at first only "the stray figure, the unattached character," of whom he was "so much more antecedently conscious . . . than of [her] setting" (6). The compositional problem is that characters cannot remain "still at large, not confined"; the author is in "the business of placing them" (8). The "house of fiction" passage arrives in the very middle of this discussion.

> The house of fiction has in short not one window, but a million—a number of possible windows not to be reckoned, rather; every one of which has been pierced, or is still pierceable, in its vast front, by the need of the individual vision and by the pressure of the individual will. These apertures, of dissimilar shape and size, hang so, all together, over the human

scene that we might have expected of them a greater sameness of report than we find. They are but windows at best, mere holes in a dead wall, disconnected, perched aloft; they are not hinged doors opening straight upon life. But they have this mark of their own that at each of them stands a figure with a pair of eyes, or at least with a field-glass, which forms, again and again, for observation, a unique instrument, insuring to the person making use of it an impression distinct from every other. He and his neighbors are watching the same show, but one seeing more where the other sees less, one seeing black where the other sees white, one seeing big where the other sees small, one seeing coarse where the other sees fine. And so on, and so on; there is fortunately no saying on what, for the particular pair of eyes, the window may *not* open; "fortunately" by reason, precisely, of this incalculability of range. (7–8)

James offers his own point-by-point decoding of the allegory: "The spreading field, the human scene, is the 'choice of subject,' while the pierced aperture . . . is the 'literary form'" (8). As James unravels the image, artistic consciousness projects *outward*. We begin from the pressing vision, and proceed to the literary form, and arrive at the choice of subject.[19] But the original description of the house, as a literal edifice, goes in the opposite direction—*inward*. In the image, the outside scene is the preexisting thing, which is seen through the window by a viewer who has been situated in advance.[20] This dialectic of determinacy prefigures the entire drama of the novel.

James relates an allegory of confinement, consciousness, and freedom whose most apparent predecessor is the allegory of the cave in Plato's *Republic*, book VII. But there are important points of difference. In Plato's cave, all of the prisoners are watching the same false or degraded pictures. It is possible to break from one's chains and to see how things really are, unmediated by illusion, but this involves leaving the cave. James's house of fiction overturns each of those features of Plato's allegory. For James, everyone is "watching the same show," but each has "an impression distinct from every other." And there is no moving around within the house or taking up a different view because every watcher is "posted." Finally, there are no "hinged doors opening straight upon life" since the house apparently has no exits or entrances.[21] One cannot escape the edifice and frolic among the Forms before reporting back to the other inmates. Everyone is stuck where they are, "disconnected." All the viewers are faced with the situation of a theatergoer who buys the cheapest tickets, discounted because of an obstructed view. It might seem then that James is assigning to each observer a sort of irrevocable fate in advance, because each is so fixed and isolated. But he does not say that the assigned perspective is a sort of trap; rather, he identifies the limitation with artistic form itself: to know what the viewer "has *been* conscious of" is to express "his boundless freedom" (8).

We have in the house of fiction allegory a résumé of Isabel's difficulties in the plot that James eventually furnishes his novel. Isabel does not see herself as falling prey to a conspiracy that circumscribes and restricts her—she does not see her perspective as being intensely determined and delimited, immovably situated at a "pierced aperture." She imagines just the opposite to be true. She conceives that she has a "hinged door opening straight upon life." Thus, when she informs her aunt that one "should have a point of view," it is with the implication that one could have a point of view *or not* (71). A point of view is something to pick up and then set down again with the fashion. She advocates instead for getting "a general impression of life," what we would call taking it all in (66). But the possibility of such unmediated access, of shuffling off the fetters of determinate consciousness, is just what James's allegory denies. For the pictorial impression of the "spreading field" set before the housed observer depends on an unseen constitutive barrier and distance that makes for the illusion of unmediated perspective. James is concerned in the plot as well as in the allegory with how consciousness encounters its determinateness as the very form of experience, not as a buckle that might be unlatched. Isabel's troubles really start here, in divorcing values (as external positivity) from the placement of subjectivity. She misrecognizes herself as unplaced, as being at large in a world where values can be read off things in their immediacy, as items in a "show"—such that freedom, too, can be located as a substantive property of her own self. In chapter 1 of *Capital*, Marx allows us to overhear commodities speak about how value belongs to them.[22] Isabel's speeches sound like if her vaunted independence could hold forth as an object, a commodity like linen or wool, about its intrinsic value.

What James presents as his compositional difficulty in the preface is therefore really a recapitulation of the novel's own plot. The story of Isabel Archer is made to mirror its own creative genesis. As he tells it, James began with "the character . . . of a particularly engaging young woman, to which . . . a setting [was] to need to be super-added" (4). Isabel is conceived independently of any "set of relations," with all the other novelistic parts sold separately (4). In the novel proper he makes no attempt to cover the tracks of its conception. He simply puts Isabel before us in all her unengaged possibility—an Albany girl waiting quietly in a room for something to happen to her—before promptly whisking her off to the international scene afoot at Gardencourt. "Placing" Isabel here means the attaching of relations, incidents, and setting. But in the narrative proper, Isabel precisely does not know when she has been *"placed"* within an environing *"architecture"* (5).

The dialogue in the novel proper produces a running commentary on this theme of placement or the absence of placement:

"We're mere parasites, crawling over the surface; we haven't our feet in the soil" (203).

"Everything's . . . a limit, a barrier, and a perfectly arbitrary one" (208).

"You can do exactly what you choose; you can roam through space." (307)

"I don't know why you call it caught."

"Because you're going to be put in a cage." (340)

"One must choose a corner and cultivate it." (340)

"You were not to come down so easily or so soon." (343)

"You talk about one's soaring and sailing, but if one marries at all one touches the earth." (346)

"But we're dreadfully fallen, I think . . . I think they ought to make [marriage] somehow not quite so awful a steel trap." (354)

So when does Isabel become definitely placed ("come down," "touch the earth")? When is she set at her pierced aperture? To borrow Ernest Hemingway's phrase from "The Killers," at what point does she "get in wrong"? Sooner than she thinks. But the novel is the record of Isabel's own shifting answer to this. We first encounter her as very much not placed, as the "not confined . . . apparition" of James's preface (8). Quite unlike the posted watchers in the house of fiction allegory, "she had no wish to look out" at the street outside her room in Albany (38). Later, she shows up at Gardencourt almost as a pair of disembodied eyes, like the ones staring out of the dark forest in Walt Disney's *Snow White and the Seven Dwarves*, "looking at everything, with an eye that denoted clear perception," and so "wide-eyed" that she "wished to check the sense of seeing too many things at once" (30, 45). She is at this point simply a vector of perception.

For her part, Isabel still considers that nothing has fixed or constrained her, and that this can be postponed indefinitely, until quite late in the book. Even once she has become engaged to Osmond, she still has the Miltonic feeling that "the world lay before her—she could do whatever she chose" (321). But, only a few pages after this, she is already speaking about her freedom in the past tense. She tells Caspar Goodwood, who is reproaching her for her choice, "I've not deceived you! I was perfectly free!" (330). As she now sees it, to stand behind and defend her engagement to Osmond, to avow her reasons, is to be determined, in every sense—placed. "The desire for unlimited expansion had been succeeded in her soul" (351). She has already "seen life," and now she can set aside "the act of . . . observing" (351). She considers that her observation until now has been unconstrained, not "placed." Furthermore, she assumes that the act of observing is a post that one can simply *resign*, as if—to return to the house of fiction allegory—one could simply step away from one's posted aperture.

But Isabel has been placed (and even "caught") long before this, by Ralph's orienting observation of her, and by his covert arrangement of her inheritance from his father, which sets her up as prey for fortune hunters. Not only that, but his direction of her destiny by his gift is misrecognized by Isabel as its opposite: as her own unbounded subjective freedom. Isabel is not simply unobservant or not attuned to the plot being laid around her. The misrecognitions that beset her could not have been avoided if she had just looked harder, or had better instruments, or had further tested out the appearances of things. Her misrecognition is rather a constitutive disjunction; it belongs to the way she takes up her subjectivity in the first place. In fetishizing her agency as unconditioned by social relations, as though Mr. Touchett's money were in some way "about" her own autonomy, she adopts an object-like view of herself, scrutinizing her capacities and obligations from the outside while unaware of the plot mechanisms that have brought them about.

On her arrival at Gardencourt, Isabel does not remain a mere pair of eyes, or a question mark, for long. She quickly comes under extensive observation by Ralph Touchett, who "surveyed" her like an "edifice from the outside" (75). The eventual irony, all told, is that her much-vaunted independence is constituted by the *concealment* of Ralph's gaze.[23] What Isabel thinks of as her unmoored free agency is an effect of being situated for viewing by Ralph Touchett. Isabel believes for most of the novel that her fate represents the promise (and failing) of an ideal and self-derived autonomy, but the recognition scene where Madame Merle gives away Ralph's secret resolves the ideal spectator of Isabel's life into this frail, dying, heartbroken man.

Early on, Ralph demurs to Henrietta Stackpole that his influence on Isabel is limited, because "I'm only Caliban; I'm not Prospero," to which she responds:

"You were Prospero enough to make her what she has become. You've acted on Isabel Archer since she came here, Mr. Touchett."

"I, my dear Miss Stackpole? Never in the world. Isabel Archer has acted on me—yes; she acts on every one. But I've been absolutely passive."

"You're too passive, then. You had better stir yourself and be careful. Isabel's changing every day; she's drifting away—right out to sea." (130)

Ralph, in being "too passive," and in observing Isabel, is paradoxically charged with having "acted on" her. What has happened is that, in "survey[ing]" and sneaking "glimpses" of Isabel, his vision has captivated and subordinated her own (70). Henrietta Stackpole detects the secret identity between the ungainly creature Caliban and the Duke of Milan who sets the whole spectacle in motion. Caliban is an object of disgust, a disturbance of the magical arrangement of the island, a deformity who makes an indecipherable streak across the field of vision. But however repudiated and spurned by the island's sovereign, he in reality stands in for Prospero's order, as the particular product of its logic. Caliban's obscene existence (indeed, his obscenity learned from Prospero) is a foul marker of Prospero's omniscience. Behind the hideous creature glower the enchanter's eyes.

The irony is that when Ralph does later play the Prospero figure, weaving Isabel's fate behind the scenes, incognito and through intermediaries, he makes a dreadful mess of the life he wants to enchant. "The direful spectacle of the wrack" of Isabel's life is all too real and, unlike in *The Tempest*, not a mirage. But Ralph is adamant that his story-function as a Proppian benefactor not appear as his own, that he not appear to be intently observing her. He persuades his father to give Isabel half of his inheritance, "without the slightest reference to [Ralph]" in the will to show that it was his idea. Even in obliging his son, Mr. Touchett remarks on the voyeuristic implications of the wish: "When I cared for a girl— when I was young—I wanted to do more than look at her" (191). But the consequence is really to conceal and disembody Ralph's surveillance of Isabel. Thus, the *seen* figure of Caliban gives way to the *all-seeing* Prospero.

Ralph's clandestine project of endowing Isabel with his father's money is misrecognized because it is reified in Marx's sense: the social relations behind value are concealed by value's form of appearance. Instead of Ralph giving Isabel her part of the money directly, as a lump sum labeled "from Ralph," the bequest from his father covers up Ralph's involvement, so that he may "see what she does with herself" without being seen to have paid steeply for that pleasure (190). He is the secret architect who "plan[s] out a high destiny" for Isabel without her knowing it, because the evidence of his intervention is wiped clean in the final version of his father's will (343). Isabel's inheritance comes before her with no (apparent) strings attached. Ralph's maneuvering is simply swallowed up in the bestowal of a fortune that bears no trace of its history.

After Ralph has directed Isabel's fate by making her a rich woman, he moves into the background, relishing the spectacle he has arranged for himself. He admits only that he knew about the will beforehand, not that it was his own suggestion (226–27). He no longer locks eyes with Isabel, or advertises his spectatorship, opting to proceed clandestinely: "when he appeared to be looking listlessly and awkwardly over her head, [he] was really dropping on her an intensity of observation" (289). Isabel of course does not see her autonomy as in any way an extension of her cousin's observation. She refuses to see anything to do with her "fate" in the quotidian person of Ralph, whose advice she shrugs off. Ralph's pleasure in tracking her suitors can only be felt as an unwelcome intrusion. When he slips up and tells Isabel that "I had treated myself to a charming vision of your future," she replies high-handedly, "I don't understand you in the least . . . Don't amuse yourself too much" (343).

Whereas the underlying arrangement between Ralph and his father is reified in a first misrecognition, Isabel then fetishizes her new fortune in a second misrecognition. For her, the money spontaneously "means freedom," in abstraction from its origins (228). She takes herself as having a vocation of independence, "the absolute boldness and wantonness of liberty," as if she were endowed with an innate and inviolable autonomy (320). She regards seventy thousand pounds as "a part of her better self; it gave her importance, gave her even, to her own imagination, a certain ideal beauty" (229). She projects self-determination, freedom, and the imperative of open-ended experience onto a self that is indistinguishable from her inheritance—indeed, *as though* spontaneously inhering in it. But, to paraphrase a famous line from *Capital*, no chemist has ever discovered autonomy or a mandate to experience in seventy thousand pounds.

Fetishism ascribes to a "sum of value . . . its *destiny*, its inner law, its tendency" to press outward and expand—a tendency which "appears as *intention*, purpose" belonging to money.[24] Isabel's subjectivity is fetishized in this sense. It is as though the picture of her destiny, of her vocation, of her limitless expansion were inscribed into her inherited fortune quite apart from its constitutive social relations. Isabel does not see any strings attached to the legacy; she takes her unlooked-for windfall as all the imperative she requires: "To be rich was a virtue because it was to be able to do" (216). Thus Ralph can instruct Isabel, misleadingly, to take the money as "a kind of compliment . . . [on her] so beautifully existing," as if it were an anticipatory reflection of what she will now make of herself (227).

But this very illusion of autonomy is itself her placement. She is slotted in a determinate perspective that dissembles itself as the very opposite: abstract, unbounded free consciousness. This misrecognition will only be undone by the novel's last recognition scene, when Madame Merle's parting shot before she leaves Europe forever is to lay bare for Isabel that "it was your uncle's money, but your cousin's idea" that set Isabel on her tragic course (551). Defeated and shamed, Madame Merle's only power is—like Toto in *The Wizard of Oz*—to yank back the curtain that hides the wizard's pathetic true identity.

The most famous scene in the novel, Isabel's extended vigil of perturbed reflections on her marriage in chapter 42, has often been taken as a recognition scene, where Isabel puts it all together for the first time.[25] The consensus critical position has been that in this scene Isabel accesses an illumination of what had been hidden from her, that she assembles the pieces of the plot against her, and that it marks a turning point in the book. But is this really so? In what follows, I will be contrarian: nothing immediately changes for Isabel because of this scene.

To be sure, James himself somewhat licenses the reading of this scene as a recognition scene since he advertises her "extraordinary meditative vigil," in the preface, in terms of recognition and identification:

> She sits up, by her dying fire, far into the night, under the spell of recognitions on which she finds the last sharpness suddenly wait. It is a representation simply of her motionlessly *seeing*, and an attempt to make the mere still lucidity of her act as "interesting" as the surprise of a caravan or the identification of a pirate. It represents, for that matter, one of the identifications dear to the novelist, and even indispensable to him. (16)

The immediate occasion for Isabel's absorbed retrospection is a perception she has of Madame Merle and Osmond together: "The impression had, in strictness, nothing unprecedented; but she felt it as something new" (404). She just sees them with each other, communing as it were. "But the thing made an image, lasting only a moment, like a sudden flicker of light. Their relative positions, their absorbed mutual gaze, struck her as something detected. But it was all over by the time she had fairly seen it" (405). What is distressing here is the feeling of having intruded on a scene of involved, hushed design that has played out before—with her own marriage. It is as if Isabel were present to witness the Norns cutting the thread of her own fate.

To take one step back, the further context for her vigil is the set of moves in the chess game of marrying off Pansy—whether Isabel will play along in pairing her stepdaughter with her own former suitor Lord Warburton (Osmond's pick), or whether she will help Pansy's candidate, Ned Rosier. Merle and Osmond obscenely want Isabel to use her old romantic influence with Warburton to "make him" propose to Pansy (409). At the same time, although Isabel is miserable in her marriage, she wants to "play the part of a good wife," and she is greatly tempted to oblige him (411). "It was surprising . . . the hold it had taken of her—the idea of assisting her husband to be pleased" (413).

To take yet a further step back, the more encompassing background is Isabel's rehearsal to herself of her escalating disappointment, regrets, and resignations in the years since her marriage. Her reservations do not break out all at once, but have been prepared in morsels of doubt. Even before she has the disturbing "impression" of Merle and Osmond, Isabel has become disenchanted with her friend, having "lost the desire to know this lady's clever trick" (399). But she still does not blame Merle for her unhappy marriage, even though Mrs. Touchett had previously intimated that "Merle took the trouble *for*" Osmond in arranging it (332). Isabel insists to herself that "Madame Merle might have made Gilbert Osmond's marriage, but she certainly had not made Isabel Archer's. That was the work of—Isabel scarcely knew what: of nature, providence, fortune, of the eternal mystery of things" (400). Her protest against shifting blame to anyone else means heaping a grandiose sense of responsibility on herself: "It was impossible to pretend that she had not acted with her eyes open; if ever a girl was a free agent she had been . . . The sole source of her mistake had been within herself. There had been no plot, no snare; she had looked and considered and chosen" (402). We know, of course, that there had been a plot.

Such is the global "situation" that Isabel is "absorbed in looking at" in the distressed contemplation of her vigil (419). Chapter 42 begins with her trying to come to grips with what would be implied by acceding to Osmond's request that she lure Warburton into marriage with Pansy, a proposal "repulsive" and "ugly." She then turns to her vision of Merle and Osmond communing with each other, and tries to take stock of how far she has come in being undeceived in her marriage, what values she can now reasonably say are her still her own, and which have "wither[ed]" and "spoil[ed]" under Osmond's touch (420). She has come to grasp Osmond's contempt and egotism, while she still incompletely gauges "the magnitude of *his* deception" (424). Her cogitations in this scene are hopelessly broken up by lacuna, like a government report that has been heavily redacted. Without knowing what is the "mysterious connection . . . between [Merle] and Pansy," Isabel cannot—could not—find her way through the dark corridors of her own history (406).

Whatever the gaps may be in Isabel's account at this juncture, where does all this immobilized thinking get her? What does it lead to? In the next chapter, she goes on as she was before, encouraging Warburton to propose to Pansy. Three chapters later, she still "had not as yet undertaken to act in direct opposition to Osmond"; she remains deeply impressed with the "sanctities of marriage." The moment is still to come when "she would have to decide," since she "wish[es] to avoid an open rupture" (457). Even after her vigil, then, she regards her marriage as "the most serious act—the single sacred act—of her life" (458). She keeps playing the required role, all the while reproaching herself: "It was what she was doing for Osmond; it was what one had to do for Osmond!" (465). So where is the supposed turning point critics have detected? For even after the supposed realizations of her vigil, "it still clung to her that she must be loyal to Osmond" (466).

I do not mean to say that Isabel's break from Osmond is mechanically achieved by the recognition scenes that follow, as if the discovered facts alone had the force to dislodge her from her marriage. She and Osmond already "had arrived at a crisis" before those disclosures (529). I am only saying that the narrative reversal, the decisive rupture with her husband, does not follow from Isabel's consolidated, retrospective insights in chapter 42. Her vigil is only the start of the tide going out, laying bare the naked shingles of her marriage. The intimations of that scene should be regarded as inaugurating the strokes and counterstrokes of the novel's endgame, rather than as a concluding enlightenment.

In other words, Isabel can only go so far on the power of her own insights. In the succeeding chapters, she arrives at two further momentous clarifications of her position. But neither of these episodes allow Isabel to achieve exit velocity. First, in chapter 48, she tells Ralph that she will come to England if he sends for her, over any possible objections from Osmond. Only at this moment does she accept whatever would be the fallout of her leaving. The critical moment comes when Ralph says: "It was for you that I wanted—that I wanted to live. But I'm of no use to you" (498). What we should notice here is that Isabel's motivation for returning to England pivots around the role Ralph has in her life, even as that role remains for the moment largely submerged. Then, in chapter 49, Madame Merle partly gives herself away to Isabel, "betray[ing]" that she had been "a powerful agent in [Isabel's] destiny," so that a "strange truth was filtering into her soul. Madame Merle's interest was identical with Osmond's" (508).

Isabel now glimpses the Sirens' rock on which she has run aground, her fatal proximity to the bones whitening on the enchanted outcrop. It comes "over her like a high-surging wave that Mrs. Touchett was right. Madame Merle had married her" (511). The nausea of this realization crests with the "conviction that the man in the world whom she had supposed to be the least sordid had married her, like a vulgar adventurer, for her money. Strange to say, it had never before occurred to her" (513). Yet if Merle "almost dropped her mask" in this scene, she does so advisedly (539). It is not a slipup. Something unholy is being revealed here, moreover something insolent to all decency.

Yet even Isabel's detection of Madame Merle's "wickedness" and Osmond's mercenary aims does not push her to leave Rome (512). Even armed with the understanding that Osmond married her for her money, in concert with Madame Merle, Isabel promptly breaks down under her husband's sophistical opposition. He succeeds in stopping her by echoing her own sense of the "traditionary decencies and sanctities of marriage" (457). Her impulse to leave him "suddenly change[s] to slow renunciation," and is "arrested" (531, 533). Balked, left with the thin consolation of moral judgment, she retires to taste afresh her acid fate. When she does leave Rome, it should now be clear, it is not prompted by "the spell of recognitions" in her fireside reflections. All the difference is made by the two recognition scenes that follow. Her scruples about breaking with Osmond then fall away. After the recognition scenes, she takes a train that same evening.

❦

Isabel's enlightenment is plotted in precise stages. It is not like a light that dawns on her in imperceptible gradations, but resembles a choreographed suite of sequential humiliations. She holds an ever-shifting set of suspicions, realizations, painful admissions, placeholder conjectures, and unfathomed depths.[26] Although James has threaded together Isabel's dawning suspicions since chapter 40, when she witnesses Merle and Osmond silently communing, these early suspicions have been indefinite—not plotted. As she now takes in their reasons, James underlines how little Isabel had really foreseen or recognized:

> "I had no idea," said Isabel presently; and looked up at her in a manner that doubtless matched the apparent witlessness of this confession.
>
> "So I believed—though it was hard to believe. Had it really never occurred to you that he was for six or seven years her lover?"
>
> "I don't know. Things *have* occurred to me, and perhaps that was what they all meant . . . Oh, no idea, for me," Isabel went on, "ever *definitely* took that form." She appeared to be making out to herself what had been and what hadn't. "And as it is—I don't understand." (536)

The Countess Gemini is casually brutal in remarking on Isabel's ignorance: "*Ça me dépasse*, if you don't mind me saying so, the things, all round you, that you've appeared to succeed in not knowing" (536). The Countess has suggested previously, "I might tell [Isabel] something that would make her worse, but I can't tell her anything that would console her" (450). In chapter 51, in the first of the novel's two recognition scenes, she now lays bare the sordid details of Osmond's past with Madame Merle, in order to give Isabel a jolt, to help pry her apart from Osmond by showing the trap that had been laid for her. Pansy is not Osmond's daughter with his first wife, but with Merle. When Osmond's wife died, he seized the opportunity of her being away in the Italian Alps and circulated the account that she died giving birth to Pansy. "The story passed, sufficiently; it was covered by the appearances so long as nobody heeded, as nobody cared to look into it" (535). At some point after this swap had been effected, Merle and Osmond broke off their affair, although she thereafter "worked for him, plotted for him" (540). But her great coup, indeed the "only tangible result she ever achieved . . . has been her bringing you and Osmond together" (538).

The Countess's narrative presents Isabel's situation "in a new and violent light" (542). Her accepted deed looks very different once it is served up to her with all its previously hidden roots still dripping. She can rightly say that she did not intend "all of that" when she made her wedding vows. But such a disavowal would pertain only to events downstream from the marriage. Her responsibility for the catastrophe would mean reflecting on how events transpired poorly, owing to colossal ignorance on her part. In other words, the illumination of the scandal behind Isabel's marriage leaves the fetishistic form of subjectivity still untouched. She is still laboring under the false self-relation by which she first got in wrong. She proceeds as if, to quote Bernard Williams, "one's life could . . . be partitioned into some things that one does intentionally and other things that merely happen to one."[27] In other words, she pulls away from the thing done, as if the act in its full array of circumstances and consequences could be refined out from the action itself, the doing: "there was more in the bond than she had meant to put her name to" (425). The sad beauty of the novel, however, is that James insists on Isabel's responsibility going all the way down to the (fetishistic) form of her agency. James is not interested in Isabel undoing her deed or halting its consequences; he is interested in her undoing her subjectivity, rewinding back to the moment of its tragic adoption.

Immediately after the scene with the Countess, Isabel faces down "the dry staring fact that she had been an applied handled hung-up tool, as senseless and convenient as mere shaped wood and iron" (545). (James adds most of this language in the New York Edition of the novel. In the 1881 first edition, Isabel is only "a dull un-reverenced tool.") She sees the degree to which she has been reified—in all possible senses. She has been manipulated and used like a dumb object, one that has now outlived its purpose. But above all reification names the misrecognition of value. Reification is a catastrophe for Isabel insofar as the project shared by most of the characters—of acquisition, valuation, and objectification—provides a cover for ugly social facts and hidden relationships.

What we need here is a balance sheet of the narrative consequences of this first recognition scene. After the Countess offers Isabel this "crude light of [her] revelation," most of the picture Isabel has of her marriage needs to be redrawn (545). But she does not yet know all. Isabel's awareness of being a manipulated "tool," while belonging to her self-reproach, does not on its own liberate her or budge the issue for her. She only breaks with Osmond (disobeys him) when she learns how far she has misrecognized the antecedent plot, the unearthed backstory of her "placement." So, what if the book were to end just after the Countess has given Isabel the impetus to start for England, but before Isabel's last meeting with Madame Merle—how would Isabel's position look to her?

I have been arguing that Isabel's misrecognition consists in the fetishism of her self-consciousness. In a first moment, she takes her own agency, capacities, and meaning to inhere spontaneously in "Isabel Archer" as given properties alongside her new financial endowment. Then, as things sour, her subsequent account of her responsibility for her fate rests on the idea that she is undetermined at first—not constrained or located—and only later (by her own regrettable action) becomes so: "One must accept one's deeds. I married him before all the world; I was perfectly free; it was impossible to do anything more deliberate" (483). The prolonged discovery of the second part of the book is that Isabel's marriage does not have the meaning for her "freedom" that she assigned it in defending Osmond against criticisms made by Caspar Goodwood (chapter 32), Mrs. Touchett (chapter 33), and Ralph (chapter 34).

The immediate upshot of the Countess Gemini's story is to push Isabel over the line to leave for England. Prior to this scene, Isabel certainly has a motivation to leave: she feels that she and Ralph owe each other something undefined, and she has promised to come back to Gardencourt if he should send for her. She also has already arrived at a perspective on the character functions of Merle and Osmond: Merle has been wicked, Osmond has been sordid, they have been "vile" together (518). But these considerations are outweighed by Isabel's repeated insistence on her responsibility for and obligations toward the marriage, on account of her exorbitant notion of her autonomy. After all, "she had looked and considered and chosen," so it must have been her own "mistake" and no one else's (402). However pregnant with meaning has been Isabel's foregoing parsing of her situation, she cannot get around this picture of her own involvement—according to which, she reasons, she has placed herself. Osmond, depending on this misrecognition of hers, can easily impede her departure. After chapter 51, Isabel can no longer deny that Madame Merle had made her marriage. Once apprised of her marriage's buried dimension of consolidated deceits and falsified history, it cannot be held up as an exhibit of being "perfectly free" and "deliberate."

Isabel's learning from the Countess Gemini of the repellant secrets Merle and Osmond have buried together is therefore a step beyond her earlier intimations. She now knows not only what was the plot (the collusion) to capture her money, she also can retrospectively plot (order on a timeline) the sequence of discrete events leading up to her crisis. The unconsoling truth relayed by the Countess definitively settles Isabel on leaving England over her husband's protests—not because it provides her with a new motivation (she already has her reasons), but because the deception practiced on her is now known to be so bad as to be exculpatory. She is thereby released from Osmond's "appeal . . . in the name of something sacred and precious" in marriage; she is excused from the grudging "observance of a magnificent form" (530).

What remains then for the other recognition scene to accomplish? For Isabel is still not all the way there to penetrating the fetish of her subjectivity. When the Countess has related to Isabel the concealed background to her marriage, her own role in that catastrophe now appears to her as a bad exercise of her agency. But her agency itself is not at that point called into question. The prominence of deception, and therefore her own ignorance, allows her to cut off the parts of her mistake where she feels no longer responsible—as if the past were a doubtful piece of fruit. In particular, she now feels comfortable blaming Madame Merle—where the function of blame is to shift anterior responsibility, but also (by effecting this transfer) to preserve her pristine agency as "free" in the sense of not being contaminated or undercut by subsequent results. One is to be responsible, that is, only where one was free. Blame is the knife that effects this saving operation.

This conception of her responsibility is overturned by the recognition scene in the following chapter. Before Isabel takes the evening train to Paris, she visits Pansy at the convent (where she is being kept in seclusion until she resigns herself to Osmond's authority). Madame Merle is there. She "guessed in the space of an instant that everything was at an end between them," but she lingers during Isabel's visit (544). Before they both leave Italy, she wants to ask Isabel "a strange question":

> "Are you very fond of your cousin?" And she gave a smile as strange as her utterance.
>
> "Yes, I'm very fond of him. But I don't understand you."
>
> She just hung fire. "It's rather hard to explain. Something has occurred to me which may not have occurred to you, and I give you the benefit of my idea. Your cousin did you once a great service. Have you never guessed it?"
>
> "He has done me many services."
>
> "Yes; but one was much above the rest. He made you a rich woman."
>
> "*He* made me—?"
>
> Madame Merle appearing to see herself successful, she went on more triumphantly: "He imparted to you that extra lustre which was required to make you a brilliant match. At bottom it's him you've to thank." She stopped; there was something in Isabel's eyes.
>
> "I don't understand you. It was my uncle's money."
>
> "Yes; it was your uncle's money, but it was your cousin's idea. He brought his father over to it. Ah, my dear, the sum was large!"
>
> Isabel stood staring; she seemed today to live in a world illuminated by lurid flashes. . . .
>
> Isabel went to the door and, when she had opened it, stood a moment with her hand on the latch. Then she said—it was her only revenge: "I believed it was you I had to thank!" (551)

This secret is not really so "lurid" as the one about Osmond's dead wife and illegitimate child. But almost the entire narrative looks different in the wake of Merle's revelation. To be sure, the reader has known from the outset that Ralph was behind Isabel's inheritance, but we only now discover that Merle, too, was in on this secret all along. Merle says that she does not "know" any of this for a fact, only that she has "guessed" it (551). It did not take her long to guess. In the scene where Mrs. Touchett first informs Merle of Isabel's new fortune, Merle silently puts together what even Ralph's own mother does not.[28]

When she tells Isabel that it is Ralph that she has "to thank," Merle bitterly exposes the fetish of Isabel's subjectivity. Ever since her marriage, Isabel has taken herself to have lost and wasted a freedom that Merle now shows was never hers to lose in the first place. We now learn that Isabel was not preyed upon *despite* Ralph's hidden intention to observe Isabel, but *because* those intentions and Isabel's misrecognition of them were immediately detected by Merle. That Ralph's involvement is hidden from Isabel is the fatal hinge of everything. Merle and Osmond did not pounce on Isabel's fortune like two adventurers spying an easy mark. On that supposition, Isabel should just have been more on her guard, clutched her purse tighter. Rather, it was specifically her blindness to Ralph's voyeuristic manipulation that is her vulnerable point. She is not entrapped by the wicked and grasping villains just because she is a headstrong American girl with too many untested ideas who has come into too much money. Isabel is caught because Merle spies Isabel's blindness to how she has been determined and "placed."

The horrible irony, then, is how Ralph's spectatorship of Isabel, figured as a "drama" for which "he was determined to sit out the performance," is somehow intuited by Merle and turned against Isabel (393). Ralph is unconsciously arming her enemies with his own private metaphors. For Osmond and Merle's conspiracy itself takes the form of a theatrical performance, staged for a captive audience of one. Isabel "sat there [watching them] as if she had been at the play and had paid even a large sum for her place" (250). Merle and Osmond "might have been distinguished performers . . . It all had the rich readiness that would have come from rehearsal" (250). Isabel is no longer a roaming eye devouring space, but a passive, seated member of the ticket-holding public, observing from amid the hushed dark, while Merle and Osmond are virtuosic actors delivering their lines rapid-fire before the footlights, with all the artificiality and stagecraft of expert direction. The unintended fallout of Ralph's plan of viewing Isabel, then, is that she is straightaway converted into a "watcher," rooted in her seat without knowing it.

When Isabel marries Osmond, James reminds the reader that we "know more about poor Ralph than his cousin" and therefore can fathom how "shocked and humiliated" he is that his project has come to this end (337). On her side, she keeps her resolution "never [to] complain of my trouble to [Ralph]" (347):

> It seemed to her an act of devotion to conceal her misery from him. She concealed it elaborately; she was perpetually, in their talk, hanging out curtains and arranging screens . . . She had told him . . . that from her at least he should never know if he was right; and this was what she was taking care of now . . . It would have been a kindness perhaps if he had been for a single instant a dupe . . . She didn't wish him to have the pain of knowing she was unhappy. (430)

We now see that Ralph has been "a dupe" after all, and not just for a "single in-stant" but for years. Osmond can factor in Ralph's interference to his plans— but not at all for the reasons that Ralph and Isabel think. Osmond does not see Ralph as Isabel sees him, as "an apostle of freedom" (457). For Osmond, who knows how internally blocked the relationship between the cousins must be, "Ralph had not now that importance . . . he had none at all" (392). He can safely assume the "gulf between" Isabel and Ralph that prevents their acting in concert to oppose him (459).

Taken together, these two recognition scenes reveal to Isabel the constitu-tive misrecognition of her own subject position that subtends her failures of independence, how she could be "soaring and sailing" one moment and "put in a cage" the next. Once all is known, her actions will henceforth be inseparable from negativity, regret, and misrecognition; what matters is that she takes this revealed ugly history as her defining placement. An abyss of social relations now opens *beneath* the fetishistic picture of her autonomy:

> Now that she was in the secret, now that she knew something that so much concerned her and the eclipse of which had made life resemble an attempt to play whist with an imperfect pack of cards, the truth of things, their mutual relations, their meaning, and for the most part their horror, rose before her with a kind of architectural vastness. (552)

To go on to define herself ever after will mean a continued engagement within that history, not cutting herself off from it as someone else's doing. The question then arises how she will revise and be responsible for "the scale of her relation to herself" in retrospection (12).

The ending of *The Portrait of a Lady* has long perplexed readers. In his note-books, James is aware that the ending will be open to the "criticism . . . that it is not finished—that I have not seen the heroine to the end of her situation."[29]

Indeed, there does not even appear to be a consensus about what happens on the last page, much less how we are to evaluate or understand it.[30] Isabel does not sit down and explicitly set out her motives before departing, the way Nora does in Ibsen's *A Doll's House*.[31] It is almost always said that she goes back to Osmond, but we do not know that for sure.[32] Nor is it at all clear what it would mean for her to do so, how that would look. All we know is that she goes back to Rome. Nonetheless, many scholars have criticized Isabel for what looks like her "renunciation," returning only to suffer in an unhappy marriage.[33] For my money, she does not go back to the marriage.

What I propose is to gather up all the threads of Isabel's responsiveness that lead to the final pages. In particular, how do the recognition scenes change things for her, and how do their effects show up in her last decisions? On my reading, Isabel's decision to go back to Rome is how she makes sense of those revelations, specifically how she revises what had been a fetishistic conception of her own agency. The conclusion of the novel is almost a handbook of annulling the constitutive determinations of reified subjectivity, bringing about the loss of its foundational supports. Such an interpretation does not, of course, yield an insider's knowledge about what Isabel really does next. My point is not to speculate on what she does after the last page, but rather to specify her agency. By going back, what had been the unconscious, manipulative, and framing social relations that determined her subjectivity, "placed" her, are opened up once more as the location where subjectivity is to be claimed and fought out.

For James's characters, one's history does not only mean "what happened," but includes the self as a fraught, untimely object of perception. W. H. Auden characterizes Jamesian consciousness as "ironic" because

> the actual self
>   Round whom time revolves so fast
> Is so afraid of what its motions might possibly do,
> That the actor is never there when his really important
>   Acts happen.[34]

That perception is overwhelmingly the business of James's people; it is the drama of the characters themselves, the issue of their assessment or paralysis about the "there" where they were to be defined. Their perennial question is something like, "What does it mean for how I now take myself to be, that I am calling my experience of what happened *this*?" To "affront [one's] destiny," then, can only be retrospective. Jamesian subjectivity is always this responsiveness (including its evasions and separations) to its own formation, taking or not taking responsibility for how it has come about. What the past will have meant is determined by what happens next, how the losses constitutive of one's history are lived forward when one is no longer blind to them.

We do not hold Isabel accountable or expect her to get things right when she is being manipulated and lied to. She is simply ignorant about how things really stand between Merle and Osmond. But her problems do not stop there. Her constitutive misrecognition is to take "Isabel Archer" as a fetish, misrepresenting her own agency as something observed from outside, a finished product. Because she does not see how her inheritance has been engineered by her cousin, she takes the apparent independence that it funds as an endowment of her spirit, as if freedom were a built-in feature of her character and destiny. The misrecognition going on, as Marx specifies in the *Grundrisse*, is that "fetishism . . . imputes social relations to things as inherent characteristics, and thus mystifies them."[35]

Because her self-relation is a relation to these immediate properties, they do not appear to be up for revision. That is why Isabel's problem at the end of the book is no longer external (the conspiracy by Merle and Osmond to deceive and entrap her), but an internal confrontation with her own agency. It is not as if Isabel just needs to discover that she is embedded in a wider set of social relations than she had glimpsed—the George Eliot move. For James, by contrast, agency is an incessant grappling not with what has been missed by the self, but with the self as what has been missed. It is not enough, then, for Isabel simply to become better informed. Fetishism's hold does not just dissipate like a mist once it has been detected.[36] Fetishism usurps the positing of values within structured social relations and displaces the origin of values onto an immediacy from which social *becoming* has vanished. It can be undone only by returning the spurious social character of value from its misattribution onto a fetishistic pseudo-subject back to the moment of its constitution, its "hidden abode." The bad manipulations in the plot are not simply left behind after they come out.

After the recognition scenes show the genesis of this peculiar item, her "destiny," Isabel does not throw out her past determinacy entirely, flinging herself into a wide-open new start, by running away with Caspar Goodwood. Nor does she accord her mistakes an irrevocable authority by returning penitent to Osmond—as if the official sanctity of the marriage, its "ghastly form" (579), were unalterable and transcendent of any profanation she might discover about the original bonds.[37] But neither can she go back to Osmond with a veil of ignorance pinned back up somehow. (As if nothing had happened!) The meaning of those determinations has already been wrested out of blindness by the recognition scenes. Isabel's old conception of her agency as an immediate property, a destiny inhering in her self rather than a constituted effect of "placement," no longer holds. For Isabel to have a defetishized sense of her past at the end of the novel means shifting her self-relation to the very site of calculating materialism where she was originally the formed and placed object.[38] Her agency now is to be formed by grasping and contesting those determinations, the previously unseen material formation of her subjective location—inclusive of the misrecognitions built into that location.

If Isabel's return to Rome means a commitment to the revision and disillusioned positing of her own agency, then it can hardly be right to call it a "renunciation." James explicitly says so: "Deep in her soul—deeper than any appetite for renunciation—was the sense that life would be her business for a long time to come" (553). As this reminds us, renunciation is a discrete act, complete in itself—not an ongoing project. (In Wagner's *Das Rheingold*, when the dwarf Alberich forswears love, renunciation is cleanly accomplished by the briefest utterance: *"so verfluch' ich die Liebe!"*[39]) Isabel is not returning in penitence or resignation. Instead, she imagines her life ahead as an open set of involvements, an unresolved "business" or interminable "scene":

"It [Osmond's retribution for Isabel leaving] won't be the scene of a moment; it will be a scene of the rest of my life." (557)

[RALPH]: "It is all over then between you?"
[ISABEL]: "Oh no; I don't think anything's over." (568)

There can be no question, then, of a definitive act that settles her fate for all time. (As James puts it in his notebooks, "I have left her *en l'air.*"[40]) After Ralph dies, Isabel begins to feel that she is only postponing an inevitable decision: "She knew she must decide, but she decided nothing; her coming itself had not been a decision. On that occasion she had simply started" (572). But when she goes back, we find again that she "started." Henrietta Stackpole tells Caspar Goodwood that "this morning she started for Rome," and he awkwardly swallows the destination: "'Oh, she started—?' he stammered . . . without finishing his phrase" (582). It is somewhat perverse that critics have silently corrected this in the direction of finality.

Isabel is going back to Rome to take up the work of redetermining her own "placement"—not in the vacuum of a specious autonomy, but also no longer blind to the moves already irreversibly played in her life. We do not know what will happen, but it is not to be anything so final as renunciation. She insists she is not going back to be buried. There is no settled meaning of her life now independently available, as if yet another substance-like self lies under the illusions she has sloughed off. For the self not to be "over" means delving into the hidden processes of her becoming, to get her hands dirty in those social relations wherein she was badly determined at the start. Isabel is looking at her scene of formation now from the lower depths of humiliation. To return to Rome, as I see it, means a struggle to be waged within the "bad" social relations she had misrecognized in the first place. She is like Rastignac throwing down the gauntlet at the end of *Père Goriot*, as he plunges back into the churning morass of the Faubourg Saint-Germain: "*À nous deux maintenant!*"[41]

When Isabel feels at last "free" and knows "where to turn" (581), she does not break from that past, from some nowhere view outside of it. Instead, she locks the door to any exit. Whatever agency she is now to have will be put together from within that past and its determinations. The mistakes and silences that "placed" her in the first place can be negated—that is to say, not deleted but restored to a retrospective coherence as the tolls of misrecognition—only with ongoing life. What will now count for her as properly valuing her own agency and others' requires contesting and staking out, for the first time in full awareness, the commitments that render one a responsible agent.

The ending of the novel cashes the check that James writes in the house of fiction allegory. The options facing Isabel are those facing the posted observer at one of the house's many windows. One option is held out by Caspar Goodwood's proposal to Isabel to run away with him. He imagines some unobstructed, unhoused view. The two of them, he says—as if they were exiting Plato's cave, unshackled, to encounter the Forms—"look at things as they are," and can "do absolutely as [they] please" (580). But James denies there is any exit or repositioning possible for the observer staring out from the house of fiction. It has no "hinged doors opening straight upon life." For Isabel to run away with Caspar would mistakenly look for some such exit, from which to jump out of her enlightenment into some stranded outer space. One cannot, in James's picture, establish direct "contact with reality—with the toiling, striving, suffering . . . world that surrounds you," as Henrietta has also coached Isabel (222). There is no such unmediated contact as this option imagines.

Critics have often seen Isabel as taking a second option, not of throwing herself into life but the opposite: a kind of martyrdom that preserves an absolute, inviolable purity not of this world.[42] Such a characterization closely corresponds to the literal description of the house of fiction. Isabel would be like one of the posted watchers, stranded at her aperture, peering down from a confinement high above life. But we have seen that in James's own gloss of the allegory, the "boundless freedom" he assigns to "consciousness" is not at all the pseudo-freedom of an isolated, self-derived subjectivity, passively withdrawn from existence (8). Rather, James decodes his allegory as the figure of an active, positing consciousness, identified with its "vision." The boundless freedom of consciousness—whether that of the artist, the posted viewer, or Isabel—consists in the "projected" determinacy of its formation as ongoing nonidentity, a self-relation that "strains, or tends to burst" its own form (7). The novel ends when Isabel takes up precisely this different relation to her own agency. The space of misrecognition itself, in which she had been unconsciously determined, is to be "a scene of the rest of [her] life."

CHAPTER 4

The Fragmentation of Subject and Object in Sherlock Holmes

> *The naked result is the corpse of the system*
> *which has left its guiding tendency behind it.*
>
> —Hegel, *The Phenomenology of Spirit*

In the preceding chapters, we have seen how novels by Charles Dickens, Anthony Trollope, and Henry James used recognition scenes to critique the position of subjectivity as a series of dislocations within capital, revealing the narrative contortions and structural misrecognitions underlying bourgeois social forms. Sir Arthur Conan Doyle's Sherlock Holmes books mark the end point and dissolution of this program. In the four Holmes novels—*A Study in Scarlet, The Sign of Four, The Hound of the Baskervilles*, and *The Valley of Fear*—and fifty-six Holmes short stories, the device of the recognition scene no longer mediates a dislocated, occluded subjectivity. Recognition scenes, in the form of the detective's solution of the precipitating mystery, become a stale, if increasingly baroque, bit of technical flair.

There is an irony here. In my account, the Holmes books figure as a *demotion* of the recognition scene, which falls off into uncritical obsolescence. But in detective fiction the recognition scene, namely, the solution at the end of each case, is also *elevated* to being the decisive principle of plot, the point of the whole exercise. The detective's retrospective account, delivered patiently to Dr. Watson for posterity, is the indispensable ingredient in the narrative formula. The reader of detective fiction, like a child groping through a box of cereal for the prize floating inside, pushes aside all the other elements of the story—character, exposition, setting—until she has clutched this item, which is its real selling point. Once it has been extracted, the rest can be safely thrown away. The supremacy of the recognition scene in detective fiction rests on this detachable and repeatable function. The form can be as stereotyped as you wish—just think of the identical drawing rooms in which Agatha Christie's Poirot assembles his suspects—but it demands a ceaseless novelty of content (the pyrotechnics of unheard-of murder instruments). The solutions demonstrate not only the virtuosity of the detective, but also of the author—who must top himself with ever more outlandish concluding explanations, for example, a rare outbreak of pseudo-leprosy or ichthyosis in Doyle's "The Adventure of the Blanched Soldier."

Because the detective's solution plays such an obvious role of unmasking and overturning false appearances, these recognition scenes have been characterized by critics like Rita Felski and Jacques Rancière as paradigms of critique. At a distance, it is not hard to see how the figure of Holmes in particular—analytical, probing, interrogating, decoding, suspicious, infallible—concentrates many of the affective postures of ideology critique, deconstruction, and so on, which Felski lumps under "critique."[1] For Rancière, the rationality of detective fiction entails a programmatic "reversal of appearances." As with Marx's famous image of the "darkroom of ideology," the truth of the detective's solution is simply the turning on their head of the illusions encountered in a first pass of visibility.[2] On these readings, detective fiction plays out the procedures of hermeneutics that one also finds in Marxian critique.

I am arguing exactly the opposite point. My claim is that the recognition scenes in Sherlock Holmes never illuminate the plot structures pertinent to Marx's critique, namely, the misrecognitions of subjectivity internal to capital. Felski's contention that "the structure of critique" is "analogous to the structure" of detective fiction, with the Holmes books as paradigm, rests on their plotting of retrospective interpretation. Specifically, the analogy with critique depends on the plot's exercise of "reason[ing] backward in order to bring a constellation of past events to light," and "expos[ing] hidden connections by moving from effects to causes."[3] Both of these hermeneutic principles are taken nearly verbatim from Holmes's many descriptions of his own investigative method.[4]

After a brief excursus on *The Valley of Fear*, the first section of this chapter questions whether the announced hermeneutic principles are carried out in the plotting of the Holmes novels and stories, or if they are merely asserted so often within the texts to pass for formal analysis. As we will see, Holmes criticism has succumbed to a fixation with Holmes's "method"—the canon of his maxims that is pasted into the stories. The aura of a precise methodology has attained a hold on criticism that obscures the inner workings of their plots. Holmes's own pronouncements therefore cannot count as evidence of an analogy with "critique" in the stories' hermeneutic structure.

The next section takes apart the plot of *A Study in Scarlet* down to its nuts and bolts. Much has been made of the temporal dislocations in detective fiction, how the teleology of the investigation is to lay out the "original" order of events (*fabula*) rather than the jumbled chronology crisscrossed by conflicting witnesses and false leads (*sjužet*). But Doyle introduces several further levels of narrative sequencing. Instead of the ultimate folding back of a splintered tale into an unbroken chain, the plotting of *A Study in Scarlet* fractures the crime and its reconstruction into isolated codes that do not communicate with one another. In his essay on reification, Georg Lukács observes how "the fragmentation of the object . . . entails the fragmentation of its subject," so that the dialectical mediations underlying each are split off into ahistorical isolation zones; consciousness thus contemplates "a perfectly closed system."[5] For us it means that the plotting of Holmes's solutions at various incompatible and unreconciled levels reproduces the specious discontinuity of bourgeois immediacy.[6]

The third section returns to the problematics of novel theory pursued throughout this book, namely, how subjectivity is mediated by its misrecognition. In previous chapters, we saw how recognition scenes in novels by Dickens, Trollope, and James are not only moments where characters find the meaning of their lives to be dislocated at their very origins. In those novels, the plotting of recognition scenes becomes freighted with the temporal hitches and blind alleys of capital's internal "plot," its contradictory self-representation in the itinerary of value. The moving parts and choreography of their recognition scenes—the hermeneutic unraveling—are themselves dialectically involved with the categories and representative modes of capital. In other words, the recovery and reconstruction of subjectivity is found to be inseparable, down to its very form of retrospection, from the balked and foreshortened mediations of capital-as-plot. The critique effected by the recognition scenes in Dickens, Trollope, and James means pulling the formal contradictions of capital over into the fraught articulation of subjectivity itself. Those authors do not back away from these contradictions, but take them into the heart of subjectivity, plotting out those repressions and usurpations as the unavoidable cost of a determinate perspective on one's history.

The plots of the Sherlock Holmes novels and stories are not like this. The misrecognitions unraveled in the detective's solution have shed the repressions and displacements our other Victorian authors included as determinations of bourgeois immediacy. Furthermore, those misrecognitions have come unglued from the retrospective positing of subjectivity, namely, the detective's reconstruction of his own cogitations and deductions. Instead of being routed through the divisions, detours, and non sequiturs that comprise capital's bad plotting, Holmes's solutions divorce the misrecognitions of the subject from the misrecognitions of the object. Each sphere is left to rotate in a kind of kaleidoscopic isolation.

Since I will mostly be looking at *A Study in Scarlet*, it is worth noting beforehand that, out of the four Sherlock Holmes novels, only *The Valley of Fear* directly represents industrial capitalism and its production relations. In short stories like "The Adventure of the Engineer's Thumb" and "The Stockbroker's Clerk," there is only a sham capitalism. Some capitalist enterprise is introduced as a front, in order to conceal noncapitalist illegality, such as counterfeiting or safecracking. In *The Valley of Fear*, however, crime is installed in the capital–labor relation itself—albeit in the "wrong" direction, as we will see.

The first part of *The Valley of Fear*, narrated by Dr. Watson, is set prior to the events of "The Final Problem," when Holmes's archenemy Dr. Moriarty had appeared to tumble to his death over the Reichenbach Falls. Setting the story earlier in Holmes's career allows Doyle to bring back Moriarty, whom he had narratively squandered in "The Final Problem."[7] Through his agents, Moriarty plots the murder of John Douglas of Birlstone Manor. Holmes investigates and discovers that the corpse, whose face had been blown off with a shotgun, is not really Douglas, who has survived the attempt on his life, but one of Moriarty's men, Ted Baldwin. Douglas had disguised the corpse as himself in the hopes that Moriarty would believe he had been killed and would stop hunting him. When Holmes discovers the ruse, Douglas hands Dr. Watson a bundle of papers relating his first entanglement with Baldwin in America, twenty years before.

The second part of the novel is not quite a transcription of Douglas's papers but apparently a recension by Watson himself, adopting an omniscient third-person mode. This flashback is set in the United States, in the iron and coal districts of the Vermissa Valley, an open battleground between monopolizing capital and criminal labor unions. The story follows Jack McMurdo (who is later revealed to be Birdy Edwards, who later becomes John Douglas), a Pinkerton agent in the pay of the big mine owners and railroad companies. McMurdo/Douglas infiltrates the Scowrers, a secret society of murderers who are the militant arm of the labor union. Doyle imagines organized labor as nothing more than an exercise in violent coercion and corruption. He even sees labor itself as responsible for the consolidation of capital against it. The rapacious union has driven out the (helpless, innocent) small mine owners and works by blackmailing and squeezing them dry; only the big companies stand a chance against its power. Militant labor is at last defeated only by a private police firm hired by the bourgeoisie.

What does any of this have to do with the mystery plot? Exactly nothing. Holmes solves the murder mystery in total ignorance of Douglas's narrative. Furthermore, none of the clues from the crime scene that do reappear in the

American flashback—a branded mark on the dead man's forearm, a calling card actually identifying the union lodge—are pertinent to Holmes's solution. The foremost clues in the solution are a missing dumbbell and a secret hiding place in the study, which have nothing to do with the Vermissa Valley, the Scowrers, or Pinkerton agents. The workings of capitalism are completely irrelevant to the mechanisms of the recognition scene here. The concealment of the crime is not in any way traceable back to the misrecognitions of capitalism. What Doyle sees as the depredations of the class struggle are merely appended onto the detective's solution after the fact. Even the connection of the murder to Moriarty, which brings the crime into the larger Holmesian mythology, is entirely external to the flashback and its solution. Moriarty has only been a paid consultant to a crime originating from and executed by the Scowrers. His involvement has been a mere assent, not deriving from his own web of operations—as if he had agreed to license the Moriarty brand name for the enterprise, without putting forward any investment of his own. Moriarty stands at the head of an all-encompassing conspiracy, but one that is nonetheless never instantiated and never mapped. In this sense Moriarty's organization is precisely analogous to the functioning of capitalism in the Holmes stories. Both are totalizing social mechanisms that somehow never enter into the inner processes of the mysteries or their solutions.

According to Pierre Bayard, "The method used by Sherlock Holmes . . . is the primary reason that these texts have become famous. But not only that: The method itself had such success that it is often referred to, well beyond the realm of literature, as a model of intelligence and rigorous thinking."[8] Indeed, one can purchase instructional books telling you "how to think like Sherlock Holmes."[9] This method, however, is not derived from an analysis of the narrative form, but from the frequent statements made by Holmes to explain his investigative procedure. It is easy to collect such specimens. The detective never tires of adumbrating the apparently rigorous axioms of this canon:

> "In solving a problem of this sort, the grand thing is to be able to reason backward . . . There are few people . . . who, if you told them a result, would be able to evolve from their own consciousness what the steps were which led up to that result. This power is what I mean when I talk of reasoning backward, or analytically." (*A Study in Scarlet*, 83–84)
>
> "The ideal reasoner," [Holmes] remarked, "would, when he had once been shown a single fact in all its bearings, deduce from it not only all the chain of events which led up to it but also all the results which would follow from it." ("The Five Orange Pips," 224–25)

Dr. Watson—who also serves as the narrator—helpfully restates Holmes's epistemological program, under the attitude of incredulity:

> "But do you mean to say," [Watson asks] "that without leaving your room you can unravel some knot which other men can make nothing of, although they have seen every detail for themselves?" (*A Study in Scarlet*, 24)
>
> I trust that I am not more dense than my neighbors, but I was always oppressed with a sense of my own stupidity in my dealings with Sherlock Holmes. Here I had heard what he had heard, I had seen what he had seen, and yet from his words it was evident that he saw clearly not only what had happened but what was about to happen, while to me the whole business was still confused and grotesque. ("The Red-Headed League," 185–86).

Nearly every story provides some new statement of the same idea: Holmes arrives at his solutions from the very same information that is set before Watson (and, by extension, the reader). We have all seen "every detail for [our]selves," we have "seen what [Holmes] had seen." No matter how confused and incomplete the data appear, Holmes, by his own account, does not require any new material to be brought in by the back door before reconstructing an astounding and improbable sequence of events.

Critics tend to take Holmes at his word, and equate the forensic premises uttered by the character with the formal operations of the plot. The bulk of Holmes criticism effectively trades out the expected analysis of the stories' plotting for the prefabricated method that Holmes claims to adhere to in his investigations and reasoning. The actual narrative operations of the stories have been overlaid with the transferred aura of a scientific and logical procedure: a "method effect" (after Roland Barthes's *effet de réel* or Althusser's *effet de connaissance*). The only trouble is that the method effect rests on and perpetuates an illusion. Holmes's investigative method does not map onto the literary hermeneutics pertaining to the mystery and its solution. As we will see, none of the Sherlock Holmes cases are solved by the logical program of deduction that is projected by the method effect.

The method effect depends not only on the apparent internal consistency of Holmes's investigative approach, but also on the many citations thrown out by Holmes that point outside the work: to scientific research, experiments, and controversies. Scholars have exercised great diligence in following up the seemingly systematic statements of Holmes's investigative procedure. Historicist critics in Victorian studies, immersed in the discursive contexts of Holmes's contemporaries, have attempted to reconstruct the influence of real developments in natural science, forensics, criminology, anthropology, and so on, on the fictional detective.[10] At times, Holmes is implicated as a more or less complicit or anxious participant in the biopolitical discourse of the British colonial apparatus, extending into identification, fingerprinting, ethnicity, and epidemiology.[11] The scientific references create an impression of contact with an extraliterary "real." Scholars have taken these citations as authenticating Holmes's methodological credentials.[12] Any given Sherlock Holmes story is stocked with such references.

For example, in *The Hound of the Baskervilles*, the murdered Sir Charles Baskerville has returned from South Africa with "much scientific information . . . [on] the comparative anatomy of the Bushman and the Hottentot" (678). Dr. Mortimer, who discovers the body, is himself the author of several articles of racial science: "Is Disease a Reversion?", "Some Freaks of Atavism," and "Do We Progress?" (671). An air of scientificity hovers on the moor no less than its native fog. However, when Holmes relates how he solved the mystery, he draws on none of these allusions.[13] What enabled him to crack the case? Two "facts": ghost dogs should not need to be given a scent (from a purloined boot) to discover their fated prey, and women leave perfume on their notes. Atavism and comparative anatomy do not figure at all in the solution. Literary form does not spring directly from extratextual scientific or philosophical citations, as if from Cadmus's teeth.

In another methodological direction, semiotic criticism has reconstructed, from Holmes's statements, a transhistorical forensic doctrine closely related to the logical studies of Charles Sanders Peirce.[14] It is only a slight exaggeration to say that these latter researches would not differ in any way had Holmes been a real person. There is even a palpable regret among the semioticians that Holmes never published his planned monograph on the whole science of detecting. As with the historicist critics, the semioticians take the translation of an external (here, philosophical) discourse into the fictional detective's reasoning to be a no-loss exchange. In other words, the crossover from, say, Peirce to Sherlock Holmes is taken not to be an aesthetic operation at all, but only a shuttling between different sites sharing the "same" discursive object.[15] What is absent—completely so—is any consideration of the plotting of the stories, or of the temporal structure of the solutions.

Even quantitative criticism, purportedly objective and scientific in its own methods, presumes (with detrimental results) the validity of Holmes's method. Franco Moretti, as an advocate of "distant reading," builds his study of the evolution of the Holmesian clue on Holmes's "method" as descriptive of the cases' plotting.[16] He argues that the formal difference setting Doyle's stories apart from his now-forgotten contemporaries is the device of clues that meet three criteria: they are necessary to the solution, visible to the reader beforehand, and decodable as to their role in the crime. The epochal discovery of Doyle was to use clues as "details open to the rational scrutiny of all" in the solution.[17] Now, this is the same "method" point about reasoning backward from available facts we have already seen emphasized by Holmes in his didactic pronouncements, and that so astonishes Dr. Watson when put into action.

Unfortunately, this shibboleth about clues being decipherable, meant to account for the evolutionary survival and propagation of the Holmesian model, is also not a property of the Holmes stories themselves.[18] "Even being generous," Moretti concedes, "there are decodable clues in no more than four of the *Adventures* (and being strict, in none)."[19] We should be "strict"—the Holmes stories do not meet the criteria of decodable clues. (I will return to the four alleged or "generous" exceptions below, to show how these phantom data points are not exceptions.) What sets the Holmes stories apart from Doyle's rivals, one might say, is not the presence but only the *aura* of decodable clues—in other words, the convincing character of the method effect.[20]

The literary evidence of how Holmes solves his cases is a definite letdown after the promises of reasoning backward and the deduction of an elaborate causality from the smallest clue. Holmes invariably relies on some information hitherto unavailable to the reader, and quite outside the *données immédiates* of the case. He possesses a specimen of black clay from an athletic track (in "The Adventure of the Three Students"), or he has taken the exact measurement of a corridor (in "The Adventure of the Norwood Builder")—evidence that is withheld from us but proves decisive. One has never "seen the same things" as Holmes, one has not "seen every detail for oneself," although the miraculous effect of Holmes's solutions depends on this ostensible parity.

It is never possible for the reader, however ingenious, to anticipate the solution based on the available information.[21] This is noticed by Holmes himself, who, more eagle-eyed than the literary scholars, occasionally criticizes the narrative double-dealing behind the construction of his "cases." He tells Watson, the supposed author of most of his adventures, "the effect of some of these little sketches of yours . . . is entirely meretricious, depending as it does upon your retaining in your own hands some factors in the problem which are never imparted to the reader" ("The Crooked Man," 412). But when Holmes takes up the narrator's duties himself, he finds another version of the same difficulty: "Alas, that I should have to show my hand so when I tell my own story! It was by concealing such links in the chain that Watson was enabled to produce his meretricious finales" ("The Adventure of the Blanched Soldier," 1007–8).

Thus the reader cannot, and is not meant to, "play along" in solving the crime. The hapless efforts of Dr. Watson to do so are a running joke, and serve as a warning by proxy against our own cleverness. One probably cannot help anticipating the answer, darting at false solutions. But only a later development of the genre will require a level playing field, where the reader must be able (if only technically) to solve the puzzle concurrently with the detective, with all the same clues and observations at her disposal. This principle is wonderfully summed up by Agatha Christie's detective, Hercule Poirot: "Of facts, I keep nothing to myself. But to everyone his own interpretation of them."[22] Yet the pleasure of reading the Holmes stories is not in being shown the answer to a brainteaser one has racked one's brain to solve. It is something else: the pleasure of witnessing an impressive and non-duplicable feat. The point is that you *could not* do it.[23]

Take, for example, the short story "The Adventure of the Cardboard Box." In this story an elderly woman receives two severed human ears through the mail, enclosed in said packaging. Holmes is called in on the case, goes down to the country, looks at the ears, looks at the box, looks at the elderly woman, asks a few questions about her family life (she has two sisters, one of whom has unhappily married a sailor with a drinking problem), and sends a telegram. He then drives around to visit her sister, finds the house closed on account of illness, and finally, upon receiving the answer to his telegram, pronounces the case solved. Holmes tells the Scotland Yard investigator where and when he may pick up his man. Everyone is astonished. So, how did he do it? What we were not shown was that the knot used to tie the box was "one which is popular with sailors" (896), and that the elderly lady's ear "corresponded exactly with the female ear" in the box (896), and that the answer to Holmes's telegram (a frequent device) showed that the brother-in-law had been in port in Belfast the day the package was sent—from Belfast (897). But this is all new information to the reader who had marveled at the case being solved on the basis of the earlier, more limited data. That does not stop Holmes from boasting to Watson that this, too, was a case where he has "been compelled to reason backward from effects to causes" (895). Undoubtedly, within the fictional world, the character Holmes reasoned backward. I am not trying to take Sherlock Holmes down a peg, although Doyle invariably gives his hero an insurmountable advantage over the reader. It is only that, if the character succeeds in imbuing senseless facticity with a chain of meanings, that is a completely separate matter than what is going on in the literary construction.

Some of the Holmes cases do come closer to being solvable puzzles than others. (Of course, many of the stories are not plotted as mysteries at all. "A Scandal in Bohemia," "The Final Problem," "The Adventure of Charles Augustus Milverton," and "The Adventure of the Illustrious Client" fall into this camp.) "Silver Blaze," from *The Memoirs of Sherlock Holmes*, initially gave me some trouble. This one does look like Holmes unraveling a problem according to his proclaimed method: by working in reverse, reconstructing a logically sound explanation of the crime only from the disjointed matter that is laid before him—and, by extension, available to the reader. In this story, a racehorse goes missing, its trainer is found dead, and the murderer turns out to be . . . the horse.

There are two points in favor of Holmes's having solved the case only by deducing from the facts presented to the reader. First, there is the famous "curious incident of the dog in the night-time" (347). Holmes points out to Watson that the watchdog at the stable did not bark when the horse was stolen. Later, Holmes shows how this indicated that the criminal was someone known to the dog and thus belonging to the stables. From this he concludes that it was an inside job. This is indeed reasoning backward. So far, so good. Second, he asks a question about the lame sheep near the stables. He explains subsequently that this pointed to the culprit being the trainer himself, because if someone wanted to lame the stolen racehorse, he would have first practiced by cutting the tendons of such animals as sheep. Both these facts are available in the lead-up to the solution, and Holmes's explanations show how decisive these seemingly minor observations were in reaching the solution. It looks like his famed technique of rational deduction is indeed at work here, and that the case rests on decodable clues.

However, a crucial part of Holmes's solution is the motive. This is where Doyle slips up. In "Silver Blaze," the criminal's motive is that he is supporting a mistress in a separate establishment under an assumed name. He needs the money to keep up this lavish double life. But this information is withheld from us until the very end. Until the last pages, the reader is led to believe that a bill discovered for an expensive gown belongs to a certain Mr. Derbyshire. Unbeknownst to us, Holmes has taken a photo of the trainer to the milliner and has ascertained that the trainer and Mr. Derbyshire are one and the same person. Holmes is therefore in possession of a motive based on information the reader and Watson know nothing about. Holmes's excursion to the milliner's does not come up until the final accounting.

It would be productive—even fun—but exhausting to examine every solution in turn. Let us take a closer look at the stories Moretti categorizes as relying on "decodable" clues. What we are looking for is a hermeneutic principle: whether the story is constructed around details made available for the scrutiny of the reader, so that the clues can be decoded and the underlying events (in principle) put back together—or if instead that interpretive activity belongs only to a character in the diegesis.

Out of the first collection, *The Adventures of Sherlock Holmes*, Moretti identifies four stories with decodable clues.[24] But in order to solve "A Case of Identity," the reader would need to detect that the same typewriter was used in two different letters—letters that we do not have before us to compare. In order to solve the case of "The Red-Headed League," we would need to see (as Holmes does) the knees of Jabez Wilson's assistant, as well as recognize in his description all the traits of one John Clay—whom Holmes has been tracking for years but who is of course unknown to us. To recognize a known criminal mastermind by sight is certainly a great advantage in "decoding" the other facts of the case! Holmes has this advantage and we do not. Next, "The Adventure of the Speckled Band," as Moretti notes, though "usually seen as a splendid cluster of clues, has been repeatedly criticized by articles pointing out that snakes do not drink milk, cannot hear whistles, cannot crawl up and down bell cords, and so on."[25] A reader would have to "know" all this bogus information that Holmes relies on in order to solve the case. The last of Moretti's exceptions, "The Adventure of the Blue Carbuncle," is solved through Holmes following the repeated sale of a goose back to its origin; the real criminal is caught because he is retracing the same tracks. This one seems to me not even close. It is really a case of legwork and not clues.

We began this inquiry by looking for evidence that the hermeneutic principles aligned with "critique" so often articulated by Holmes—reasoning backward, discovering hidden connections leading to ultimate causes—are operative in the plotting of his solutions. It has turned out otherwise. When Holmes sees that, for example, one ear (on a head) looks like another ear (in a box), this can hardly be taken to demonstrate the workings of "critique."

Rather than identifying Holmes with critique, I concur with the older Marxist criticism on Doyle, which sees the Holmes books as instead ratifying bourgeois apologetics and providing an ideological cover through their reductive and superficial assignment of social causality. However, this criticism itself tends to be too "sociological" and lacking in formal precision. For example, Raymond Williams sees the detective's solution, in analytically isolating a single bad actor rather than a systemic complexity, as furnishing an alibi to vindicate a localizable apparatus of legalistic power. He describes the ending of the stories as fixing on a narrow point of culpability, of "local agency" abstracted away from broader mystifications.[26] Moretti, in an earlier study of Holmes, theoretically oriented toward Frankfurt School Marxism, argues that the rigidly formulaic solutions of the Holmes stories, their mechanistic technique or "syntax," function as bearer of a flattening hegemonic imperative.[27] Detective fiction, he claims, by enforcing a gulf between its "deep structures" and the "surface laws" of its plotting, functions as an instance of *cultural fetishism.*"[28]

The problem for both Williams's and Moretti's Marxist readings is that they understand Holmes's solutions to fold any overdetermination or complexity into an ultimately limited, determinate identification, when Holmes collars the individual culprit. They consider the solution to eliminate any "leftover." That is what

I want to argue against. For this picture is not borne out in numerous cases. Often Holmes's arrest of the criminal opens an eruptive trauma, such as the intergenerational and intercontinental revenge flashbacks in *A Study in Scarlet* (in Mormon Utah) or *The Sign of Four* (the 1857 Indian mutiny), which are "settled" by the crime but utterly ignored by Holmes, and do not form any part of his solution.

I do not mean to celebrate the messiness and formal badness of the Holmes cases as being somehow subversive of a total ideological closure. Quite the opposite. Both Williams and Moretti identify, correctly in my view, the bourgeois-aligned ideological dimension of the detective's solutions, how they are sundered from the real, material processes of history. But they see those processes as being entirely swallowed up (or cathected) in the solution—or banished altogether, which is what we find in Agatha Christie's chamber pieces. As we will see in analyzing *A Study in Scarlet*, instead of collapsing all of the social and historical dimensions of a case into a finite point, Doyle splits the backstory of the crime into several strands that never get knotted together. The misrecognition belonging to the crime (how to read the clues and so on) is just not mediated by the larger history that is arbitrarily set next to it. "History" persists in the Holmes stories, but as a foreign body, just one fragmentary sequence among others.

❦

A Study in Scarlet is probably most memorable to its readers for first bringing Holmes and Watson together, and setting them up in lodgings at 221B Baker Street. But the proper action begins when an American is found dead, with no marks of violence, in an unfurnished room in Brixton. The Scotland Yard investigator calls on Holmes, the world's only consulting detective, for assistance. Despite the word "Rache" being written in blood on the wall, the murder has nothing to do with a "Rachel" nor with German socialists, which are the two official theories. Holmes gives an astonishingly precise description of the murderer, though he does not prevent a second murder. The victim this time is another American, the secretary of the first man. Holmes's method of investigating is entirely opaque to Watson (and to the reader). After asking seemingly irrelevant questions and making brusque pronouncements with no apparent basis, he abruptly claps handcuffs on a complete stranger who comes up to their rooms of his own will, and declares this unknown cabdriver, Jefferson Hope, to be the murderer. So ends part I of the novel.

Immediately following this, Doyle drops the "reminiscences" of Dr. Watson, and begins a long third-person narrative entitled "The Country of the Saints," set in Mormon Utah. The main character of this section is neither Holmes, nor Watson, nor even the murder victim, nor even our recent acquaintance Jefferson Hope, but someone we have never heard of, one John Ferrier. The historical setting is 1847 (and subsequently 1860), while the murder under investigation in London takes place in the early 1880s. This John Ferrier and his adopted daughter are saved from starvation by Mormons while migrating westward, but on the condition that they join the faith. When they arrive in Salt Lake City, Ferrier prospers and the girl Lucy grows up to be a beauty, fought over by the sons of the Mormon Elders. Ferrier, disgusted by the practice of bigamy, refuses to let Lucy marry into the Mormon elite, and together they escape from Salt Lake City with the help of Lucy's non-Mormon fiancé Jefferson Hope. The Mormons, not to be put off so easily, murder Ferrier and take Lucy back to Salt Lake City, where she is forced into a bigamous marriage but dies soon after. Jefferson Hope vows revenge for this double murder and follows Lucy's two Mormon suitors across America and then across Europe. He finally catches up with them in England, with the murderous results already seen.

The material in the flashback (taking up roughly one-third of the novel) does not correspond exactly with what was to have been explained—namely, how the murder was committed. Notwithstanding this positive flood of material from the past, the flashback does not advance the case's solution proper, but instead shelters a vast horde of irrelevancies. The Mormon drama does not figure at all in Holmes's investigation.[29] On one hand, the third-person narration cuts off when Jefferson Hope arrives in London: the story is not carried up to the murder itself. On the other hand, the most important elements (such as the motive) are recounted still once more when the story resumes in Watson's hand.

It might appear that, after the protracted flashback, there is not much left for Holmes to add. After all, we have already been transported to 1850s Utah, we have heard Jefferson Hope's confession at the police station—how he planted false clues at the crime scene, the chemical makeup of the poison he used, the connection to the second murder, and so on. But a great deal apparently remains for Holmes to clear up. In fact, the main event has yet to be narrated, for only now does Holmes rehearse his own process of reasoning. This is the payoff. (Conspicuously, Holmes makes not a single reference to the strange life of John Ferrier, which we have just had at great length.) It is as though everything has to be observed twice: once for the mystery of the crime itself, and again for the equally mysterious method of Holmes's solution. In its insufficiency to either task, Watson's account, that famous device of internal focalization, turns out to be only holding at bay until the final chapter the unadulterated stream of the detective's own observing consciousness.

Taken together, the flashback, the murderer's confession to the police, and Holmes's own reconstruction of the case overwhelm the novel with retrospection. The second half of the novel takes on the inverse characteristics of that psychological type recognizable from Dostoevsky or psychoanalysis, the innocent person who will not stop confessing to heinous crimes out of all proportion to his real culpability. In *A Study in Scarlet*, it is as if no crime can be quite solved enough, with the result that the initial crime scene becomes just such a minor appendage to a growing corpus of explanations.

We are now in a position to pull apart the different temporal sequences operating in the plot—leaving aside for now the extraneous Mormon flashback. In "The Typology of Detective Fiction," Tzvetan Todorov uses the sturdy distinction taken from the Russian formalists, between *fabula* and *sjužet*, as the starting point for a narratological analysis of detective fiction.[30] *Fabula*, the underlying or inciting event, means here the raw occurrence of the crime—this is what the detective is trying to piece together. Viktor Shklovsky, in his discussion of the Holmes stories, calls this their "temporal transposition": we see the bloody consequences of the crime but the commission of the crime is omitted.[31] *Sjužet*, on the other hand, refers to the digressive and baffling progress of the detective's questioning and pursuit, often in the footsteps of the original actors. In *Reading for the Plot*, Peter Brooks interprets the Holmes case "The Musgrave Ritual" as an exemplary instance of plot as the hermeneutic work upon the *fabula* accomplished in the *sjužet*.[32]

This is a start. But the sequences of *fabula* and *sjužet* really cover only a part of the plot structure. There is more cognitive doubling back in a detective story than just the investigation and the solution.

- For the narratologists, the crime is the *fabula* to be reconstructed. It takes place first but is not narrated until later. Let us call this the *Crime* sequence.
- The *sjužet*, meanwhile, begins with the body being found, the detective being called in, the study of the crime scene, and ends with the arrest and identification of the criminal. Let us call this the *Investigation and Arrest* sequence. Here we see all of the evidence—the crime scene, the clues—out of order, awaiting reassembly in the solution. At that point Holmes pronounces the story of the crime.

These two sequences do not exhaust the different orderings we see in *A Study in Scarlet*.

- While Holmes succeeds in putting the events of the crime into their proper order, his logical deduction, the way that he eliminates successive improbabilities, takes a different route from both the step-by-step commission of the crime and the zigzag retracing of the investigation. The logical articulation does not coincide with these chronological ones. This is the *Logical* sequence.

- Then there is the flagging of clues within the hermeneutic code, the moment when an item in the narrated world properly comes into its own as a clue and is available (or visible) for the reader in all its relevant dimensions. The Investigation and Arrest sequence may present the items belonging to the Crime sequence in one order, as merely occurrent entities, but delay making them available (potentially decodable) to the reader except in a transposed order. As Holmes remarks to Watson elsewhere, "Now you clearly see the sequence of events, though you see them, of course, in the inverse order to the way in which they presented themselves to me" ("The Adventure of the Six Napoleons," 594). This inverted order is the *Availability to the Reader* sequence.

- Finally, there is the order in which he narrates the solution. Moretti says that Holmes "narrates the *fabula*."[33] In fact, Holmes often prefers to replay the order of the *sjužet*. He goes back through the events of the investigation as Watson narrated them in the first place. Now he adds his commentary along the way; the important difference is that clues are made available to him in yet another sequence. He is free to jump around between his initial suspicions, his legwork and clever ploys, and his privileged information. This is the *Reconstruction* order. (In stories without a third-person flashback, Holmes might use this space to parachute in a full recounting of the backstory leading up to the crime, as we see with the prior history of the black pearl of the Borgias in "The Adventure of the Six Napoleons." In *A Study in Scarlet* that duty is handed over to an outside narration, which arrives in the dead middle of the book.)

These sequences can be put into their own meta sequence. Crime obviously starts everything off. Next, the Investigation and Arrest, which other critics take as the *sjužet*, itself acts as a new *fabula* the subsequent sequences overcode in turn. Then, the Logical order determines what clues will count as being relevantly Available to the Reader. The Reconstruction comes last and replays the Investigation in its annotated hermeneutic fullness; Holmes goes back and notices for our benefit what Watson had missed.

Each sequence organizes the pertinent information in the case in a different way. There are only three pieces of information that Holmes requires to arrest the murderer. (This does not include, strangely enough, knowing the identity of the murderer. Holmes claps handcuffs on whatever cabdriver walks through his door, once his trap has been laid. Doyle does not require that the culprit should have already fallen under suspicion by the reader.) These items are:

> "a cab had made two ruts with its wheels close to the curb" in front of the house where the body was found (32)
>
> "Having sniffed the dead man's lips I detected a slightly sour smell, and I came to the conclusion that he had had poison forced upon him" (84)
>
> "a ring tinkled down and rolled across the floor . . . a woman's wedding-ring" (29–30)

Just as any good mystery contains a number of red herrings or false leads, so *A Study in Scarlet* introduces many brilliant deductions by Holmes that do not end up leading anywhere. They are window dressing, irrelevant to the solution. I am thinking of Holmes's impressive foreknowledge of the murderer's height, his florid face, the observation that the horse driving the cab has three new shoes and one old one, the particularities of the cigar ash at the scene, and so on. None of that matters. All that is needed is the cab tracks, the poison, and the ring.

In the Crime sequence, these clues are left during the deed itself. First, the cab is left standing in front of the house by the murderer; then, the poison is forced on the victim; finally, the wedding ring is dropped in the exultation over the dead body. So the sequence here is cab tracks, poison, ring.

The Investigation and Arrest sequence is focalized through Watson, who performs several narrative functions. He gathers in all the details of the scene at Number 3, Lauriston Gardens, without any filter: the background information to the case (like the content of the victim's pockets that give his name, Enoch Drebber, and his address), a description of the setting, the various bad theories put forward by the official police, and his own recapitulation of the apparent difficulties of the case. Most importantly, Watson records the steps of the strange pantomime that Holmes performs in his study of the crime scene: his scrutiny of the path leading up to the house, his examination and sniffing of the body, and his peregrinations and obscure measuring of odd marks about the room using his magnifying glass. After the examination of the crime scene, the chapters leading up to the murderer's arrest at the end of part I follow each of the three clues in turn. Chapter 4 introduces Holmes's observations about the ruts made by the cab wheels in the mud. In chapter 5, Holmes places an advertisement about the lost ring meant to lure its owner out of hiding. In chapter 7, Holmes comes into possession of the pills, which have been left behind at the scene of a second murder. So the order presented to Watson is cab tracks, ring, poison.

The first point in the Logical sequence is the murder by poison. Holmes is fond of remarking that "when you have excluded the impossible, whatever remains, however improbable, must be the truth" ("The Adventure of the Beryl Coronet," 315). Suicide is ruled out by another set of footprints and the writing scrawled in blood on the wall. The use of poison is indicated by there being no marks on the body, and confirmed when Holmes smells the dead man's lips. "I came to the conclusion that he had had poison forced upon him . . . By the method of exclusion, I had arrived at this result, for no other hypothesis would meet the facts" (49). Once the nature of the crime is in place, Holmes is in a position to interpret the "single real clue which was presented," namely, the ruts left by the cab wheels (49). These "showed . . . that the horse had wandered on in a way which would have been impossible had there been anyone in charge of it. Where, then, could the driver be, unless he were inside the house?" (85). Along with the footprints found all around the room, this drifting horse indicates that the killer had been some time about his business. "It must have been a private wrong, and not a political one, which called for such a methodical revenge" (84). Furthermore, if "one man wished to dog another through London, what better means could he adopt than to turn cabdriver?" (85). Once revenge is established as the motive, the discovery of the ring is logically subordinate; it merely "settled the question. Clearly the murderer had used it to remind his victim of some dead or absent woman" (85). The Logical order is poison, cab tracks, ring.

Clues become Available to the Reader in a still different order than their first mention in the course of the Investigation. Watson introduces clues in a sort of coarse focus, but the case usually turns on a detail that is brought out by the finer focus of Holmes's eye. As he puts it to Watson: "You see, but you do not observe." ("A Scandal in Bohemia," 162–63). Where Watson only sees "many marks of footsteps upon the wet clayey soil," Holmes observes a complex dance of different boots and different strides: "Patent-leather boots had gone round, and Square-toes had hopped over," or "Patent-leathers stood still while Square-toes walked up and down" (A Study in Scarlet, 28, 33, 34). What I count as the first appearance of a clue is the moment when the reader has not only seen some item in its mere presence, but when its salient dimension—how it will fit into the puzzle—becomes available. As we have seen, most of Holmes's astonishing productions depend on some observed detail that he keeps in hand, so that this sequence is necessarily wrenched from the order of Watson's narration. Of the three clues here, only the wedding ring, which falls away from the body when it is being carried to the morgue, is decodable on its first appearance (29). Holmes asserts the use of poison as a parting shot while leaving the crime scene (32). But this point only becomes fully available to us eleven chapters later, when he tells Watson that he smelled poison on the victim's lips (84). We find the same transposition when Holmes first describes the cab tracks in some detail (32). The important point—that the wheels had drifted, suggesting that the horse was unattended—is not made available to the reader until ten chapters later (85). The order, then, is ring, poison, cab tracks.

The Reconstruction sequence, given in the detective's solution, is properly the recognition scene, albeit in a deficient mode. In *A Study in Scarlet*, Holmes begins the Reconstruction by lecturing Watson about his analytical method of reasoning backward: "this was a case in which you were given a result and had to find everything else for yourself" (84). We are told that "the whole thing is a chain of logical sequences without a break or flaw" (85). But in explaining the case to Watson he does not proceed backward at all, rewinding from the results to causes. Instead, he provides a running commentary on what he observed and how he responded, in the *same* order we have already seen in Watson's narration of the Investigation and Arrest. We now learn what Holmes was thinking at moments when his behavior or pronouncements were obscure to Watson. The links between Holmes's virtuosic explanations and his observed research are now provided. This means bringing back in all the old irrelevant clues. How did Holmes arrive at the idea of the murderer's florid complexion? Because the blood at the scene must have "burst from the murderer's nose in his excitement," and that only happens with "ruddy faced" people (85). Furthermore, Holmes does not follow "the different steps in [his] reasoning" in a linear fashion, as promised (84). The steps of Holmes's reasoning are still being presented out of order, apart from their analytical determinations. Consequently, he introduces the same clue, the cab tracks, in two different places—dividing his "impression" as if it was two separate events. He examines the tracks only once; by that point he has "already determined in [his] own mind" the relevance of the cab drifting into the road (85). But he holds back from presenting that determination in its proper place, as a "step" in his reasoning; he mentions it only after he has telegrammed to Cleveland, asking about the victim's marriage, and received back the name of the murderer. The first incomplete observation about the cab tracks is now repeated, but as it were "enlarged," so that Holmes might deduce that Jefferson Hope is working as a cabdriver.

Why does Holmes intrude the irrelevant clues and the repetition of the cab tracks clue into the supposedly flawless, unbroken Reconstruction sequence? Because the datum to be explained is not the occurrence of the crime at all. The object of Holmes's concluding narration is not primarily to reassemble the chain of events (the rather outré crime) that produced the crime scene with its confusing array of clues and misdirection—as Todorov, Moretti, and Brooks argue. It is rather to provide a rationale for his own inscrutable behavior as already observed during the investigation, for example, his focus on seemingly unimportant matters, his silences, his prophetic descriptions pulled out of thin air. Wherever Watson (or the attending official police) cannot follow Holmes's questions and deductions, that is where Doyle is planting a marker for the hermeneutic code to come back and pick up later. The locus of mystery in this sequence is not, therefore, the who of the crime under investigation, but the how of his solution.

In other words, the denouement allows Holmes to treat the coherence of his own actions as the object of inquiry and reconstruction. We first follow his pursuit of the criminal in the dark, and it is this pursuit that is illuminated after the fact by Holmes—the murder itself having been narrated by Jefferson Hope. The mystery that Holmes has to unravel, in the chapter titled "Conclusion," is not the mystery of the crime. Consequently, the misrecognitions involved are both trivial and external. Trivial, because the interpretation of something like the murderer's florid face has no bearing on the ultimate mystery. (Another way to put this is that the crime itself dwindles in importance next to Holmes's process of reasoning.) External, because the misrecognition concerning Holmes's reasoning—his queries seem like non sequiturs, he fixates on whimsical or inscrutable points of detail—is only a misrecognition *for us*, to use Hegel's distinction; there is no misrecognition of his reasoning *for itself*. Holmes is not laboring under any confusion about what he is up to. Things are opaque only because we are locked into Watson's perspective and Holmes prefers to keep him in the dark. "I'm not going to tell you much more of the case, Doctor. You know a conjuror gets no credit when once he has explained his trick" (33).

There is neither a subjective nor objective dialectic of misrecognition here. When it comes to Holmes's own consciousness, the whole idea is that he is infallible, never taken in. Certainly, Holmes will never find himself behind the curtain of the mystery, like what we see in Wilkie Collins's *The Moonstone*, where the investigating protagonist Franklin Blake learns that he himself committed the crime in an opium-induced unconscious state. Neither is there any internal mediation on the side of the crime, which is straightforward enough in its execution; its enigmatic shadow does not cloak any constitutive misrecognition. That is to say, the crime and its history are not a tangled sequence *for the criminal*. In *A Study in Scarlet*, when Holmes follows up the clue of the wedding ring, this produces only the name of the killer. Cleveland does not have to telegraph back to him the entire text of part II of the book. For Holmes's purposes, the clue is simply not that deep. The further elaboration of its history in "The Country of the Saints" is not immanent to its function within the plot, but only a kind of bad infinity of more and more backstory. Just as Holmes's own (subjective) impression of the cab tracks could be split off into separate moments, so the (objective) history of the ring is fragmented into a separate narration.

According to Ernst Bloch, the *"most decisive* criterion" of the detective novel is "the *un-narrated factor* and its *reconstruction . . .* the discovery of something that happened *ante rem."*[34] Many of Holmes's cases do involve long flashbacks that precede the commission of the crime, and these never figure as pertinent misrecognitions in the solution. That is to say, Holmes does not piece together the backstory by way of solving the crime. It is just something tacked on and not incorporated.[35] Such long retrospections set apart from Holmes's interpretive work are especially a feature of the novels. In *A Study in Scarlet*, the interpolated narrative does not belong to Watson's written account, and it takes up five chapters, or 34 percent of the total pages. In *The Sign of Four*, the interpolated narrative is recounted in dialogue to Holmes, and it takes up one chapter, or 19 percent of the total pages. In *The Valley of Fear*, the interpolated narrative is related in the third person by Watson, as his reconstruction of a collection of papers discovered at the crime scene, and it takes up seven chapters, or 52 percent of the total pages.

Instead of completing or deepening the solution, the Holmesian flashback merely attaches additional material to the investigation, not so much reconstructing the past as annexing an adjacent narrative. The flashbacks are set outside the course of Watson's narration of the investigation proper and intrude rudely on the self-contained "given facts" of the case. Often, these supervening flashbacks import into the stories a distinctive generic content as well. They are drawn fully formed from the generic worlds of romance or adventure. In *A Study in Scarlet*, the flashback is a historical romance; the flashback in *The Sign of Four*, set during the 1857 Indian Rebellion, is plainly lifted from *The Moonstone*; in "The Adventure of the Cardboard Box," it is a domestic melodrama of adultery; in "The *Gloria Scott*," a tale of mutiny on the high seas; in *The Valley of Fear*, something like an industrial novel. It is as though Doyle were conducting, in the margins of the detective genre, a revue of the literary variety of which he was capable and from which the public's demand for more Sherlock Holmes was keeping his talents. At the same time, the stories include the past only as discrete miniatures—far from being "dialogical," such inclusions are strictly partitioned off from Holmes himself.[36] Holmes himself has no interest in the past as such. "His clear and logical mind would not be drawn from its present work to dwell upon memories of the past" (*The Hound of the Baskervilles*, 761). His cases begin only when his doorbell rings or he receives a telegram—they have no prior existence. As soon as one case has terminated, his focus on the next one "has a curious way of blotting out what has passed . . . So each of my cases displaces the last" (*The Hound of the Baskervilles*, 761).

When the past is summoned up in the stories, it is as a preserved repository. No matter how far back the cases reach, their temporality remains static. One of Doyle's favorite scenarios is a revenge from long ago. Three of the novels, *A Study in Scarlet*, *The Sign of Four*, and *The Valley of Fear*, depict the prosecution of an ineradicable—though long past—grievance.[37] No one in this universe ever forgives and forgets. Revenge brooks every delay: the true meaning of Satan's "immortal hate" in *Paradise Lost*. Once the wheels of vengeance have been set in motion, no number of disguises, no amount of globetrotting, and no passage of time can ever diminish the revenge motive. In the Sherlock Holmes stories, there can be no forgiveness, nor wearing away. Doyle will often prefer to let an elaborate revenge scheme play out fully, rather than have his detective intervene and prevent the crime. For example, at the end of part I of *A Study in Scarlet*, the arrest of Jefferson Hope is held up as an astonishing success, even though it arrives when there is no risk of any further murders—he has succeeded in murdering everyone he had intended to—and too late for justice to be served, as Hope dies of a heart attack before he can even stand trial. The case is solved—but only insofar as there is a new and equally unknown name and face to put to the crime. At the end of the investigation, the detective merely produces before us a character we have never seen nor heard of previously. In this sense the arrest also "arrests" the temporality of interpretation. The flashback to Mormon Utah remains a leftover, an overcompensating superfluous illumination that has another try at folding the *fabula* into the *sjužet*, but never intersects with the detective's reasoning in his solution.

The Sherlock Holmes cases, as a paradigm of detective fiction, occupy a privileged place in narratology, where they are taken to strip the story down to the barest mechanisms of its plot.[38] Novel theory, narratology's disciplinary cousin, has had less to say about the four Holmes novels that Doyle wrote (*A Study in Scarlet*, *The Sign of Four*, *The Hound of the Baskervilles*, and *The Valley of Fear*), except to disdain considering them as capital-N "Novels." Moretti asserts that at root "detective fiction is radically anti-novelistic"; no matter whether a story is "ten or two hundred pages . . . detective fiction always has the structure of the short story."[39] D. A. Miller likewise draws a distinction between "the detective novel" and "the novel *tout court*."[40] This interpretation goes as far back as the Russian formalists. In distilling the regimented script followed by the Holmes short stories, Shklovsky does not even address the novels, as if they were just padded-out versions of the same formula.[41]

My claim is that the Sherlock Holmes novels should be considered in light of the problematics of novel theory—and not merely by pointing out that the first two novels precede any of the stories. (If anything, the stories are derivative of the novels, which show the underlying seams of their construction much more.) After all, the central situation of each of Holmes's cases makes concrete the lofty ontological theme articulated by Lukács in *The Theory of the Novel*: "the refusal of the immanence of being to enter into empirical life."[42] Every "clue" overlooked at the scene of the crime is a reminder that essential meanings no longer shine forth from things in their immediacy. In detective fiction, there is no longer any "spontaneous totality of being," only the hermeneutic labor to work up the past from its leavings.[43]

Lukács suggests that the depletion of meaning from reality in the novel reflects "a world that has been abandoned by God."[44] This is another version of Max Weber's sociological remarks on the "disenchantment of the world."[45] Undoubtedly Sherlock Holmes is one of the colossal and even mythical figures of the kind of disenchantment Weber has in mind.[46] In every instance, the detective purports to install a meaningful pattern, a coherent sequence, a motive, in place of a confused heap of facticity. What has been inexplicable becomes obvious, even banal, in his demonstrations. *"Omne ignotum pro magnifico [est]"* (177). On the other hand, Holmes's prodigious efforts to heave up a clutch of commonplace items into proof of conspiracy and outlandish evil keeps prosaic reality from "disintegrat[ing] into the nothingness of inessentiality."[47] Nothing remains entirely innocent, for what is overlooked might be the key to apprehending a criminal enterprise. The most tedious possible task, the copying out of the *Encyclopedia Britannica* in "The Red-Headed League," may be resolved into the most exhilarating: an underground tunnel burrowing into a bank vault.

For our purposes, what is decisive in considering the Sherlock Holmes cases in light of the theory of the novel is the problematic of sundered, out-of-place subjectivity. Holmes and Watson can say in truth what Oedipus says in error, that they are "strangers to the deed" they are tasked with investigating.[48] The possibility that the two could, like Oedipus, be unwittingly investigating themselves is briefly raised in "The Adventure of Charles Augustus Milverton," only to be set aside as a bit of comedy when Holmes discounts a vague description of a suspect: "Why, it might be a description of Watson!" (582).

In the plotting of the Holmes mysteries, consciousness itself is utterly passive until jolted from outside. Holmes would remain in a stupor of cocaine, scraping dreamily at his violin, were it not for the welter of inciting stimulations that flood into his sitting room, stirring him to vital motion. Like a good empiricist subject, Holmes begins "with [his] mind entirely free of impressions" (84). To fill the mind's blank slate, he therefore requires an unbroken influx of arousing sensations, or "an impact operating from without."[49] Subjectivity is cordoned off from any implication in the temporality of the misrecognitions that it comes on from outside. The detective is inoculated from the imperatives to unmake or revise his own subjectivity because he comes to each mystery from the outside, without grave implications for his own life. He is able to leave his work at the office, so to speak. The misrecognitions pertaining to subjectivity here are not mediating because they are simply the sleight of one hand (Holmes) hiding from the other (Watson) what it is doing. Subjectivity thus remains stunted—insatiable, yet complete in itself. The opposing world, meanwhile, is nothing but the discontinuous arising of failed actions, which Holmes bats away one case at a time. It never coalesces into a totality or coherent pattern, since the "deeper" misrecognition—the severed historical dimension—is uncoordinated with the crimes to be solved. Subject and object, then, are split off not only from each other, but each side is fragmented, ramifying into noncommunicating cul-de-sacs.

Holmes is a calibrated machine of observation and analysis. From the moment we first meet Holmes in *A Study in Scarlet*, he is complete. Like Athena, he is born fully armed. The thousand pages that follow only fill in superficial qualities (e.g., the name of his brother). This completeness means, of course, that he is violently incomplete as a person or realistic character. He has forcibly, purposefully reduced himself to the thinking machine that he is. He is utterly sealed off as a human being.

> His ignorance was as remarkable as his knowledge. Of contemporary literature, philosophy and politics he appeared to know next to nothing. Upon my quoting Thomas Carlyle, he inquired in the naïvest way who he might be and what he had done. My surprise reached a climax, however, when I found incidentally that he was ignorant of the Copernican Theory and of the composition of the Solar System. (21)

Holmes has instrumentalized every relation and activity; he has no acquaintance whom he cannot call upon to play some part in a case, no hobby that he does not turn to some surprising use. He is a monomaniac, like Don Quixote or Captain Ahab, who each sees in the world only the distorted image of his own idée fixe. As Lukács writes of the former, "he is incapable of any contemplation; he lacks any inclination or possibility of inward-turned activity."[50] Holmes's character is leveled down by his constant pursuit of the same thing, to something less than human (an asocial drug addict) and also more than human (his incredible feats of memory, the ability to forgo sleep when on a case). As we have seen, his solutions relocate the locus of mystery from the crime itself to a second-order recapitulation of his own thought process. Thus, he discovers only himself over and over again.

The world upon which Holmes hurls himself is a discontinuous tumult of facts and impressions. History appears only as an arbitrary eruption, in numerous undigested, generically disruptive flashbacks that do not develop or lend coherence to the crimes in which they result. When the backstory is thus dilated, the result is an arbitrary yoking of incompatible meanings and genres; the different scales of the past do not inform one another. Instead of rooting the mystery within its long-term conditions and environment, Doyle leaves the short-term misrecognition stranded in history, rattling around in history like a pea in its shell. Unfolding the crime does not lead to the unfolding of the backstory, the recounting of which is a separate affair. Whatever may be the threads of concealed truth in the crime scene that allow Holmes to solve the immediate mystery, pulling on those threads will never bring him face to face with history. That dimension of the past is not repressed, it is simply "off-site."[51]

Whenever a totalizing movement is mentioned, such as the vast conspiracy with Dr. Moriarty at its head, this is only abstractly asserted. We never see the intervening links of social reality put into play. As Lukács describes "abstract idealism" in the novel, "outside reality is no more than a sluggish, formless, meaningless mass."[52] Although Holmes's career is an unbroken string of successes, the world of crime remains untouched and undiminished. Whatever his objective of ending all crime, "he cannot, with all his negating, get so far as to annihilate it outright and be done with it."[53] The fantasy of retirement he outlines in "The Final Problem" is of course unrealizable: "if I could beat [Professor Moriarty], if I could free society of him, I should feel that my own career had reached its summit, and I should be prepared to turn to some more placid line in life . . . I could continue to live in the quiet fashion which is most congenial to me, and to concentrate my attention upon my chemical researches" (470). Even though, as we have seen, Holmes defeats his "Napoleon of crime" in "The Final Problem," neither the death of this archvillain nor Holmes's own apparent death are sufficient to put an end to his crime-solving activities (471). In a novel like George Eliot's *The Mill on the Floss* or Dickens's *Our Mutual Friend*, when characters meet their death clasped in each other's arms, this represents a symbolic and emotional finality, perhaps artificial but an appropriate conclusion. When Sherlock Holmes (apparently) and Moriarty (actually) plunge to their deaths, it is felt as an abrupt and arbitrary termination, not as a resolution and culmination of forces long at work. The Holmes saga can only come to a halting and abortive stop (as in "The Final Problem") or be cut off mid-reel, as it were—such that the last stories, in *The Case Book of Sherlock Holmes*, give no indication of *being* the last stories. There are even more Holmes stories published after the "final" one than came before.[54] The cases are without real temporality, "a motley series of isolated adventures complete in themselves."[55]

Objective, outside reality therefore has neither permanence nor immanence in itself, but is only a "bad" infinity of perpetually arising collisions against Holmes's consciousness. All of Victorian England crops up in his cases only as a string of crimes and infamies. At most, we can see Watson reading a newspaper or coming back from a patient before the story's client sends up his card at 221B Baker Street or (in the later stories) before Watson is called away from his wife by Holmes's summons. The little down time that *is* visible in the stories is anathema to Holmes, as we see in *The Sign of Four*:

> [WATSON]: "May I ask whether you have any professional inquiry on foot at present?"
>
> [HOLMES]: "None. Hence the cocaine. I cannot live without brainwork. What else is there to live for? Stand at the window here. Was ever such a dreary, dismal, unprofitable world? See how the yellow fog swirls down the street and drifts across the dun-colored houses. What could be more hopelessly prosaic and material? What is the use of having powers, Doctor, when one has no field upon which to exert them? Crime is commonplace, existence is commonplace, and no qualities save those which are commonplace have any function upon earth." (93)

The "dismal, unprofitable world" is, however, rarely seen. Holmes's world is as suffocating as Hamlet's Elsinore. He prefers the blinds to be drawn. "He loved to lie in the centre of five millions of people, with his filaments stretching out and running through them, responsive to every little rumor or suspicion of unsolved crime" ("The Adventure of the Cardboard Box" 888). Watson only takes up his pen to describe the brief periods of crime-solving that dot an otherwise commonplace (and unnarrated) existence. So, on one hand, the world reveals itself only in snatches of opposition to Holmes, as a field on which he can exercise his talents. On the other hand, it is the very ruptures in the prosaic world (its nonidentity) that call Holmes forth, set him into motion. For the big events of history or any superordinate logic of society also fall outside of his concern. He is interested in the newspaper only for its agony column ("The Adventure of the Noble Bachelor," 288). Watson tells us, "I was aware that by anything of interest, Holmes meant anything of criminal interest. There was the news of a revolution, of a possible war, and of an impending change of government, but these did not come within the horizon of my companion" ("The Adventure of the Bruce-Partington Plans," 913).

We have seen that the flashbacks are not yoked to the explanation of the crime, but subsist in an annex of mere occurrence. This arbitrariness and disconnection is also true of each of the cases in relation to almost any other. Holmes is given to repeating the choice maxims concerning his method, in case the reader has missed them elsewhere. Even the characterization of Professor Moriarty in *The Valley of Fear* presumes no readerly acquaintance with his earlier presentation in "The Final Problem." The stories are chronologically out of order, but this, too, is a kind of pointless quirk—there is no good reason a given story could not as well have taken place in 1887 as in 1903. The order in which one reads the stories, the year in which they are set, whether Holmes is thought to be alive or the story has been drawn from a posthumous archive—all of this is totally arbitrary.

The narrative form of subjectivity is therefore fetishized, insofar as consciousness is unmediated by history or materiality; and it is reified, insofar as the processes of history and social conflict glimpsed at the margins of the cases are not sublimated into factors of consciousness, but merely terminate in (without being taken up by or resolved into) the covering superficiality of a number of arbitrary crimes. The crime is never shown as repressing its historical preconditions, which are tacked on to add pathos, or flair, or just additional pages. That is to say, the Holmes mysteries are not uncritical, ideological productions only in their content (since they never approach the insight common to Honoré de Balzac and Bertolt Brecht that the mystery underlying the gleaming innocence of capital is the greatest crime of all) but down to the novelistic problematic undergirding their plotting of subjectivity and misrecognition.

The Sherlock Holmes mysteries more or less kill off recognition scenes in the English novel outside of detective fiction. Of course, literary forms do not have absolute dates of expiration. The appearance of *A Study in Scarlet* in *Beeton's Christmas Annual* in 1887 was not an extinction event. But if you are looking for novelistic recognition scenes outside of detective fiction, they really are much harder to find after its publication. Just the year before, Thomas Hardy's *The Mayor of Casterbridge* and Robert Louis Stevenson's *The Strange Case of Dr. Jekyll and Mr. Hyde* both employed recognition scenes to unmask a corrosive deceit implicit in the bourgeois self-image. (Elizabeth-Jane is not Henchard's own daughter! Dr. Jekyll *is* Mr. Hyde!) But Hardy's subsequent novels *Tess of the D'Urbervilles* (1891) and *Jude the Obscure* (1895) do not include any recognition scenes. The decisive moments in characters' destinies, instead of being illuminated after the fact, remain unknown to them, or are merely compulsive, or go unrepresented. In *The Picture of Dorian Gray* (1891), as if to cement its status as a plotless "novel of ideas," Oscar Wilde gives away the dramatic secret of Dorian's unfading youth—his portrait ages, he does not—at the very outset, instead of disclosing it at the end.[56] There is certainly suspense over whether Dorian will get caught, but there is no longer mystery, as there was in *Dr. Jekyll and Mr. Hyde*.

To be sure, Henry James's later fiction does contain some remarkable recognition scenes, especially in *The Ambassadors* (1903). But in this respect, at least, one can draw a hard line between the late James and his successor, Joseph Conrad. The humiliating and disillusioning discovery made by Lambert Strether is brought home with a nearly unbearable intimacy. Conrad does preserve some of the tricks of temporality and epistemological reversals belonging to recognition scenes, but without dislocating subjectivity in misrecognitions outside of itself. The temporal transpositions found in *The Secret Agent* (1907) or *Under Western Eyes* (1911) are situated outside of any character's consciousness. They are not involved in the novelist's formal pyrotechnics. In *The Secret Agent*, none of the characters ever holds all the threads of the story in their hands. In *Under Western Eyes*, Razumov at least knows about himself that he has made a deal with the tsarist police; the reader is in the dark only because that scene is cut off and not revealed until the last part of the book.[57] The narrative sleight of hand is not, for us, a misrecognition in the plot itself.

Of course, recognition scenes do not get wiped out entirely. They persist in the generic enclave of detective fiction, where they become increasingly refined—largely by expelling the social content that the Holmes cases still appended to their solutions. Detective fiction becomes more and more a locked-room scenario in every sense, an intellectual puzzle formulated outside of any impure social complications. As Raymond Williams has observed, "the true fate of the country-house novel was its evolution into the middle-class detective story," with its "isolated assembly of a group of people whose immediate and transient relations were decipherable by an abstract mode of detection rather than by [any] full and connected analysis."[58] This isolation and abstraction goes hand in hand with the technical advance made on Doyle's management of his recognition scenes by later mystery authors. For Christie's recognition scenes are much cleaner and more contained. Her detectives, Poirot and Mrs. Marple, do not (like Holmes) hold back the decisive observation that would in principle allow the reader to solve the case on her own. They are puzzles in a sterilized laboratory setting. At the same time, Christie eschews even the uncoordinated narrative parataxis of Doyle's interpolations; she brackets history altogether, whereas Doyle strains to keep Sherlock Holmes unstained by a history that is leaking everywhere into narrative form.

The familiar version of this story runs something like this: sometime after the turn of the century, literature grew up, and respectable novels left behind the improbable coincidences and tidy conclusions of the "awful Victorian plot." Consequently, "modern writers look contemptuously at the old-fashioned, complicated methods by which the old novelists set their plots into motion."[59] No more madwomen stowed away in the attic, no more forged wills, no more secret mothers. Modernist fiction is positioned at a complete remove from the arcane devices rigged up in a novel by Dickens or Collins or Eliot. The so-called "genuine artist" is now presumed "to be above the 'long-lost heir' trick or the complicated substitutes for the old-fashioned device."[60] This objection survives unchanged in Fredric Jameson's criticism of the "mechanical practice of dé-nouement, the final tying together of the loose ends, the fulfillment of all the carefully planted clues and secondary characters, the great recognition scenes as well (Mamma! Papa! Our son!),," which modernist authors can no longer take seriously.[61] If a modernist work like *The Heart of Darkness* does resemble old-fashioned detective fiction, as Peter Brooks contends, it does so only by turning the genre on its head, producing "a tale of inconclusive solutions to crimes of problematic status."[62]

The standard account just rehearsed begins from the presumption that, by giving up the plotting of recognition scenes and leaving them to detective fiction, authors like Wilde and Conrad cast off what was most regrettable and hack-neyed in the Victorian novel. But what has really vanished, in Wilde and Con-rad, just as much as in the Holmes mysteries, is the dialectical mediation of subjectivity that had been the achievement of the recognition scenes in Dick-ens, Trollope, and James. In other words, works like *The Picture of Dorian Gray*, *The Heart of Darkness*, *The Secret Agent*, and *Under Western Eyes* have more in common with degraded genre fiction like *The Hound of the Baskervilles* than they know. Following the Holmes model, literary fiction also removes the pro-duction of meaning from an internal process; what is misrecognized no longer works its way into being in the plot, but is sealed off as a deplorable, jagged confusion—unable to take a hand in its own becoming. Wilde's philosophical novel and what Brooks calls Conrad's "unreadable reports" share with the de-graded detective novels that meaning is only assigned by, or is a problem for, an outside observer.[63] For example, Dorian Gray's involvement in the story is structurally dependent on his untouched removal; he can never "have" the ex-periences he is living out, except by relocating them to the magical portrait, which undergoes them in his place. The overall consequence is, in Lukács's vocabulary, a "contradictory subjectivism . . . which simulates a kind of dialec-tic in its dividedness, but which, in reality, only mirrors the disunity of the ob-server's standpoint."[64]

After the Victorian period, then, fiction might be said to arrive at a compro-mise. On one hand, recognition scenes are allowed, but confined to detective novels. On the other hand, while modernist literature disdains recognition scenes, it nonetheless preserves the fragmented formatting of subjectivity and objectivity that so prominently structures the Sherlock Holmes mysteries. In either case, plot no longer pulls in the contradictory involvements of historical subjectivity that were cast as misrecognitions in the Victorian novels by Dickens, Trollope, and James studied here. The recognition scenes in those novels critique capital as an immediacy in which subjectivity's misrecognitions are excised. The work of subjectivity—its meaningful transpositions and retrospective temporality—is revealed to be bound up in bourgeois social relations that misrepresent that work as either belonging to a falsely autonomous, dislocated subjectivity, or else they bury it under an inert, thinglike form. In those books, concealed relationships unfold from misrecognition; significance is consolidated from the wreckage of the past by an extensive process of hard revisions and confessed losses. When the Victorian novel form is at last superseded, the surviving parties conspire to banish henceforth the dialectical mediations that were really the achievement of those "awful" plots.

Conclusion
From Reification to the Theory of the Novel

These things were here and but the beholder
Wanting.

—Gerard Manley Hopkins, "Hurrahing in Harvest"

The claim of this book is that the problematic of misrecognition in the novel is specifically conditioned by the misrecognitions at work in capitalism. Even—or especially—where subjectivity in the novel is spared any contaminating involvement with capital, that very separation should be interpreted as part and parcel of reification and fetishism. For the outcome of these capitalist misrecognitions is the immediacy of subjectivity untethered from its material determinations—in Georg Lukács's terms, "the divorce of the phenomena of reification from their economic bases."[1] That is what is pernicious about any attempt to root out the corrupting traces of capital from the subject. Capital itself wants nothing more than to furnish a subjectivity purged of its unhappy determinacy.

Plot is where novelistic subjectivity, defined here in terms of misrecognition, happens. A "plot hole" in capital is another way of describing how capital vacates its constitutive temporality and voids the inner sequence of its formation. The most consequential way that capitalism shows up in the novel is therefore in the formal dimension of plot. That is where subjectivity takes up, or better, repeats for itself its own (constitutive) absence or deletion from capital. The very absence of subjectivity from the inner workings of capital can only be detected in subjectivity's modes of *not* finding itself there. And this is where not just formalism but the theory of the novel comes in.

In *The Theory of the Novel*, Lukács defines the novel in terms of its specific "metaphysical dissonance."[2] He presumes an irreparable schism or "incommensurability" between the soul and the world.[3] In this scheme, subjectivity by definition has to remain outside of and beyond the external world to which it is opposed. From this summary it can be seen what is missing in Lukács's theory: the possibility of misrecognition. Neither of his terms—soul or world—can be mistaken or misrepresented by the other, once they are situated on incommensurable ontological levels. For this reason, the soul never undergoes a detour or submergence in the world. In *The Theory of the Novel*, subjectivity is instead primordially split off from benighted reality. There is an unbridgeable hiatus between the two realms.

The Theory of the Novel cannot countenance, therefore, what is the basic premise of *History and Class Consciousness*: the constitutive misrecognition of subjectivity. For the Marxist Lukács, the "dissonance" is no longer between the subject and the object world. In capitalism, the subject is determined *as* and structured *by* the non-subjective. Thus, "it is precisely the conscious activity of the individual that is to be found on the object-side of the process."[4] The constitutive moment of the subject is locked up in mute otherness, and subjectivity assumes, in Karl Marx's term, an unrecognizable and "fantastic form." This all depends, not on ideology or the pervasiveness of power, but on the concealment of social relationships structuring the commodity form of value.

What does the theory of the novel require from Marxism? According to Jay Bernstein, "What is revealed [in the novel] is the activity of the self in giving form to experience."[5] The contribution of Marxism is to demonstrate how that activity unfolds within the structures of capitalism. The task for novel theory is therefore to give an account of its categories as emerging in tension with capitalism's determinations of subjectivity. Yet the misrecognition of subjectivity in the commodity-form, which is the overwhelming topic of Lukács's study of reification, has been neglected by subsequent Marxist theories of the novel, in favor of attention paid to abstraction and totality.

The concept of misrecognition laid out in this book is not specific to the novel form. It is indissociable from subjectivity as such. The significance of the novel is that the structure of misrecognition at work in subjectivity is therein yoked to the misrecognitions of capital. Prior structures of misrecognition are subsumed into the inversions of reification and fetishism. In the novel, one no longer finds misrecognition "in the wild," untouched by the representational structures induced by the capitalist value-form. I will come back to this literary history in a moment.

Apart from Marxism, psychoanalysis offers perhaps the most significant theoretical articulation of the role of misrecognition in the formation of subjectivity. Specifically, misrecognition is central to Freud's case study of the "Wolf-Man" and in the analysis of fantasy in "'A Child is Being Beaten.'" In the Wolf-Man's dream, several wolves are sitting in a tree outside of his window. The wolves are completely still and looking directly back at the dreamer. But in the interpretation of the dream, these silent observers are resolved into so many avatars of the child who is witnessing the primal scene: "The attentive looking, which in the dream was ascribed to the wolves, should rather be shifted on to him. At a decisive point, therefore, a transposition has taken place."[6] The unsettling gaze which is outside, enigmatic, and confrontational, turns out to be the gaze of the subject himself, at the very moment (albeit retrospectively) of his coming into being as a vector of desire. The dream retrospectively casts the formative moment of subjectivity into a dislocated position, a kind of mirroring that cannot be deciphered as such.

Something similar happens in the fantasy described in "'A Child is Being Beaten.'" In this article, Freud excavates the origins of a beating fantasy which undergoes several stages of repression. The transformations of the fantasy transpose the recipient of the beating from another child (in the first phase) to the child who is producing the fantasy (in the second phase) and then back to another child (in the final phase). What is important is that the masochistic dimension, which lies under the most essential repression, is transposed by misrecognition. The subject is nominally absent from the scene: "The figure of the child who is producing the beating-phantasy no longer itself appears in it."[7] But the act of looking on at the anonymous beating, which is admitted at last, is itself only a cover for a regressive, masochistic pleasure: "only the *form* of this phantasy is sadistic."[8] The subject here plays, in various disguises and grammatical inversions, all the parts of the scene. Desire is dislocated across every position of the structure.

In the psychoanalytic theory of neurosis, what is repressed is a libidinal cathexis. Repression operates on an ideational content, excluding it from the conscious system. What is repressed, however, soon avails itself of a substitutive formation. While the psychical representative of the instinct is denied entrance to consciousness, it circumvents this expulsion by means of distorted and disguised derivatives. The repressed material finds its way back into expression (the "return of the repressed") by translating itself into unrecognizable form.

Misrecognition, in the Marxist theory articulated here, involves an additional twist beyond the psychoanalytic account. In reification, the repression of the social dimension of value, its historicity and temporality, is accomplished by subjectivity itself, in the very form of its activity. Value-positing labor, mediated by the commodity-form, is *self-repressing*. It heaps up the produced commodities

which misrepresent it. Living labor becomes dead labor only through its specifically capitalist mode of being living labor. The misrecognitions of capitalism are
thus not submerged, veiled, or concealed under a false outer covering, the way
that Ariel is imprisoned in the pine tree by Sycorax, awaiting the magical staff of
Prospero to be released. Although bourgeois economic categories mystify the
social constitution of value, the mystification is built into the value-form itself.[9]
What is concealed or repressed in capitalism cannot therefore be brought to
light apart from its misrepresentation.[10] The commodity, in other words, is at
once the "veil" whose form conceals and mystifies, at the same time that it assumes the very subjectivity that it occludes.

Before the modern novel, structures of misrecognition abound in literature. For
example, the apostle Peter's denial of Jesus appears in all four Gospels. After
Jesus has been arrested, Peter is warming himself over a fire in the courtyard of
the high priest, where Peter is recognized by a nosy maid as one of Jesus's fol-
lowers. He denies knowing anything about it and moves away. Someone else
sees him and calls over some bystanders to lay hands on this wanted accomplice.
Again, Peter denies knowing Jesus. He is found out a third time, by his Galilean
accent. He begins to invoke a curse on himself and to swear that he does not
know the man they are talking about, when the cock crows. Then Peter remem-
bers that Jesus had predicted to him that the cock would not crow until Peter
had denied him three times. Peter breaks down and weeps bitterly. The misrecognition, of course, is not on the side of those accosting Peter, identifying
him as if he were in a police lineup. The misrecognition is all on Peter's side. He
is enacting his fate unawares. He only wishes in this scene to become untethered
from the catastrophe that has descended, to tear himself away. But the misrecognition is not only his breathless, automatic denials. Earlier that night, when Jesus
had predicted all this to Peter on the Mount of Olives, Peter had said he would
die with Jesus before he would deny him. What Peter has gotten shamefully
wrong—first in declaring to Jesus that he would not deny him, and then in denying him—is his inability to bear the loss taken on by Jesus. It is as if any separation were total, whereas all there is is fragility and endurance.

    In *Jersualem Delivered*, Torquato Tasso's sixteenth-century chivalric epic,
there is a curious and devastating misrecognition, which Freud singles out as
"the most moving picture" of fated and unconscious repetition.[11] In a night
battle, the knight Tancred has mistakenly slain the maiden warrior Clorinda,
whose identity is concealed by a suit of unmarked armor. He is stricken with
"woeful knowledge" when he lifts her visor and sees his dying beloved.[12] After
Clorinda is buried, Tancred enters a wood that has been enchanted by the

sorcerer Ismen, where he hacks at a cypress tree which then speaks in the voice of Clorinda:

> "Enough, enough!" the voice lamenting said,
> "Tancred, thou hast me hurt, thou didst me drive
> Out of the body of a noble maid . . .
> And now within this woeful cypress laid,
> My tender rind thy weapon sharp doth rive,
> Cruel, is't not enough thy foes to kill,
> But in their graves wilt thou torment them still?"[13]

For Tancred it seems as if wounding Clorinda over and over were his vocation, as if everything he strikes will turn out to be his beloved in some vulnerable form. But the voice is only the impersonation of an evil spirit: "All were illusions false by witchcraft wrought."[14] Freud wants to emphasize the sense of blind harm, that Tancred's every movement is steered back to the same catastrophe. But the important point about misrecognition is that Tancred's real grief is preserved, even if in a false form. Indeed, like the dead son in the dream of the burning child in *The Interpretation of Dreams*, the illusion (that Clorinda is magically imprisoned in a tree) shows her "as once more alive."[15] The disturbing misrecognition is to take what is being grieved as gone forever, unrecoverable, when, in fact, the lost beloved returns in unbearable proximity, horribly reanimated.

The history of the novel is marked from the beginning by misrecognitions that are knotted together with incipient structures of representation in capitalism. The tightening grip of capital's misrecognitions over the novel does not come from outside, but from inside, as an evasion that only replicates, *as its own form*, that from which it would flee. The first modern novel, Miguel de Cervantes's *Don Quixote*, historicizes the transition from an early modern conception of values, as substances fixed in a rigid order, to bourgeois value as the reflexivity of social representations, a play of mirrors. The book is from start to finish nothing but a series of misrecognitions. Our hidalgo is not living in a chivalric romance. The windmills are not giants. The barber's basin is not a golden helmet. In part I of the novel, published in 1605, these misrecognitions only ever concern the dissemblance of an underlying reality. Don Quixote is in this sense a fetishist who endows things with a magical substantiality. One thing is converted into another—"every thing belonging to knight errants . . . being metamorphosed into the reverse of what it is" without ever losing its real identity.[16] But in part II of the novel, published in 1615, the misrecognitions are a riot of unsubstantiated reflections. There is no longer the possibility of an "outside view" from which to sort out the perceptions of any character from what is "false, fictitious, and apocryphal."[17] None of the characters can draw a clean line between what is a reflection and what is original reality. Substance has been dissolved into reflections, which have no independent being apart from their social construction. We have here a kind of aesthetic premonition of what Marx will later describe as commodity fetishism. Cervantes seems to intuit that modern rationality will eventually fall prey to misrecognizing its own representations, taking for "enchantments" what are elaborate aesthetic constructions—owing to their apparent autonomy.

The most important progenitor of the English novel, John Bunyan's *The Pilgrim's Progress*, also involves its protagonist in a continual misrecognition. In the literal narrative, Christian finds himself in a social landscape where unchecked aristocratic dominion and rampant commoditization are allied against him. He is *"a Man cloathed with Raggs,"* who is at every turn the prey of grasping "Merchandizers" on one side, and the oppressive claims of the aristocracy on the other—not only the fiend Apollyon but also "the Lord *Old Man*, the Lord *Carnal delight*, the Lord *Luxurious*, the Lord *Desire of Vain-glory*, my old Lord *Lechery*, Sir *Having Greedy*."[18] But for the reader, these profane appearances of the literal narrative are themselves misrecognitions. The reader is enjoined to decode everything in the story, an allegory "delivered under the Similitude of a Dream," into its spiritual significance. As Bunyan advises in the concluding poem to part I, the allegorical *"figure, or similitude"* is merely *"the out-side of my Dream,"* the *"Curtains"* or *"Vail"* hiding *"the substance of my matter"* (155). However, what is concealed by the innumerable commodities sold at Vanity Fair is only their decoded spiritual significance, in which "Houses, Lands, Trades, Places, Honors, Preferments, Titles, Countreys, Kingdoms, Lusts, Pleasures, and Delights of all sorts, as Whores, Bauds, Wives, Husbands, Children, Masters, Servants, Lives, Blood, Bodies, Souls, Silver, Gold, Pearls, Precious Stones, and what not" are interpreted solely as sensualities, as tempting use-values (86). Commodities here are as bad as you like, but they do not function in the allegorical sense as a misrecognition of social relations. For Bunyan, to demystify the commodity, to pull back the curtain, is to unveil a spiritual not a material significance.

In Daniel Defoe's *Robinson Crusoe*, as in Cervantes and Bunyan, misrecognition continues to be dualistic, an ontological separation between a higher-order interpretation of events and the debased contingencies of plotted action. After his religious conversion, Robinson interprets everything that befalls him as "Dispositions of Providence," so that the mute hostility of the solitary wilderness into which he is thrown is replete with signs directed toward his salvation.[19] The work of Robinson's subjectivity is to impose its meaning retrospectively by finding God's purpose and judgment in every turn of his narrative. What originally presents itself as wreck and isolation has to be wrenched into a spiritual accounting and recast as blessing and deliverance. The crucial event in this process is a recognition scene, when Robinson finds a man's footprint on the beach. At first this appears as evidence of something wholly unassimilable, not to be converted back into a sign of Providence. The eventual discovery and rescue of Friday, however, restores and writes back Robinson's own subjectivity into the event after the fact. For when he delivers Friday from the other cannibals, this unfolds just as he has dreamed it previously. What had sprung up as something unrecoverable by the conversions of providential reading is thus once more rendered in terms of Robinson's own teleological subjectivity. The footprint is revealed as a projection of his own sovereign dominion of the island and his ultimate release. That is to say, the plot disallows the recognition scene from functioning as such; the footprint does not count as a hermeneutic reversal, but only as further evidence of a prior interpretation.

In this connection, Marx's remarks on "alienation" in *Robinson Crusoe* are very instructive, even though Marx is not really considering it as a novel, rather as a just-so story beloved by political economists. For Marx, Robinson's activities on his island—taming goats, building fortifications, bookkeeping—are instances of non-alienated labor, since he is "one and the same Robinson" in each of his various functions.[20] That would be true if the novel only detailed Robinson's projects of survival, his subjectivity *for* itself. But there is also the providential perspective of the narrating moment, taken as his subjectivity *in* itself. There is not "one and the same Robinson," but always a divide and tension between the misrecognized spiritual accounting and an empirical, successive ordering of events.

We saw earlier that in Henry Fielding and Ann Radcliffe, recognition scenes come to the forefront of novelistic construction. Intricate sequences of revelations now become the all-in-all of plotting. These discoveries prompt the retrospective interpretation of ambiguous hermeneutic signals that now radiate back across the whole novel. The endings of *Joseph Andrews, Tom Jones, The Mysteries of Udolpho, The Italian,* and other works thereby effect a point-by-point revision of the misrecognitions of a "first pass" coherence by another (true) sequence, which envelops and resituates the elements of the prior version. Here subjectivity undergoes every imaginable convolution, putting on and taking off a series of wrong identities, only to be completely restored at the end. The important point here is that subjectivity is not mediated by the forms of its misrecognition, which leave subjectivity intact and unmarked.

In *Tom Jones*, money (i.e., currency) becomes the subject of a perfectly Aristotelian recognition scene. The recognition by Squire Allworthy of his stolen banknotes by their identifying marks is reminiscent of Fielding's previous novel, *Joseph Andrews*, where Joseph is identified by his strawberry-shaped birthmark. "With the recognition of the money," Deidre Lynch writes, "Fielding moves readers back into a romance universe in which the foundling is always found out . . . and in which banknotes, as well as long-lost relations, can be the subjects . . . of anagnorisis."[21] But this function of currency is very distinct from the role of money as capital in the novel. Capital occupies a realm separate from the plotting of subjectivity and its vindications. Unlike a banknote—and unlike Tom Jones—capital does not have a fixed value that will eventually emerge from the play of false appearances. Money as capital, according to the "wise Tenets, which are so well inculcated in that Politico-Peripatetic School of *Exchange-Alley*," is nothing but self-difference. "The just Value and only Use of Money [is] to lay it up," subject to "Reversions [and] Expectations."[22] As things unfold, the arbitrary "Reversions" and vicissitudes of capital—as an unstable, unnatural registration of "real Value"—stand in an incommensurable relation to the constancy of inner value that Tom exemplifies.[23] In other words, Fielding keeps the arbitrariness and misrepresentation innate to capital quite apart from the plotting of subjectivity; one is not routed through the other.

In Radcliffe's Gothic recognition scenes, the final "explanation of the deception, which had given . . . so much superstitious terror," invariably reveals precapitalist social forms—feudal, patriarchal, and priestly domination—to be the real causes of illusory terrors.[24] In *The Mysteries of Udolpho*, Emily St. Aubert finds herself imperiled and enshrouded by secrets that seem to haunt her own past. She projects all manner of implications and secrets behind the black veil, presaging her doom. But there is no dead body there: "Had she dared to look again, her delusion and her fears would have vanished together, and she would have perceived, that the figure was not human, but formed of wax."[25] The figure is itself a piece of "monkish superstition," to which some ancestral lord of Udolpho had been condemned to do penance.[26] It is a colossal piece of irrelevance.[27] Emily's mistake is to posit some aspect of her own subjectivity as being repressed in the machination of the plot. It is not. Nothing can be learned about the self from the parade of spooky mystifications. What is concealed in all the drama of uncanny resemblances and burned manuscripts and haunted chambers has nothing to do with the veil that conceals it. The contrast with Marx's program of demystifying bourgeois illusions is absolute. In capitalism, the misrecognitions of value are built into the very reality that they disguise. The mystifications of bourgeois society are materially mediated by commodity exchange. Gothic mystifications, however, conceal directly coercive forms of domination and dependence that are not mediated by the misrecognitions staged in Radcliffe's plots. The upshot is to separate out the concealments and dislocations belonging to subjectivity from the dimension of the historical social forms.

In *The Theory of the Novel*, Lukács trains a withering glance at the notorious recognition scene in Goethe's *Wilhelm Meister*, in which Wilhelm's destiny is revealed to him in a showy presentation by the clandestine Society of the Tower. Where Wilhelm's life had appeared as nothing "but error on the back of error, deviation following deviation," the hand of the Tower is now to be discerned in the management of his fate, his unconscious "apprenticeship."[28] "In very many actions of his life, in which he had conceived himself to be proceeding freely and in secret, he had been observed, nay guided" (455). Lukács regrets that Goethe resorted to the "fantastic apparatus" of the secret society's all-seeing initiates; the revelations concerning Wilhelm are "arbitrary and ultimately inessential," "a disrupting dissonance" that yields only "a mystification without hidden meaning."[29] It is true that the recognition scene can hardly be taken seriously. But what is clumsy and unconvincing is not Goethe; it is the Tower itself. Wilhelm does not find the event very enlightening, and he gives what amounts to a bad review: "we are just as wise as we were [before]" (490). We expect that a recognition scene will put an end to misrecognition. Mystifications will be dispelled and illusions will burn off like mist, leaving only the real disposition of things, where before there were misleading outlines, looming shadows, and fragments poking through. But the work of the Tower appears to be to sow misrecognition—and little else. The recognition scene accomplishes all of the expected gestures of revelation, retrospection, demystification, and enlightenment—yet without canceling or disabling the original misrecognitions at work. The subject recruited into the Tower is not at all delivered from illusions and misrepresentations. Wilhelm is being recruited into a sort of self-dissembling activity. The primary activity of the Tower is the concealment of its social aims and the opaque organization of its interventions, through "juggleries and every sort of hocus-pocus" (491). The mystifications and false appearances whose revelations it engineers are of its own making.

But this misdirection is precisely its direction, its staging. The Tower's role in the novel's recognition scene is to perform the office of an opaque, alien formation that does not coincide with Wilhelm's *own* sequence of non-self-coinciding performances. *Bildung* here means the succession of manufactured forms of the self's own nonidentity, its sequence of roles assumed and dropped. The self *is* this dissemblance—the state of being immersed in directing illusions of which one is also the observer.[30] That is to say, the Tower is finally only a moment of Wilhelm's aesthetic self-mediation. The theatrics of the recognition scene postulate the overcoming of aesthetic self-loss as a form of its persistence—so that Wilhelm's *Bildung* does not catch itself in the act. Subjectivity is allowed here to fabricate the outside agency under which it will be rebuked, and its impulses reappropriated, thereby shuffling off the obvious pathology of individuality. Illusion is spoiled, so that it may continue all the more thoroughly. The recognition scene proper effects a double move: on one hand, it is a spectacular announcement of the renunciation Wilhelm has acceded to, but on the other hand, it exemplifies the degraded aesthetic form that is being set aside. The Tower announces to Wilhelm its distance from his erroneous subjectivity, the better to serve as the sublimation and efflorescence of what is (officially) being given up. The abandonment of aesthetic immersion and its continuance are one. Misrecognition no longer is a mistaken detour, but belongs to the self-mediation of subjectivity, its necessity of finding its own forms as sheer exteriority.

From Cervantes to Radcliffe, what is enchanted or illusory is *only* misrecognition, error. Subjectivity is purged of these misrecognitions—as so much "dross," in Bunyan's words, "To throw away."[31] When we turn to the period from Goethe to Walter Scott, we find subject formation being accomplished through the working through of dissemblance by the plot. In *Wilhelm Meister*, as also in postgothic novels like *Ivanhoe* and *Caleb Williams*, subjectivity is mediated by hermeneutic retrospection. But this conjunction is merely formal, external. Subjectivity is harnessed to repression as though repression were the engine of its formation. But repression is carefully denied as being the subject's point of origin. The assembling of retrospective coherence, reconfiguring the past in a different life shape, is somewhat of a non sequitur to the story's action, the narrative hustling of the hero from pillar to post. The plot as it were stands in for the subject's self-difference, but that mediation is kept at an internal distance, the left hand of the plot not knowing what the right hand is doing. Subjectivity incorporates negativity as a formative moment, part of a story of its development. The self is no longer exonerated from the grit and murk of its becoming.

But that process of mediation—subjectivity's structural inaccessibility to itself and its temporal revision—does not occur *within* the plotting of repressed secrets and false identities in these books. There is only a kind of parataxis conjoining subjectivity's ironies and the hermeneutic pyrotechnics of the plot, without an inner relation between the two moments. Wilhelm Meister's aesthetic education requires the theatrical enactment of misrecognized destiny, but only as a moment of his own theatrical self-dissemblance. In *Caleb Williams*, when Squire Falkland reveals his stage-managing of Caleb's persecution and deliverance, this uncouples the political critique of repression from the plotting of secret guilt stowed in the fatal trunk. In Scott, the misrecognition of the historical in-itself of emergent classes is inaccessible to the plotting of disguised identities that draw the nominal hero further into the ruses of ironic action. In all these works, *Bildung* is set up so as never to catch itself in the act. Subjectivity as an achieved result is held aloof from all the tawdry fakery of the plotting, like the hocus-pocus of the Society of the Tower in *Wilhelm Meister*, or the cat and mouse game played by Squire Falkland, or the little cloths covering the heraldic devices on shields in *Ivanhoe*.

❦

Novelistic form is not a timeless invariant. It cannot be removed from the permutations of social and historical misrecognition, whether they be the mystifications of feudal ideology or the incipient commodity-form. On the other hand, neither is the novel a mere instantiation of illusions that are promulgated elsewhere and imported into literary structure from "real" history. The problematic of novelistic form is of course unresolvable. If subjectivity could leap out of the muck of its occlusions and temporal dispersals to coincide with itself without further ado, then it would no longer be subjectivity, it would be a formal self-identity, a thing.

What happens to barred, dislocated subjectivity after the misrecognition has been uncovered and dispelled? Is subjectivity healed, restored, reunified, reconciled? No. The subject is like Humpty Dumpty in this respect; there is no putting it back together again. What happens next has different names. Psychoanalysis calls it "working through." As Jacques Lacan puts it, the "subject is open to taking on the variable, broken, fragmented, sometimes even unconstituted and regressive, images of himself."[32] Lukács insists that the aftermath of recognition "is no single, unrepeatable tearing of the veil that masks the process."[33] In the *Oedipus Tyrannus*, Oedipus wishes only that he could entomb his knowledge, "to shut up" the agonizing truth.[34] In *Little Dorrit*, there is only a "vanishing-point" in which the unsealed truth is sealed up again in forgiveness and mercy. In *The Last Chronicle of Barset*, it is true that Mr. Crawley is (like Job) restored to a greater prosperity: "the living of St. Ewolds, which was, after some ecclesiastical fashion, attached to the rectory of Plumstead," bringing in £350 a year, is conferred on him.[35] But there is not to be restitution or "reinstitution" of the parish that Crawley resigned. In *The Portrait of a Lady*, Isabel Archer finds that there is no clean exit from her mortification; there is finally no "knowledge that was not pure anguish," except the facing of it, that particular Jamesian abandonment in the face of total conflagration.[36] Perhaps the most bitter expression of this unending humiliation of misrecognized agency is uttered by the god Wotan, in Richard Wagner's *Die Walküre*, when confronted with his powerlessness to create a free being: "With disgust I find only myself, over and over, in everything I create."[37]

One more image from Lukács: At the end of the reification essay—subjectivity having earlier recognized itself in the commodity-form, discovered itself as a "pure, naked object"—what remains is a disenchanted encounter with the "emptied and bursting husks" of those earlier determinations.[38] This image is incomplete. For those husks are not fragments of an otherness that is now to be left behind, relics of an extraneous deviation. The spent husks are being itself, laid bare. The waste and disarray left over after every exposure—is our own. Whatever is to be meaningful going forward just has to be hauled in from what had been misrecognized and now appears as so much stray damage.

Notes

Introduction

1. George Orwell, "Charles Dickens," in *Dickens, Dali & Others* (San Diego: Harcourt Brace Jovanovich, 1973), 46, 47.

2. Roland Barthes, *S/Z*, trans. Richard Miller (New York: Hill & Wang, 1974), 76.

3. D. A. Miller, *The Novel and the Police* (Berkeley: University of California Press, 1988).

4. Gillian Rose, *Hegel Contra Sociology* (London: Athlone, 1981), 60.

5. Charles Dickens, *Great Expectations* (Oxford: Oxford University Press, 1953), 303. Cited parenthetically after this.

6. Karl Marx, *Capital*, vol. 1, trans. Ben Fowkes (New York: Vintage, 1977), 256.

7. Rose, *Hegel Contra Sociology*, 164, 182.

8. Rose, *Hegel Contra Sociology*, 218.

9. G. W. F. Hegel, *The Phenomenology of Mind*, trans. J. B. Baillie (New York: Harper & Row, 1967), 259.

10. On the "constitutive . . . *function of misrecognition*" in the mirror stage of ego development, see Jacques Lacan, "The Mirror Stage as Formative of the *I* Function," in *Écrits*, trans. Bruce Fink (New York: Norton, 2006), 80. On the role of misrecognition in ideological representations, see Louis Althusser, "Ideology and Ideological State Apparatuses," in *On the Reproduction of Capitalism*, trans. G. M. Goshgarian (Brooklyn: Verso, 2014), 232–72. See also the discussions of Lacanian and Althusserian misrecognition in Slavoj Žižek, *The Sublime Object of Ideology* (London: Verso, 1989), 2, and Judith Butler, *The Psychic Life of Power: Theories in Subjection* (Stanford, CA: Stanford University Press, 1997), 95–97. All of these conceptualizations owe a great deal to Alexandre Kojève, *Introduction to the Reading of Hegel*, trans. James H. Nichols Jr. (Ithaca, NY: Cornell University Press, 1980).

11. Jacques Lacan, *The Seminar of Jacques Lacan, Book I: Freud's Papers on Technique, 1953–1954*, trans. John Forrester (New York: Norton, 1991), 283. Translation modified.

12. Georg Lukács, *History and Class Consciousness: Studies in Marxist Dialectics*, trans. Rodney Livingstone (Cambridge, MA: MIT Press, 1971), 168.

13. If Marx's commodity analysis has a narrative dimension, it has usually been understood as being about character—not plot. After all, Marx first introduces commodity fetishism with an unforgettable minor character: that convivial eccentric, the wooden table that "stands on its head, and evolves out of its brain grotesque ideas." *Capital*, 1: 163. Later in *Capital* we meet "Monsieur le Capital and Madame la Terre" stepping forth in their impersonation as "social characters." These spurious characters give the lie to

the effulgent individuality of bourgeois personhood. Their spectral autonomy casts a shadow over the self that has become another itemized entry in an inventory of objects. Marx's point is that these fetishistic characters that populate capitalism's categories of appearance arise when social processes lose their back story. In other words, the bare construct of "character" is what happens when you take away their plot. Indeed, these characters collapse, like bundles of clothes and hats that had been propped up on stilts, once the perambulations of value are set into narrative sequence, their real plot, and revealed as "simply a metamorphosis of forms." *Capital*, vol. 3, trans. David Fernbach (London: Penguin, 1991), 969.

On Marx and the theory of character, see Alex Woloch, *The One vs. the Many: Minor Characters and the Space of the Protagonist in the Novel* (Princeton, NJ: Princeton University Press, 2003), 26–30.

14. Marx, *Capital*, 1: 279.

15. Rose, *Hegel Contra Sociology*, 217.

16. On the derivation of forms of subjectivity from the commodity-form, see Lukács, *History and Class Consciousness*; Rose, *Hegel Contra Sociology*; Alfred Sohn-Rethel, *Intellectual and Manual Labor: A Critique of Epistemology*, trans. Martin Sohn-Rethel (Atlantic Highlands, NJ: Humanities Press, 1978); Moishe Postone, *Time, Labor, and Social Domination: A Reinterpretation of Marx's Critical Theory* (Cambridge: Cambridge University Press, 1993); and Étienne Balibar, "The Social Contract Among Commodities: Marx and the Subject of Exchange," in *Citizen Subject: Foundations for Philosophical Anthropology*, trans. Steven Miller (New York: Fordham University Press, 2017), 185–202.

17. Samuel Johnson, *A Dictionary of the English Language* (1755), s.v. "Plot."

18. I am indebted to two other studies that "read" the inner logic of capital as somehow novelistic: Ann Cvetkovich, *Mixed Feelings: Feminism, Mass Culture, and Victorian Sensationalism* (New Brunswick, NJ: Rutgers University Press, 1992), 165–98; and Anna Kornbluh, *Realizing Capital: Financial and Psychic Economies in Victorian Form* (New York: Fordham University Press, 2014). Whereas I concentrate on plot, Cvetkovich focuses on the "melodramatic or sentimental spectacle of the worker" (165), while Kornbluh focuses on the "rhetoric" and "tropological movement" of financial capital (3).

19. Marx, *Capital*, 3: 969.

20. Marx, *Capital*, 1: 167.

21. Marx, *Capital*, 1: 135.

22. Fredric Jameson, *The Political Unconscious: Narrative as a Socially Symbolic Act* (Ithaca, NY: Cornell University Press, 1981), 242. The allegorical rewriting that Jameson develops in this text necessarily leaves behind a narrative's original plot as so much sloughed-off skin. According to this method, the structural determinations of the capitalist mode of production are to be grasped through interpretation of a textual unconscious: its contradictions and semantic possibilities. What we are left with in *The Political Unconscious* are modes of historical (and collective) form-giving no longer recognizable or inhabitable as such, but only available as "sedimented" interpretations.

23. Georg Lukács, *The Theory of the Novel*, trans. Anna Bostock (Cambridge, MA: MIT Press, 1971). Lukács defines the novel in terms of its specific "metaphysical dissonance," namely, "the refusal of the immanence of being to enter into empirical life" (71).

24. For instance, Mary Poovey traces the "aesthetic agenda" by which literature demarcates an ethical and moral space ultimately distinct from the representational techniques of finance. *Genres of the Credit Economy: Mediating Value in Eighteenth- and Nineteenth-Century Britain* (Chicago: University of Chicago Press, 2008). Catherine Gallagher argues that the aesthetic and the novelistic in particular operate as a form of "suspended animation" that removes value from its bodily and material determinants. "The Bioeconomics of *Our Mutual Friend*," in *The Body Economic: Life, Death, and Sensation in Political Economy and the Victorian Novel* (Princeton, NJ: Princeton University Press, 2006), 86–117.

Anna Kornbluh's recent account of the trope of "fictitious capital" complicates the picture drawn by Poovey and Gallagher. She argues, in the opposite direction from the historicist critics, that Victorian novels ironize and interrupt political economy's separation of capital from fiction. Capital cannot be divided cleanly from the aesthetic, because it "is always already fictitious." *Realizing Capital*, 7. Kornbluh's description of her method as "financial formalism" might also describe my own approach (15). However, I am making a rather different argument about the role of subjectivity in capitalism. In Kornbluh's reading of Marx, capital is a figure of self-constituting subjectivity (114, 125). She therefore sees subjectivity, or "psychic economy," as a spurious grounding of capital. To base capital in subjectivity—belief, interiority—is "the ultimate ideological alibi" (3). She sees the attempt to ground financial capital in psychic structures as a way of exculpating the financial vicissitudes of capital by turning the economic into a matter of the inner self.

25. Aristotle, *Poetics*, trans. James Hutton (New York: Norton, 1982), 1450b20. Citations are to the standard Greek text.

26. See Sianne Ngai, *Theory of the Gimmick: Aesthetic Judgment and Capitalist Form* (Cambridge, MA: Harvard University Press, 2020). Ngai's definition of the gimmick requires that it be "labor-saving"—in other words, that the aesthetic "contrivance" is cutting corners somewhere (1). A recognition scene *as such* is therefore not a gimmick, since by definition what is recognized is at last restored, the past put back in its proper place. Recognition scenes, so to speak, obey the law of the conservation of matter. A recognition scene only becomes a gimmick in Ngai's sense when there is a gaping plot hole, where the construction is shoddy. In the gimmicky recognition scene, the connections to the past are really no-thoroughfares, or the foundations for its revelations have not been properly laid. Consequently, its plot "mechanics" are felt to be working too hard, too noisily.

27. Aristotle's remarkable discussion of plot is to be found in chapters 6 through 16. Plot itself is defined as "the combination of the events" in "the imitation of the action" (1450a4–5).

28. Aristotle, *Poetics*, 1452a19.

29. Aristotle, *Poetics*, 1452a30.

30. Aristotle, *Poetics*, 1452a33.

31. Aristotle, *Poetics*, 1455a17.

32. Aristotle, *Poetics*, 1454b20–1455a21.

33. Aristotle, *Poetics*, 1452b2, 1452a36.

34. Terence Cave, *Recognitions* (Oxford: Oxford University Press, 1988), 9.

35. Cave, *Recognitions*, 222.

36. Cave, *Recognitions*, 1.

37. Northrop Frye, *Anatomy of Criticism: Four Essays* (Princeton, NJ: Princeton University Press, 2000), 212.

38. Northrop Frye, *The Educated Imagination* (Bloomington: Indiana University Press, 1964), 55.

39. On recognition in Hegel, see Kojève, *Introduction to the Reading of Hegel*; Axel Honneth, *The Struggle for Recognition: The Moral Grammar of Social Conflicts*, trans. Joel Anderson (Cambridge, MA: MIT Press, 1995), 1–63; Robert B. Pippin, *Hegel on Self-Consciousness: Desire and Death in* The Phenomenology of Spirit (Princeton, NJ: Princeton University Press, 2011); and Robert Brandom, *A Spirit of Trust: A Reading of Hegel's* Phenomenology (Cambridge, MA: Harvard University Press, 2019).

40. See the translator's note to Honneth, *The Struggle for Recognition*, viii.

41. Hegel, *The Phenomenology of Mind*, 490, 740.

42. Cave, *Recognitions*, 156.

43. Paul Ricoeur, *The Course of Recognition*, trans. David Pellauer (Cambridge, MA: Harvard University Press, 2005), 75–79.

44. Bernard Knox suggests that the *Oedipus Tyrannus* is not really an "example" of plot for Aristotle. Rather, Aristotle reverse engineered his definition of plot starting from Sophocles's play. *Oedipus at Thebes: Sophocles' Tragic Hero and His Time* (New Haven, CT: Yale University Press, 1957), 31.

45. Aristotle, *Poetics*, 1454b27, and Erich Auerbach, *Mimesis: The Representation of Reality in Western Literature*, trans. Willard R. Trask (Princeton, NJ: Princeton University Press, 1953), 3–7. There are several scenes in the *Odyssey* where the returned Odysseus is "recognized." He variously makes himself known to his swineherd, his son, the suitors, his wife. In book 19, the servant Eurycleia identifies the palace beggar as her absent lord, from a scar he bears on his thigh. However, this scene of discovery is not shared by the audience. We already know that the beggar is Odysseus in disguise. Whatever is awakened of unknown wells of tenderness or regret in the characters when Eurycleia's aged and rough hands feel the seam of his old wound, the discovery itself cannot be shared by the audience. Indeed, Auerbach stresses that it would be utterly contrary to Homer's procedure to keep the reader "in darkness" (3). For this reason, Cave observes that Auerbach's discussion of the scene "evades *anagnorisis*." *Recognitions*, 22.

46. Sophocles, *Oedipus the King*, trans. David Grene (Chicago: University of Chicago Press, 2010), line 1068. I have matched the line numbering with the standard Greek text throughout.

47. Bernard Williams, *Shame and Necessity* (Berkeley: University of California Press, 2008), 71.

48. Peter Brooks, *Reading for the Plot* (Cambridge, MA: Harvard University Press, 1992), 117.

49. See the terminology of "equivocation," "snare," "partial answer," "suspended answer," and "jamming" in Barthes, *S/Z*, 75.

50. Karl Reinhardt, *Sophocles*, trans. Hazel Harvey and David Harvey (New York: Barnes and Noble, 1979), 119.

51. See Sigmund Freud, "Screen Memories," in *The Standard Edition of the Complete Psychological Works of Sigmund Freud*, vol. 3, trans. and ed. James Strachey (Vintage: London, 2001), 299–322.

52. On the doubling of Oedipus, see Knox, *Oedipus at Thebes*, 149; and René Girard, "Oedipus Analyzed," in *Oedipus Unbound: Selected Writings on Rivalry and Desire*, trans. Mark R. Anspach (Stanford, CA: Stanford University Press, 2004), 31–36.

53. Sophocles, *Oedipus the King*, line 475.

54. Sophocles, *Oedipus the King*, line 745.

55. Sophocles, *Oedipus the King*, line 220.

56. Marx, *Capital*, 1: 166.

57. Marx, *Capital*, 1: 164–65. My emphasis.

58. Marx, *Capital*, 1: 166.

59. Marx, *Capital*, 1: 165. My emphasis.

60. Marx, *Capital*, 1: 139.

61. Marx, *Capital*, 1: 166–67.

62. Even the best readers of Marx have conflated reification and fetishism. See, for example, Lukács, *History and Class Consciousness*, 83–86; and David Harvey, *A Companion to Marx's* Capital (London: Verso, 2010), 41.

63. On the unhappy afterlife of "reification," see Gillian Rose, *The Melancholy Science* (London: Verso, 2014), 35–66. "Reification" in German is either *Verdinglichung* or *Versachlichung*. The former term is used by Georg Lukács in the title of his important essay, "Reification and the Consciousness of the Proletariat," in *History and Class Consciousness*, 83–222. But there is no conceptual difference whatsoever between Marx's usage of *Verdinglichung* and *Versachlichung*. It is true that Marx uses *Verdinglichung* only once, in *Capital*, 3: 969. But in the same passage he switches over to *Versachlichung* without change of meaning. My position is that reification is conceptually (if not terminologically) at issue *whenever* Marx discusses surplus-value production as the inversion of persons-as-things and things-as-persons.

64. See, for example, Jürgen Habermas, *The Theory of Communicative Action*, vol. 1, trans. Thomas McCarthy (Boston: Beacon, 1984), 355–65; Seyla Benhabib, *Critique, Norm, and Utopia: A Study of the Foundations of Critical Theory* (New York: Columbia University Press, 1986), 182–85; Andrew Feenberg, *The Philosophy of Praxis: Marx, Lukács, and the Frankfurt School* (Brooklyn: Verso, 2014), 66–69, 71–73. The latter-day Frankfurt School theorist Axel Honneth tendentiously interprets reification as a bad "habit" that leads to the forgetting of a normative attitude of "empathetic engagement." *Reification: A New Look at an Old Idea* (New York: Oxford University Press, 2008), 35.

65. The definitive work on the conceptual indeterminacy of reification is Timothy Bewes, *Reification, or The Anxiety of Late Capitalism* (London: Verso, 2002).

66. Lukács takes up the commodity-form according to the issues of German philosophical idealism, where the central question is about the subject's role in the conceptual determinations that allow for our experience of objects. In the commodity, the objectivity of value is divorced from its historical and social determinations, and leads an autonomous life apart from our activity. The categories of social existence thus appear as alien impositions. Objects are unmediated, "torn from the complex of their true determinants and placed in artificial isolation," so that "reality" confronts us as if "cocooned by . . . concepts" not of our making. *History and Class Consciousness*, 163, 129.

67. The value-positing role of labor-power as a commodity, "its ability to yield surplus produce . . . is submerged without a trace in the quantitative exchange categories

of capitalism," yet in its very "absence of consciousness acts as an unacknowledged driving wheel in the economic process." Lukács, *History and Class Consciousness*, 169.

68. In the Frankfurt School interpretation of fetishism, the properties of objects that are socially constituted are misrepresented as possessing an ahistorical, formal objectivity. Fetishism on this reading describes how we are ruled by a sterile, impersonal apparatus of social facts falsely attributed an a priori validity. See, for instance, Theodor W. Adorno, *Negative Dialectics*, trans. E. B. Ashton (New York: Continuum, 1973), 189–90; Susan Buck-Morss, *The Origins of Negative Dialectics: Theodor W. Adorno, Walter Benjamin, and the Frankfurt Institute* (New York: The Free Press, 1977), 26; Rose, *The Melancholy Science*, 60; Benhabib, *Critique, Norm, and Utopia*, 108.

69. Marx's explicit reference is to the "misty realm of religion," with its seemingly "autonomous figures" of man-made divinity, "endowed with a life of their own, which enter into relations both with each other and with the human race." *Capital*, 1: 165.

70. "The capital fetish in its consummate form [is] the idea that ascribes to the accumulated product of labor . . . the power of producing surplus-value in geometric progression by way of an inherent secret quality, as a pure automaton." Marx, *Capital*, 3: 523.

71. See Žižek, *The Sublime Object of Ideology*, 14–26, 30–34. However, as Žižek would concede in a subsequent piece of self-criticism, "Marx *never* referred to commodity fetishism as ideology—for the simple reason that it is an 'illusion' which is not part of any 'ideological superstructure,' but located in the very heart of the capitalist 'economic' base." Slavoj Žižek, *Living in the End Times* (Brooklyn: Verso, 2010), 186n.

72. Karl Marx, *Theories of Surplus Value*, part 3, trans. Jack Cohen and S. W. Ryazanskaya (Moscow: Progress Publishers, 1971), 296.

73. Positing [*setzen*] is especially central to the philosophy of J. G. Fichte: "At certain points in the *Science of Knowledge* Fichte writes almost as if *setzen* and its compounds were the only verbs in the German language." Peter Heath and John Lachs, Preface to *Science of Knowledge*, by J. G. Fichte, trans. Peter Heath and John Lachs (Cambridge: Cambridge University Press, 1982), xiii.

74. Karl Marx, *Grundrisse*, trans. Martin Nicolaus (London: Penguin, 1973), 307.

75. Marx, *Capital*, 1: 680.

76. Karl Marx, *Theories of Surplus Value*, part 1, trans. Emile Burns (Moscow: Progress Publishers, 1968), 390.

77. Marx, *Grundrisse*, 454.

78. Marx, *Capital*, 1: 1054.

79. Marx, *Capital*, 1: 757.

80. Marx, *Grundrisse*, 454.

81. Marx, *Grundrisse*, 470.

82. Marx, *Capital*, 1: 163.

83. Marx, *Grundrisse*, 308.

84. Marx, *Grundrisse*, 831.

85. Marx, *Grundrisse*, 452–53.

86. Marx, *Capital*, 1: 1056.

87. Marx, *Capital*, 1: 255.

88. Marx, *Grundrisse*, 450.

89. What comes "first" and "second" here are dialectical moments; this is not to suggest that capital proceeds stage by stage, like the Stations of the Cross. At every turn, fetishism might precede or initiate reification.

90. In much recent scholarship, critique has been served notice of its obsolescence. For critique's detractors, see Eve Kosofsky Sedgwick, "Paranoid Reading and Reparative Reading," in *Touching Feeling: Affect, Pedagogy, Performativity* (Durham, NC: Duke University Press, 2003); Bruno Latour, "Why Has Critique Run out of Steam?" *Critical Inquiry* 30, no. 2 (Winter 2004); Stephen Best and Sharon Marcus, "Surface Reading: An Introduction," *Representations* 108, no. 1 (Fall 2009); Rita Felski, *The Limits of Critique* (Chicago: University of Chicago Press, 2015). The discussion of Marx in this body of work is grossly inadequate. For instance, there is only one place where Felski attends to the specificity of Marx's critique. (Otherwise it is always "Marx, Freud, and Nietzsche.") She characterizes "the Marxist idea of critique as an 'inversion of an inversion' (bourgeois ideology perceives reality upside down, argues Marx, so that it must be flipped right side up to arrive at the truth.)" *Limits of Critique*, 128. But Marx never says that critique is an inversion of bourgeois ideology. Felski has mixed up two different methodological statements, one from *The German Ideology* and one from the Afterword to *Capital*.

91. Lukács, *History and Class Consciousness*, 83. Emphasis removed.

92. Marx, *Capital*, 3: 969. Translation modified.

93. Hegel, *The Phenomenology of Mind*, 212–13.

1. Financial Crisis and the Partitions of Subjectivity in *Little Dorrit*

1. For Viktor Shklovsky, the form of the "mystery novel allows [Dickens] to interpolate into the work large chunks of everyday life, which, while serving the purpose of impeding the action, feel the pressure of the plot and are therefore perceived as a part of the artistic whole." *Theory of Prose*, trans. Benjamin Sher (Normal, IL: Dalkey Archive Press, 1991), 145. George Orwell, for whom Dickens's narrative procedure is the paradigm of the "awful Victorian 'plot,'" complains of the "needless ramifications" and creaking "machinery" into which characters get "sucked" like so many injured limbs. "Charles Dickens," in *Dickens, Dali & Others* (San Diego: Harcourt Brace Jovanovich, 1973), 46, 47. D. A. Miller identifies this compulsive narrative procedure with "the police model of closure" that installs a localizable form of order, literally arresting the narrative's hermeneutic indeterminacy. *The Novel and the Police* (Berkeley: University of California Press, 1988), 93.

2. As Catherine Gallagher puts it, Dickens "must create a belief that dark things (plots, conspiracies, vices) lurk everywhere, needing to be revealed. The belief in secrets creates the need to expose, but the need to expose is reciprocally dependent on the invention of secret plots." Catherine Gallagher, "The Duplicity of Doubling in *A Tale of Two Cities*," *Dickens Studies Annual* 12 (1983): 134.

3. On the permeable border between social-systemic and psychic structures in Dickens, see John Kucich, "Repression and Representation: Dickens's General Economy," *Nineteenth-Century Fiction*, 38, no. 1 (June, 1983): 66; Eve Kosofsky Sedgwick, *Between Men: English Literature and Male Homosocial Desire* (New York: Columbia University Press,

1985), 164–65; Ian Duncan, *Modern Romance and Transformations of the Novel: The Gothic, Scott, Dickens* (Cambridge: Cambridge University Press, 1992), 225.

4. On the role of money, banking, debt, the finance of investment, liability, and speculation in Dickens's other novels and his journalism, see Patrick Brantlinger, *Fictions of State: Culture and Credit in Britain, 1694–1994* (Ithaca, NY: Cornell University Press, 1996), 157–62. See also the older account in Humphrey House, *The Dickens World* (Oxford: Oxford University Press, 1942), 58–59.

5. Charles Dickens, *Little Dorrit* (Oxford: Oxford University Press, 1953), 710. Hereafter cited parenthetically.

6. It should be noted that the specific economic meaning of "speculation" originally refers to commodity futures. See Adam Smith, *The Wealth of Nations*, ed. Edward Cannan (New York: Random House, 1994), 131.

7. For a reading of *Little Dorrit* that emphasizes the perspective of systemic critique and the comprehension of social totality, rather than the bifurcated structure that I am laying out, see Amanda Anderson, *The Powers of Distance: Cosmopolitanism and the Cultivation of Detachment* (Princeton, NJ: Princeton University Press, 2001), 63–90. The critical omniscience that Anderson sees as granted to the embittered characters Rigaud, Henry Gowan, and Miss Wade, however, does not extend to the secrets of Merdle's schemes. Ironically, the novel's most corrosive characters are among the most innocent of involvement in the financial ruin.

8. For a different reading of the convergence and separation of the plotting of approved erotic subjectivities (as "ownership") from the sins of instrumental exchange and "acquisition" (paradigmatically, Merdle), see Jeff Nunokawa, *The Afterlife of Property: Domestic Security and the Victorian Novel* (Princeton, NJ: Princeton University Press, 1994), 19–39. For Nunokawa, the work of the novel's conclusion is to maintain the former category as pristine and removed at a safe distance from the dirty work of the latter (28–31). I am claiming the converse. When Amy Dorrit burns the codicil to the will, this has the ironic result of preserving capital as untarnished by subjectivity, and preventing the flow of any rich interior content into the blankness of capital accumulation.

9. For the argument that the Merdle plot is recovered into the novel's larger project of moral and aesthetic closure, see Mary Poovey, *Genres of the Credit Economy: Mediating Value in Eighteenth- and Nineteenth-Century Britain* (Chicago: University of Chicago Press, 2008), 374–77. On this reading, Clennam's "being in debt is equivalent to Merdle's forgeries and theft," so that a substitutionary atonement for the financial losses can be brought about by Clennam's moral rehabilitation (377). I claim that the novel only raises the possibility of "conversion" between moral and financial domains in order to refute any such equivalency.

10. For a negative assessment of this recognition scene as "thoroughly unconvincing" and a "forced imposition of meaning," see George Levine, *Darwin and the Novelists: Patterns of Justice in Victorian Fiction* (Chicago: University of Chicago Press, 1991), 174.

11. Sigmund Freud, "Miss Lucy R," from *Studies on Hysteria*, in *The Standard Edition of the Complete Psychological Works of Sigmund Freud*, vol. 2, trans. and ed. James Strachey (Vintage: London, 2001), 117n. This edition hereafter *SE*.

12. Most critics of the novel have noticed some version of this point, that the prison in *Little Dorrit* extends far beyond the walls of the Marshalsea, and encompasses a kind of spiritual imprisonment. See F. R. Leavis and Q. D. Leavis, *Dickens the*

Novelist (London: Chatto & Windus, 1970), 222–23; Edmund Wilson, "Dickens: The Two Scrooges," in *The Wound and the Bow* (New York: Farrar, Straus & Giroux, 1978), 46; and J. Hillis Miller, *Charles Dickens: The World of His Novels* (Bloomington: Indiana University Press, 1969), 228–32.

13. Karl Marx, *Capital*, vol. 1, trans. Ben Fowkes (New York: Vintage, 1977), 928.

14. Orwell, "Charles Dickens," 5.

15. "In mental life nothing which has once been formed can perish . . . Everything is somehow preserved and . . . in suitable circumstances . . . can once more be brought to light." Sigmund Freud, *Civilization and Its Discontents*, SE 21: 69.

16. Trilling remarks on the novel's circularity in this regard, where "the secret of [Arthur Clennam's] birth, of his being really a child of love and art" is itself the starting point for his "ethical will" to unconceal these very facts. Introduction to Dickens, *Little Dorrit*, xii.

17. *The Red Shoes*, directed by Michael Powell and Emeric Pressburger (The Archers, 1948).

18. 2 Corinthians 13:8.

19. Eve Kosofsky Sedgwick, "Paranoid Reading and Reparative Reading," in *Touching Feeling: Affect, Pedagogy, Performativity* (Durham, NC: Duke University Press, 2003).

20. For a list of the passages in which this mystery is developed, see Shklovsky, *Theory of Prose*, 130–31.

21. Marx, *Capital*, 1: 279.

22. See William Pietz, *The Problem of the Fetish*, ed. Francesco Pellizzi, Stefanos Geroulanos, and Ben Kafka (Chicago: University of Chicago Press, 2022).

23. Marx, *Capital*, 1: 165.

24. Poovey, *Genres of the Credit Economy*, 375.

25. Fredric Jameson, *The Antinomies of Realism* (Brooklyn: Verso, 2013), 211.

26. Marx, *Capital*, 1: 381.

27. Marx's ideas about crisis, not really a complete theory, are scattered throughout his work. See especially *Capital*, vol. 3, trans. David Fernbach (London: Penguin, 1991), 349–75; and *Theories of Surplus Value*, part 2, trans. S. W. Ryazanskaya (Moscow: Progress Publishers, 1968), 492–535. Commentaries that I found useful on this topic include Ernst Mandel, Introduction to *Capital*, vol. 3, by Karl Marx, trans. David Fernbach (London: Penguin, 1991), 3: 38–53; Ben Fine and Alfredo Saad-Filho, *Marx's* Capital (London: Pluto Press, 2010), 76–86; David Harvey, *Limits to Capital* (London: Verso, 2006), 190–203, 300–29, 424–38.

28. Marx, *Capital*, 1: 279.

29. I mean by this something different from Georg Lukács's interpretation of crises as eruptions of an irrationality banished by the rigid formalism of the bourgeois ideological horizon. *History and Class Consciousness: Studies in Marxist Dialectics*, trans. Rodney Livingstone (Cambridge, MA: MIT Press, 1971), 105. Lukács leans here on Hilferding's thesis that crises result from the disproportional toggling of production ratios, rather than from absolute overproduction. See Rudolf Hilferding, *Finance Capital: A Study of the Latest Phase of Capitalist Development*, ed. Tom Bottomore (London: Routledge & Kegan Paul, 1981). Capitalist crises are creatures of reification, but not because they are irrational in Lukács's sense.

30. "The barriers within which the maintenance and valorization of the capital-value has necessarily to move—and this in turn depends on the dispossession and impoverishment of the great mass of the [workers]—therefore come constantly into contradiction with the methods of production." Marx, *Capital*, 3: 358.

31. Marx, *Capital*, 3: 366.

32. Marx, *Theories of Surplus Value*, 2: 495.

33. On Victorian conceptions of "fictitious capital," see Anna Kornbluh, *Realizing Capital: Financial and Psychic Economies in Victorian Form* (New York: Fordham University Press, 2014), 21–44. The villain of Kornbluh's account is the ideological trope of "psychic economy," which (illegitimately) posits interiority as the ground of capital, and which supplants an earlier critique of fictitious capital and its role in capitalist crises, which Kornbluh links with Marx. Though Kornbluh does not discuss *Little Dorrit*, the novel's publication in 1857 would situate it in the middle of her narrative. While Dickens does show Mr. Merdle's enterprises to be utterly fictional in the sense of being fraudulent scams (and therefore not really capital at all), the crash itself is not attributed to psychological causes. The money is really gone. My view is that Dickens's criticism of speculation in the novel, especially where it touches on "fictitious capital," has the downside that it also denies the capitalist mode of production. Capital is thereby dismissed as *merely* fictitious, nonexistent, so that the causes of crisis do not reside (as I am arguing) in capital's reification of social antagonisms within production, but in its (to quote the novel) unfounded "spr[inging] from nothing" (709).

34. Karl Marx, *Capital*, vol. 2, trans. David Fernbach (London: Penguin, 1992), 137.

35. Marx, *Capital*, 1: 255.

36. Dickens is devastating in showing how Clennam & Co. is built on a rotten foundation of secret wrongs—but the firm itself is a relic that has not kept "the track of the time," and has "been left far behind" as a "mere anomaly and incongruity" (46).

37. For this reading, see Hillary M. Schor, *Dickens and the Daughter of the House* (Cambridge: Cambridge University Press, 1999), 124, 144–47.

38. For a version of this argument, see Miller, *Charles Dickens*, 246.

39. Elaine Hadley, "Nobody, Somebody, and Everybody," *Victorian Studies* 59, no. 1 (Autumn 2016): 83.

40. "Clennam appears to have spent most of the novel searching for a way to get himself locked up in the Marshalsea." Ruth Bernard Yeazell, "Do It or Dorrit," *Novel: A Forum on Fiction* 25, no. 1 (Fall 1991): 40.

41. For a reading of Dickens's perspectival metaphor here, see Garrett Stewart, "Dickens and the Narratography of Closure," *Critical Inquiry* 34, no. 3 (2008): 538–39.

2. Interest-Bearing Capital and the Displacement of Affect in *The Last Chronicle of Barset*

1. Anthony Trollope, *An Autobiography* (London: Penguin, 1996), 84.

2. Trollope, *Autobiography*, 165.

3. Anthony Trollope, *Barchester Towers* (Oxford: Oxford University Press, 1989), 143.

4. "Important information [in Trollope] never remains hidden, as it might in the novels of Balzac or James, but always becomes a matter of unrestricted knowledge.

This manifestation of the truth in events is symptomatic of a much larger convergence of aesthetics with moral and social symbolic structures." John Kucich, *The Power of Lies: Transgression in Victorian Fiction* (Ithaca, NY: Cornell University Press,1994), 49.

5. On Trollope's method as novelist, see Walter Kendrick, *The Novel-Machine: The Theory and Fiction of Anthony Trollope* (Baltimore: Johns Hopkins University Press, 1980).

6. Trollope, *Autobiography*, 149.

7. Trollope, *Autobiography*, 109–10.

8. Trollope felt that the plot of *The Last Chronicle* was doubly improbable, or required at least some suspension of disbelief: "I cannot quite make myself believe that even such a man as Mr. Crawley could have forgotten how he got it; nor would the generous friend who was anxious to supply his wants have supplied them by tendering the check of a third person. Such fault I acknowledge,—acknowledging at the same time that I have never been capable of constructing with complete success the intricacies of a plot that required to be unraveled." *Autobiography*, 176.

9. Northrop Frye, *Fables of Identity: Studies in Poetic Mythology* (New York: Harcourt, Brace and World, 1963), 29.

10. Frye, *Fables of Identity*, 29.

11. Frye, *Fables of Identity*, 28.

12. Frye, *Fables of Identity*, 28.

13. Mary Poovey, *Genres of the Credit Economy: Mediating Value in Eighteenth- and Nineteenth-Century Britain* (Chicago: University of Chicago Press, 2008), 407, 393.

14. Poovey, *Genres of the Credit Economy*, 400.

15. Poovey, *Genres of the Credit Economy*, 404.

16. On the interplay between reflective and unreflective postures toward institutions, beliefs, and practices in Trollope, see Amanda Anderson, "Trollope's Modernity," *ELH* 74, no. 3 (Fall 2007): 509–34.

17. "Anxiety is therefore the universally current coinage for which *any* affective impulse is or can be exchanged if the ideational content attached to it is subjected to repression." Sigmund Freud, *Introductory Lectures on Psycho-Analysis*, in *The Standard Edition of the Complete Psychological Works of Sigmund Freud*, vol. 16, trans. and ed. James Strachey (Vintage: London, 2001), 403–4. This edition hereafter *SE*. Timothy Bewes connects anxiety to reification, drawing on Søren Kierkegaard's conception of anxiety as fear lacking any definite object. *Reification, or The Anxiety of Late Capitalism* (London: Verso, 2002), 245–47.

18. Patrick Brantlinger, *Fictions of State: Culture and Credit in Britain, 1694–1994* (Ithaca, NY: Cornell University Press, 1996), 168, 171–72.

19. Because the ambiguities of the initial suspicion and explanations are crucial to the eventual solution, I have given the summary in quotations as much as possible. All references to the novel will be given parenthetically from Anthony Trollope, *The Last Chronicle of Barset*, ed. Stephen Gill (Oxford: Oxford University Press, 1980). I have silently Americanized "cheque" to "check."

20. In chapter 32, Mr. Toogood, a character apparently on loan from *The Pilgrim's Progress*, takes it upon himself to reopen the inquiry, only to meet with the same information already out in the world. In chapters 40 and 42, he turns up the information that will eventually hold the mysterious events together, namely, the role of the

Dragon of Wantly inn—but none of this information can be fitted together at present (410). It appears to Toogood that Crawley will have to play a sob story in court. "One wants sympathy in such a case as that—not evidence" (438).

21. Anthony Trollope, *The Way We Live Now*, ed. Frank Kermode (London: Penguin, 1994), 184.

22. See, for instance, chapter 46, where Mr. Butterwell loans Crosbie money at a lower, "gentlemanly" rate of interest than the going rate, and chapter 48, where John Eames asks for leave from his office, and the choreography of power in that environment.

23. Martin Heidegger, *Being and Time*, trans. John Macquarrie and Edward Robinson (New York: Harper Collins, 1962), 231.

24. Sigmund Freud, *The Interpretation of Dreams*, SE 5: 460. In the original, the entire quotation of the dream-report is italicized.

25. Freud, *Interpretation of Dreams*, SE 5: 461.

26. Freud, *Interpretation of Dreams*, SE 5: 462.

27. Freud, *Interpretation of Dreams*, SE 5: 462.

28. Freud, *Interpretation of Dreams*, SE 5: 460.

29. For a different interpretation of the psychology of investments in Trollope, tying anxiety to the vicissitudes of the stock-market graph, see Audrey Jaffe, "Trollope in the Stock Market: Irrational Exuberance and *The Prime Minister*," *Victorian Studies* 45, no. 1 (2002): 43–64.

30. On a "transgressive dishonesty" built into the domain of bourgeois morality, see Kucich, *The Power of Lies*, 41–74.

31. On capital as tautological, see Karl Marx, *Capital*, vol. 1, trans. Ben Fowkes (New York: Vintage, 1977), 250–51, 320. On the function of tautology in Trollope, see Aviva Briefel, "Tautological Crimes: Why Women Can't Steal Jewels," *Novel: A Forum on Fiction* 37, no. 1/2 (2003): 135–57; and Daniel Wright, "Because I Do: Trollope, Tautology, and Desire," *ELH* 80, no. 4 (Winter 2013): 1121–43. For Briefel, discussing *The Eustace Diamonds*, tautological means "redundant" (151). For Wright, discussing *Can You Forgive Her?* and *The Way We Live Now*, tautology is something good in Trollope when it functions as "social refusal," an exit from the coercive public space of giving reasons (1141), but tautology is something bad when it appeals to the ideological self-evidence of "rationalistic language" (1132). This distinction, however, depends on Wright being able to identify which ideologies are "insidious" and which are not (1140).

32. Karl Marx, *Capital*, vol. 3, trans. David Fernbach (London: Penguin, 1991), 515.

33. Marx, *Capital*, 3: 515.

34. Marx, *Capital*, 3: 516.

35. Marx, *Capital*, 3: 517.

36. Marx, *Capital*, 3: 515.

37. John Milton, *Paradise Lost*, book 5, line 860.

38. Marx, *Capital*, 3: 516.

39. Marx, *Capital*, 3: 550.

40. Marx, *Capital*, 3: 468.

41. Marx, *Capital*, 3: 517.

42. Marx, *Capital*, 3: 517.

43. There are two other moments, apart from Crawley's statements, where the true solution can be discerned. But they cancel each other out. First, Mr. Harding writes to his daughter, Mrs. Arabin, about the case: "It has something to do with the money which was given to Mr. Crawley last year, and which if I remember right, was your present" (432). If we read between the lines and see "your" as meaning "Mrs. Arabin," and "money" as not just bank notes but also the included check, we have arrived at the solution. But these hints are taken back in a second moment shortly thereafter. Mr. Toogood tells John Eames that his belief is "That the money was her [Mrs. Arabin's] present altogether, and not his. It seems that they don't mix their money" (504). Putting these two pieces of information together, the reader will now interpret "your present" to refer to bank notes ("money") furnished by Mrs. Arabin—not to the present of a check.

44. At the very end of the novel, Mr. Toogood marvels that Crawley "knew where he got the check as well as I know it now, [but] he wouldn't say so, because the dean had said it wasn't so" (819). This is following Crawley's reflections, after he has been cleared, that he knew the real explanation all along, but "postponed the elaborated result of my own memory to [Arabin's] word" (794). But this is not so; Crawley has previously said several times that the money came in the envelope from Arabin.

45. Shklovsky, *Theory of Prose*, trans. Benjamin Sher (Normal, IL: Dalkey Archive Press, 1991), 107–8.

46. It later comes out, due to some amateur detection on the part of Mr. Toogood, that one Mr. Scuttle stole this check from Mr. Soames while driving him to the above-named inn, this Scuttle having subsequently lived up to his name and fled to New Zealand (781).

47. The only new clue that will form part of the eventual explanation is when Mr. Toogood notices that there was "a queer lot about the house" at the Dragon of Wantly (410). See preceding note.

48. Marx, *Capital*, 1: 757.

49. Quoted in Trollope, *Autobiography*, 96.

50. D. A. Miller sees Trollope's Barchester as "an imbricated social-institutional surface," any departures from which serve only to more firmly cathect or anchor the individual subject within the closure of social normativity. *The Novel and the Police* (Berkeley: University of California Press, 1988), 129. Amanda Anderson has observed how Trollope's "characters barometrically exhibit the pressure of the conditions of modernity," especially when they seem "trapped . . . by their own psychological postures." It is as if such characters redouble their own situatedness—not content with being merely embedded, they must forcefully determine themselves by further digging in. "Trollope's Modernity," 512, 511. Nicholas Dames, writing about the function of the career in Trollope, stresses how characters' desires and the shape of their lives are formed within—and conditioned by—the "boundaries" and "exterior strictures" of the professional domain. The self is not prior to this "syntagmatic field," but rather is articulated as a series of positions inside it, whether in the office, the Cathedral close, or the halls of Parliament. "Trollope and the Career: Vocational Trajectories and the Management of Ambition," *Victorian Studies* 45, no. 2 (Winter 2003): 267, 271, 253.

51. J. Hillis Miller, *Communities in Fiction* (New York: Fordham University Press, 2014), 92.

52. Miller, *Communities in Fiction*, 85.

53. Miller, *Communities in Fiction*, 89.

3. The Fetishism of the Subject and Its Secret in *The Portrait of a Lady*

1. Kenneth Burke, *A Grammar of Motives* (New York: Prentice-Hall, 1945).

2. Henry James, "The Beast in the Jungle," in *The Portable Henry James*, ed. John Auchard (New York: Penguin, 2004), 280–81.

3. Henry James, "The Jolly Corner," in *The Portable Henry James*, 312, 318, 312.

4. For Dorothy Van Ghent, James is revealing how "the shadow of spiritual dispossession is the somber shape under the money outline." *The English Novel: Form and Function* (New York: Harper & Row, 1961), 213.

5. For a discussion of fetishism in James that departs from Marx's emphasis on the immaterial abstractions of the commodity's value-form to focus on the excessive materiality or objecthood of "things," see Bill Brown, *A Sense of Things: The Object Matter of American Literature* (Chicago: University of Chicago Press, 2003). See especially pp. 27–30 for Brown's careful distinction of his own account of commodity fetishism, as an aesthetic fascination with things, from Marx's definition. For a discussion of James's aestheticism in terms of "commodity fetishism," see Jonathan Freedman, *Professions of Taste: Henry James, British Aestheticism, and Commodity Culture* (Stanford, CA: Stanford University Press, 1990), xix–xxii.

6. Henry James, *The Portrait of a Lady* (Oxford: Oxford University Press, 2009), 207. All subsequent references to the novel will be given parenthetically from this edition.

7. Raymond Williams, *The English Novel from Dickens to Lawrence* (New York: Oxford University Press, 1973), 135; Terry Eagleton, *Criticism and Ideology* (London: Verso, 1978), 145; Fredric Jameson, *The Political Unconscious: Narrative as a Socially Symbolic Act* (Ithaca, NY: Cornell University Press, 1981), 221–22. For a dissenting view, arguing that James is a historical materialist, see Slavoj Žižek, *The Parallax View* (Cambridge, MA: MIT Press, 2006), 124–44.

8. Karl Marx, *Capital*, vol. 1, trans. Ben Fowkes (New York: Vintage, 1977), 167n.

9. For a reading of James as a capitalist who subjects Isabel to commodification, see Michael Gilmore, "The Commodity World of *The Portrait of a Lady*," *The New England Quarterly* 59, no. 1 (1986): 51–74. For a reading of "objectification" in terms of *Portrait*'s textuality, or how characters are made readable to others, see Laurel Bollinger, "The Ethics of Reading: The Struggle for Subjectivity in *The Portrait of a Lady*," *Criticism* 44, no. 2 (2002): 139–60.

10. Freedman, *Professions of Taste*, 153, 157, 162, 158.

11. Ross Posnock, *The Trial of Curiosity: Henry James, William James, and the Challenge of Modernity* (New York: Oxford University Press, 1991), 261, 330n.

12. Freedman, *Professions of Taste*, 165, 166; Posnock, *The Trial of Curiosity*, 330–31.

13. Roger Luckhurst calls *The Portrait of a Lady* "the pivotal novel" in the "transition from Victorian to Modernist novel forms." Introduction to *The Portrait of a Lady*, by Henry James (Oxford: Oxford University Press, 2009), vii. For Michael Gorra, *Portrait* is "the bridge across which Victorian fiction stepped over into modernism." *Portrait of a Novel: Henry James and the Making of an American Masterpiece* (New York: Liveright, 2012), xvi. David Kurnick, in looking at Jamesian style, asks us "to step to

the side of James's plots." "What Does Jamesian Style Want?" *Henry James Review* 28, no. 3 (2007): 214. For the contrary view, which orients James (and particularly his recognition scenes) not toward modernist style but toward an earlier tradition of melodrama, see Peter Brooks, *The Melodramatic Imagination: Balzac, Henry James, and the Mode of Excess* (New Haven, CT: Yale University Press, 1995).

14. Most critics prefer to subtly downgrade the novel's late revelations (the ones in chapters 51 and 52), situating them as secondary to a drama of consciousness accomplished elsewhere. If critics discuss a "recognition scene" in the novel, it is usually the scene in chapter 42. A more extreme critical position is to leave out the recognition scenes altogether. For example, Dorothy Krook does not mention Isabel's discovery that there has been a deceitful conspiracy against her. *The Ordeal of Consciousness in Henry James* (Cambridge: Cambridge University Press, 1962). Neither does Yi-Ping Ong, in *The Art of Being: Poetics of the Novel and Existentialist Philosophy* (Cambridge, MA: Harvard University Press, 2018). In Ong's Kierkegaardian account, it is as if the facts of the case about Merle and Osmond simply do not change anything, are not relevant to Isabel's crisis. For a defense of James's recognition scenes, see Van Ghent, *The English Novel*, 216; and Gorra, *Portrait of a Novel*, 275–79.

15. For the contrary view, that the preface to *Portrait* and the novel are incompatible projects, see Sharon Cameron, *Thinking in Henry James* (Chicago: University of Chicago Press, 1991), 54.

16. Here are three examples. Krook cites (to explain Isabel's last move) the passage *just prior* to the Countess Gemini's revelations, when Osmond impresses on Isabel the serious commitment of marriage, as "command[ing] her most inward assent; and it is this fact that finally compels her to go back to him." *The Ordeal of Consciousness*, 362. Gilmore also quotes from Isabel's earlier debate with Osmond, over whether she can *leave* Rome, how he apparently stops her in her tracks—as if this had any bearing on her *return* to Rome. Since Isabel does go on to disobey Osmond, that earlier scene can hardly motivate what Gilmore sees as her eventual submission and "renunciation of action." "The Commodity World," 73. J. Hillis Miller writes about her own implication in the bad marriage, that Isabel "has not been entrapped by Madame Merle, as she admits to herself at one crucial moment of self-understanding," meaning the moment when she says there had been no plot against her. *Literature as Conduct: Speech Acts in Henry James* (New York: Fordham University Press, 2005), 58. But Isabel is just *wrong* when she says that there was "no plot, no snare" (402). She later appreciates that Merle had been "deeply false . . . deeply, deeply, deeply" (512). The Countess Gemini says Merle "plotted" for Osmond (540).

17. Marx, *Capital*, 1: 279.

18. On James's "house of fiction," see Sara Blair, "Henry James and the Paradox of Literary Mastery," *Philosophy and Literature* 15, no. 1 (April 1991): 89–102; Dorothy Hale, *Social Formalism: The Novel in Theory from Henry James to the Present* (Stanford, CA: Stanford University Press, 1998), 25–26; and Anna Kornbluh, *The Order of Forms: Realism, Formalism, and Social Space* (Chicago: University of Chicago Press, 2019), 34–55.

19. You might expect James to say that the constrained viewpoint—the window or opening—was the "choice of subject," so that the consciousness of the artist was derived from the limited outlook on reality available to him/her. But what he says instead is much stranger. The "pierced aperture" is the literary form; the "choice of

subject" is what can be seen *with* (or from) that literary form; the consciousness of the artist is then a consequence of *this* seeing.

20. On the "tension between projection and reception" in James's prefaces, see Hale, *Social Formalism*, 27.

21. J. Hillis Miller rightly notes that the house of fiction is reminiscent of "the house of suffocation" in Isabel's experience of her marriage. But Miller thinks that what is bad and suffocating is being in the position of the one surveilled. Miller, *Literature as Conduct*, 71. I do not see how that could be. Much more obviously suffocating is being the "posted" viewer, unable to move around because perched at some hole in a "dead wall," in a house with no doors.

22. Marx, *Capital*, 1: 176–77.

23. In the case of Caspar Goodwood, whose scrutinizing perspective is (unlike Ralph's) out in the wide open, Isabel equates "being out of your sight"—not feeling that "you were watching me"—with her own "liberty" and "personal independence" (169).

24. Marx, *Capital*, 1: 976.

25. For discussions of chapter 42 as a recognition scene or *anagnorisis*, see Terence Cave, *Recognitions* (Oxford: Oxford University Press, 1988), 430, and Miller, *Literature as Conduct*, 72.

26. For both the Countess and Madame Merle's revelations, James apparently gives away ("spoils") the twists beforehand. We already know that Ralph persuaded his father to remake his will, and we have seen Madame Merle plotting with Osmond to manipulate Isabel and marry her for her money. This should disqualify them as recognition scenes, by my own definition. But, like a magician, while James seems to be showing us everything, the deception that is really going on is taking place somewhere other than what we are seeing. James has not in either case given away the main thing—only enough to stoke the suspense of wondering when things will come crashing down around the oblivious Isabel. We do not learn that Pansy is Madame Merle's child from her affair with Osmond until the Countess Gemini tells all. And the reader learns that Merle had guessed about Ralph's involvement at the same time that Isabel learns it. That is all to say, in both scenes James withholds a further turn of the screw from the reader who thinks she already has the secret in hand.

27. Bernard Williams, *Shame and Necessity* (Berkeley: University of California Press, 2008), 70.

28. "'What does your son think of it?' [Madame Merle] abruptly asked.

"'He left England before the will was read . . . But it's not likely he'll ever object to anything done by his father.'

"'Didn't you say his own share had been cut down?'

"'Only at his wish. I know that he urged his father to do something for the people in America. He's not in the least addicted to looking after number one.'

"'It depends upon whom he regards as number one!' said Madame Merle. And she remained thoughtful a moment, her eyes bent on the floor." (316)

29. Henry James, *The Notebooks of Henry James*, ed. F. O. Matthieson and Kenneth B. Murdock (Chicago: University of Chicago Press, 1981), 18.

30. For the view that Isabel at the end of the novel is dutifully accepting the consequences of prior actions, see Krook, *The Ordeal of Consciousness*, 360; Terry Eagleton, *The English Novel: An Introduction* (Oxford: Blackwell, 2005), 231; Sigi Jottkandt, *Acting*

Beautifully: Henry James and the Ethical Aesthetic (Albany, NY: SUNY Press, 2005), 84. For the view that we have no way of knowing why Isabel made her choice, or that it could have any number of meanings, see R. P. Blackmur, *Studies in Henry James* (New York: New Directions, 1983), 195, 200; Freedman, *Professions of Taste*, 166; and Miller, *Literature as Conduct*, 79. For the view that Isabel's decision does not so much *have* a meaning as it *denies* the circumstances as being capable of positive meaning, see Arnold Kettle, *The English Novel*, vol. 2 (New York: Harper, 1960), 29–34. For a more positive view of Isabel's decision, as self-determined, responsive to others, and unburdened of her earlier illusions, see Robert B. Pippin, *Henry James and Modern Moral Life* (Cambridge: Cambridge University Press, 2000), 142–43.

Patrick Fessenbecker sorts out the mass of critical responses to the novel's ending into three categories: her reasoning is just bad; her only option is a bad one; or her action is in some sense the "right" one. "Freedom, Self-Obligation, and Selfhood in Henry James," *Nineteenth-Century Literature* 66, no. 1 (2011): 69–95. This division permits a convenient survey of critical positions, but when all is told, the vocabulary of what is "explicable" and "justifiable" is question-begging. Fessenbecker's own interpretation seems only to say that her choice is justified *because* it is explicable. He writes, "when Isabel chooses to stay with Osmond at the novel's end, it is simply because to do anything else would be to violate her self" (86). On this reading, she has made her volitional bed, so to speak, and must sleep in it or else betray herself. But in James reasons only have the authority given to them from within one's own history; the role of the ethical self is to say in the present what the meaning of the (past) made bed is and what will *now* count as betraying or violating that meaning.

31. For a discussion of Ibsen's "discussions," see George Bernard Shaw, "The Technical Novelty," in *The Quintessence of Ibsenism* (New York: Hill & Wang, 1957), 171–84.

32. Harold Bloom surely speaks for many readers when he writes, "I both aesthetically approve yet humanly resent and am saddened by Isabel's return to Osmond." Harold Bloom, "Introduction," in *Henry James*, ed. Harold Bloom (Broomall, PA: Chelsea House, 2002), 10.

33. Jean-Christophe Agnew, "The Consuming Vision," in *Henry James: A collection of Critical Essays*, ed. Ruth Bernard Yeazell (New York: Prentice Hall, 1994); Eagleton, *The English Novel*, 231; Gilmore, "The Commodity World," 73; Kettle, *The English Novel*, 2: 31, 86; Miller, *Literature as Conduct*, 79.

34. W. H. Auden, "At the Grave of Henry James," in *Selected Poems*, ed. Edward Mendelson (New York: Vintage, 2007), 129.

35. Karl Marx, *Grundrisse*, trans. Martin Nicolaus (London: Penguin, 1973), 687.

36. Marx, *Capital*, 1: 169; see also Georg Lukács, *History and Class Consciousness: Studies in Marxist Dialectics*, trans. Rodney Livingstone (Cambridge, MA: MIT Press, 1971), 177.

37. The strongest evidence that Isabel *does* go back to her unhappy marriage out of some sense of obligation occurs after Ralph's death but before her encounters with Lord Warburton and Caspar: "She had a husband in a foreign city, counting the hours of her absence; in such a case one needed an excellent motive. He was not one of the best husbands, but that didn't alter the case. Certain obligations were involved in the very fact of marriage, and were quite independent of the quantity of enjoyment extracted from it" (572). The open question is what those obligations are. There

is no warrant that "certain obligations" refers to the kind of total, self-immolating renunciation that readers have wished to impose on Isabel. Compare the two other examples of married women in the novel: Mrs. Touchett, who lives apart from her husband, and the Countess Gemini, whose adulterous husband "had given his wife every pretext," yet keeps her on a short leash (282). There is no straightforward rule that Isabel could impose on herself here.

38. Most obviously, Isabel must now see her responsibility to Pansy, and her interference in Osmond's plans to marry her off without regard to her own heart, quite differently. Previously it has looked like an ethical obligation that fell into her lap: "She had said to herself that we must take our duty where we find it . . . Here was an opportunity, not eminent perhaps, but unmistakable" (402). But after the recognition scenes, Isabel must see Pansy not by contrast to herself any longer but as a repetition of her own fate. Isabel can no longer say of Pansy that the girl *only* "was a passive spectator of the operation of her fate" (239).

39. Richard Wagner, *Das Rheingold*, scene 1, in *The Ring of the Nibelung*, German text with English translation by Andrew Porter (New York: Norton, 1977).

40. James, *The Notebooks*, 18.

41. Honoré de Balzac, *Le Père Goriot*, ed. P.-G. Castex (Paris: Garnier Frères, 1963), 309.

42. Kettle, *The English Novel*, 2: 29–34; Gilmore, "The Commodity World," 73.

4. The Fragmentation of Subject and Object in Sherlock Holmes

1. On detective fiction as paradigm of critique, see Rita Felski's chapter, "An Inspector Calls," in *The Limits of Critique* (Chicago: University of Chicago Press, 2015), 85–116.

2. Jacques Rancière, *The Edges of Fiction*, trans. Steve Corcoran (Cambridge, UK: Polity Press, 2020), 83, 84.

3. Felski, *Limits of Critique*, 91, 92.

4. The formula "to reason backward from effects to causes" can be found in the short story "The Adventure of the Cardboard Box," but variations on these sayings abound, somewhat like the pronouncements of Christ in the synoptic Gospels. Arthur Conan Doyle, "The Adventure of the Cardboard Box," in *The Complete Sherlock Holmes*, 2 vol. (Garden City, NY: Doubleday, 1930), 895. Hereafter individual works in this collection cited parenthetically. Note: the pagination is continuous.

5. Georg Lukács, *History and Class Consciousness: Studies in Marxist Dialectics*, trans. Rodney Livingstone (Cambridge, MA: MIT Press, 1971), 89.

6. "Under capitalism . . . the different strands of the economy achieve a quite unprecedented autonomy . . . As a result of the objective structure of this economic system, the surface of capitalism appears to 'disintegrate' into a series of elements all driven towards independence." Georg Lukács, "Realism in the Balance," trans. Rodney Livingstone, in *Aesthetics and Politics*, ed. Ronald Taylor (London: Verso, 2007), 32.

7. The inconvenience of this retroactive chronological shuffling is, of course, that Watson has never heard of Moriarty in "The Final Problem," and now hears about Moriarty "first" in *The Valley of Fear*.

8. Pierre Bayard, *Sherlock Holmes Was Wrong: Reopening the Case of* The Hound of the Baskervilles, trans. Charlotte Mandell (New York: Bloomsbury, 2008), 30.

9. Maria Konnikova, *Mastermind: How to Think Like Sherlock Holmes* (New York: Penguin, 2013).

10. Sometimes Holmes explicitly cites the forerunners of his own investigative approach: Winwood Reade in *The Sign of Four* (137), Georges Cuvier in "The Five Orange Pips" (225), and Alphonse Bertillon in "The Naval Treaty" (460). But historicism discovers a further, vast referential context in Holmes's fleeting hints and allusions—as if an iceberg of erudition stretched out below his explicit citations. Holmes thus becomes a putative reader of Charles Lyell, Charles Darwin, John Tyndall, E. B. Taylor, Thomas Huxley, Francis Galton, William Whewell, and so on. See Lawrence Frank, *Victorian Detective Fiction and the Nature of Evidence: The Scientific Investigations of Poe, Dickens, and Doyle* (New York: Palgrave Macmillan, 2003), 176, 203.

11. Ronald R. Thomas, *Detective Fiction and the Rise of Forensic Science* (Cambridge: Cambridge University Press, 1999), 220–39; Susan Cannon Harris, "Pathological Possibilities: Contagion and Empire in Doyle's Sherlock Holmes Stories," *Victorian Literature and Culture* 31, no. 2 (September 2003): 447–66; John McBratney, "Racial and Criminal Types: Indian Ethnography and Sir Arthur Conan Doyle's *The Sign of Four*," *Victorian Literature and Culture* 33, no. 1 (March 2005): 149–67; and Jesse Oak Taylor, "Ritual and the Liminality of Sherlock Holmes in *The Hound of the Baskervilles* and *The Sign of Four*," *English Literature in Transition* 48, no. 1 (2005): 55–70.

12. Rosemary Jann sees Holmes's immersion in contemporary (Victorian) scientific and pseudo-scientific theories as playing an important role in Doyle's narrative construction. "Sherlock Holmes Codes the Social Body," *ELH* 57, no. 3 (Autumn 1990): 685–708. But Jann does not make any distinction between the information that is re-sequenced in Holmes's solutions, and the *extra* information that Holmes incessantly registers and comments on. A case in point: she pays considerable attention to Holmes's analytic processes in *The Hound of the Baskervilles*, but does not mention the two clues that actually solve the case. My view is that the scientific references do not play a "methodological" role in the narrative construction.

13. On the limited relevance of the scientific context to Holmes's solutions, see Stephen Knight, *Form and Ideology in Crime Fiction* (London: Macmillan, 1980), 85–86.

14. Umberto Eco and Thomas A. Sebeok, eds., *The Sign of Three: Dupin, Holmes, Peirce* (Bloomington: Indiana University Press, 1988).

15. As Michel Foucault observes, an object constituted in one discourse is not transferable to another as though still maintaining its original reference. What happens in one discourse "is far from relating itself to one sole object formed once and for all, and from conserving it indefinitely in its horizon of inexhaustible ideality," across different discourses. Rather, each zone has its own rules for the constitution and emergence of objects. *L'archéologie du savoir* (Paris: Gallimard, 2008), 48–49. My translation.

16. Franco Moretti, "The Slaughterhouse of Literature," *Modern Language Quarterly* 61, no. 1 (2000): 207–27.

17. Moretti, "Slaughterhouse," 216.

18. Whenever a story does not meet the above criteria, Moretti presents this as a deviation from protocol, as if Doyle forgot the mechanism he had invented. To explain this inconsistency, Moretti postulates a productive tension for Doyle, who oscillates between clues as "mere ornament" and clues as "puzzle-solving mechanism."

However, there is no such tension or oscillation because Doyle never discovers this latter function of clues. Moretti, "Slaughterhouse," 215.

19. Moretti, "Slaughterhouse," 215.

20. A perhaps more obvious explanation for the success of Doyle's stories over those of his "rivals" apparently does not occur to Moretti: they have the character of Sherlock Holmes, and the others do not.

21. Régis Messac observes about Holmes's solutions: "We are impressed, but we would be less so if we had been kept informed of all the results of Holmes's sorties . . . [which] he tells us only at the end." This is judged to be a "convenient fault, which permits the author to hold us rapt with a banal mystery whose solution we would too quickly make out, if he were to communicate all the facts to us." Le "Detective Novel" et l'influence de la pensée scientifique (Paris: Honoré Champion, 1929), 610, 611. My translation.

22. Agatha Christie, The Murder of Roger Ackroyd (New York: Harper, 2011), 238.

23. Doyle acknowledges that the Holmes stories are not always puzzles, solvable only by Holmes. Watson concedes that there is a literary "Scylla and Charybdis" he faces, between depicting feats of reasoning (possibly banal) and stories of adventure (without analysis). "For in those cases in which Holmes has performed some tour de force of analytical reasoning, and has demonstrated the value of his peculiar methods of investigation, the facts themselves have often been so slight or so commonplace that I could not feel justified in laying them before the public. On the other hand, it has frequently happened that he has been concerned in some research where the facts have been of the most remarkable and dramatic character, but . . . the share which he has himself taken in determining their causes has been less pronounced than I, as his biographer, could wish." "The Resident Patient," 422.

24. Moretti, "Slaughterhouse," 213.

25. Moretti, "Slaughterhouse," 215.

26. Raymond Williams, The Country and the City (New York: Oxford University Press, 1973), 227.

27. Franco Moretti, "Clues," trans. Susan Fischer, in Signs Taken for Wonders: On the Sociology of Literary Forms (London: Verso, 2005), 130–56.

28. Moretti, "Clues," 152.

29. Messac calls the Mormon interlude "parasitic." Le "Detective Novel," 591.

30. Tzvetan Todorov, The Poetics of Prose, trans. Richard Howard (Ithaca, NY: Cornell University Press, 1977), 42–52.

31. Viktor Shklovsky, Theory of Prose, trans. Benjamin Sher (Normal, IL: Dalkey Archive Press, 1991), 101.

32. Peter Brooks, Reading for the Plot (Cambridge, MA: Harvard University Press, 1992), 23–29. I should mention what Brooks does not: that he has picked a too-convenient example for himself. For "The Musgrave Ritual" is one of the very few cases where Watson does not tag along. Watson is present only in the narrative frame, to prompt Holmes to an uninterrupted narration of a case that predates his amanuensis. The awkward result is that Holmes, not having withheld anything from the reader, is as baffled as we are when it comes to the final links in the "long chain of surmise and of proof" (397). So Musgrave himself supplies the two decisive points: the dating of the coins, and his ancestor being a Royalist after the English Civil War. Doyle was well

aware of the disadvantage of having Holmes narrate his own investigation. In "The Adventure of the Blanched Soldier," the detective touches on the aesthetic problem of giving his own account: "And here it is that I miss my Watson. By cunning questions and ejaculations of wonder he could elevate my simple art, which is but systematized common sense, into a prodigy. When I tell my own story I have no such aid" (1011).

33. Moretti, "Clues," 148.

34. Ernst Bloch, "A Philosophical View of the Detective Novel," in *The Utopian Function of Art and Literature: Selected Essays*, trans. Jack Zipes and Frank Mecklenberg (Cambridge, MA: MIT Press, 1988), 255.

35. Rancière observes that "the story of the crime and that of its reasons are two different stories," because while the rationality of detective fiction has "tightened to the utmost . . . the chain of efficient causes," doing so only "drove it apart more radically still from the order of final causes." *The Edges of Fiction*, 86, 87.

36. Contrast this gesture of distance with Agatha Christie's oriental novels, *Murder in Mesopotamia*, *Murder on the Orient Express*, and *Death on the Nile*. These works are so exactly like Christie's novels set on English country estates that it is almost only a matter of changing a few place-names. A "locked room" mystery is the same everywhere. Whereas Doyle is at great pains to import the generically exotic into 221B Baker Street, Christie ingenuously flaunts her ability to set an identically English mystery virtually anywhere—as long as it is a place frequented by the English bourgeoisie.

37. Contrast this with the extremely complicated temporal logic of forgiveness in Thomas Hardy's novels of the same period, *The Mayor of Casterbridge*, *Tess of the D'Urbervilles*, and *Jude the Obscure*. The latter novels revolve around reconciliations that had better not have taken place, after a long passage of time and the wearing-away of painful memories—and the disastrous forgiving of things that had better not have been forgiven (wife-selling, rape, bigamy).

38. See Brooks, *Reading for the Plot*, 18, 25, 244.

39. Moretti, "Clues," 137, 146.

40. D. A. Miller, *The Novel and the Police* (Berkeley: University of California Press, 1988), 51.

41. Shklovsky, *Theory of Prose*, 101–16.

42. Georg Lukács, *Theory of the Novel*, trans. Anna Bostock (Cambridge, MA: MIT Press, 1971), 71.

43. Lukács, *Theory of the Novel*, 38.

44. Lukács, *Theory of the Novel*, 88.

45. On the "disenchantment of the world," see Max Weber, "Science as Vocation," in *From Max Weber: Essays in Sociology*, trans. H. H. Gerth and C. Wright Mills (New York: Oxford University Press, 1946), 155.

46. For Catherine Belsey, "The project of the Sherlock Holmes stories is to dispel magic and mystery, to make everything explicit, accountable, subject to scientific analysis." The point of Holmes's solutions is therefore "to dispel any magic from the deciphering process." *Critical Practice* (London: Routledge, 2002), 91–92, 94.

47. Lukács, *Theory of the Novel*, 88.

48. Sophocles, *Oedipus the King*, line 220.

49. G. W. F. Hegel, *The Phenomenology of Mind*, trans. J. B. Baillie (New York: Harper & Row, 1967), 279.

50. Lukács, *Theory of the Novel*, 99.

51. My point is that history is not a repressed dimension of the stories; it is never brought into the structures of misrecognition. For a discussion of repression in detective fiction, see Jacques Lacan's "Seminar on 'The Purloined Letter'": "What is hidden is only ever *what is missing from its place*, as it says on the call slip of a volume mislaid in a library. And even if the book were on the next shelf or in the next case, it would still be hidden, however visible it may seem there. For it can literally be said of something that it is missing from its place only if it can change places—that is to say, of the symbolic." *Écrits*, trans. Bruce Fink (New York: Norton, 2006), 17. Translation modified.

52. Lukács, *Theory of the Novel*, 100.

53. Hegel, *Phenomenology of Mind*, 235.

54. When Doyle first resurrects Holmes, he sets his investigation (*The Hound of the Baskervilles*) in 1889, prior to "The Final Problem," such that the latter story still marks a limit point—May 1891—the Holmesian "end of history," after which no real action is possible. However, even this pretense is soon abandoned, and Holmes is corporeally brought back to life in "The Empty House," and thereafter Holmes is more active than ever. Watson tells us in "The Adventure of the Solitary Cyclist": "From the years 1894 to 1901 inclusive, Mr. Sherlock Holmes was a very busy man. It is safe to say that there was no public case of any difficulty in which he was not consulted during those eight years, and there were hundreds of private cases, some of them of the most intricate and extraordinary character, in which he played a prominent part" (526).

55. Lukács, *Theory of the Novel*, 130.

56. Yet Wilde brings out all the hoariest tropes of dramatic *anagnorisis* in his play *The Importance of Being Earnest* (1895).

57. For a discussion of post-Victorian recognition scenes in the late James, and also in Joseph Conrad's *Under Western Eyes*, see Terence Cave, *Recognitions* (Oxford: Oxford University Press, 1988), 428–88.

58. Williams, *The Country and the City*, 249.

59. Georg Lukács, "Narrate or Describe?" in *Writer and Critic and Other Essays*, ed. and trans. Arthur D. Kahn (New York: Grosset & Dunlap, 1970), 134.

60. Leslie Stephens, *George Eliot* (London: Macmillan, 1902), 150.

61. Fredric Jameson, *The Modernist Papers* (New York: Verso, 2007), 180.

62. Brooks, *Reading for the Plot*, 238.

63. Brooks, *Reading for the Plot*, 238.

64. Georg Lukács, *The Historical Novel*, trans. Hannah Mitchell and Stanley Mitchell (Boston: Beacon Press, 1963), 179.

Conclusion

1. Georg Lukács, *History and Class Consciousness: Studies in Marxist Dialectics*, trans. Rodney Livingstone (Cambridge, MA: MIT Press, 1971), 95.

2. Georg Lukács, *The Theory of the Novel*, trans. Anna Bostock (Cambridge, MA: MIT Press, 1971), 71.

3. Lukács, *The Theory of the Novel*, 98.

4. Lukács, *History and Class Consciousness*, 165.

5. J. M. Bernstein, *The Philosophy of the Novel: Lukács, Marxism, and the Dialectics of Form* (Minneapolis: University of Minnesota Press, 1984), 187.

6. Sigmund Freud, "From the History of an Infantile Neurosis," in *The Standard Edition of the Complete Psychological Works of Sigmund Freud*, vol. 17, trans. and ed. James Strachey (Vintage: London, 2001), 34–35. This edition hereafter *SE*.

7. Sigmund Freud, "'A Child is Being Beaten': A Contribution to the Study of the Origin of Sexual Perversions," *SE* 17: 185-6.

8. Freud, "'A Child is Being Beaten,'" *SE* 17: 191.

9. As Moishe Postone observes, the "impersonal and abstract social forms [of value production] do not simply *veil* . . . the 'real' social relations of capitalism," rather these forms of appearance "*are* the real relations of capitalist society." *Time, Labor, and Social Domination: A Reinterpretation of Marx's Critical Theory* (Cambridge: Cambridge University Press, 1998), 6.

10. Marx understands the "visible surface phenomena" to arise historically *before* the "invisible essence" that is to be disclosed. Karl Marx, *Capital*, vol. 3, trans. David Fernbach (London: Penguin, 1991), 184.

11. Sigmund Freud, *Beyond the Pleasure Principle*, *SE* 18: 22.

12. Torquato Tasso, *Jerusalem Delivered*, trans. Edward Fairfax (New York: Capricorn, 1963), canto 12, stanza 67, line 8.

13. Tasso, *Jerusalem Delivered*, canto 13, stanza 62.

14. Tasso, *Jerusalem Delivered*, canto 13, stanza 64, line 8.

15. Sigmund Freud, *The Interpretation of Dreams*, *SE* 5: 510.

16. Miguel de Cervantes, *The History and Adventures of the Renowned Don Quixote*, trans. Tobias Smollett (New York: Modern Library, 2001), 246.

17. Cervantes, *Don Quixote*, 1005.

18. John Bunyan, *The Pilgrim's Progress*, ed. W. R. Owens (New York: Oxford University Press, 2003), 10, 88, 92. Hereafter cited parenthetically.

19. Daniel Defoe, *Robinson Crusoe*, ed. Michael Shinagel (New York: Norton, 1994), 79.

20. Karl Marx, *Capital*, vol. 1, trans. Ben Fowkes (New York: Vintage, 1977), 169.

21. Deidre Lynch, *The Economy of Character: Novels, Market Culture, and the Business of Inner Meaning* (Chicago: University of Chicago Press, 1998), 97.

22. Henry Fielding, *Tom Jones*, ed. Sheridan Baker (New York: Norton, 1973), 211.

23. Capital is a thing not of "nature," but a denial of it. Old Mr. Nightingale, at least, "had conversed so entirely with Money, that it may be almost doubted, whether he imagined there was any other Thing really existing in the World: This at least may be certainly averred, that he firmly believed nothing else to have any real Value." Fielding, *Tom Jones*, 591.

24. Ann Radcliffe, *The Mysteries of Udolpho*, ed. Bonamy Dobrée (Oxford: Oxford University Press, 1966), 635.

25. Radcliffe, *The Mysteries of Udolpho*, 662.

26. Radcliffe, *The Mysteries of Udolpho*, 662.

27. Radcliffe corrects Emily's perception of the object behind the black veil solely for our benefit, since Emily has no further opportunity of verifying Udolpho's inventory of curiosities. The disclosure of Signora Laurentini's true history is also (somewhat) withheld from Emily, for "the narrative of the abbess [related to her] was . . . deficient in many particulars." *The Mysteries of Udolpho*, 655.

28. Johann Wolfgang von Goethe, *Wilhelm Meister's Apprenticeship*, trans. Thomas Carlyle (New York: Collier, 1962), 405. Hereafter cited parenthetically.

29. Lukács, *Theory of the Novel*, 142.

30. On *Bildung* in the novel as "an uncanny moment" of "radical self-loss," see Marc Redfield, *Phantom Formations, Aesthetic Ideology and the Bildungsroman* (Ithaca, NY: Cornell University Press, 1996), 76.

31. Bunyan, *The Pilgrim's Progress*, 155.

32. Jacques Lacan, *The Seminar of Jacques Lacan, Book I: Freud's Papers on Technique, 1953–1954*, translated by John Forrester (New York: Norton, 1991), 158.

33. Lukács, *History and Class Consciousness*, 199.

34. Sophocles, *Oedipus the King*, trans. David Grene (Chicago: University of Chicago Press, 2010), line 1388. Translation modified.

35. Anthony Trollope, *The Last Chronicle of Barset*, ed. Stephen Gill (Oxford: Oxford University Press, 1980), 869. It is also emphasized that Crawley comes into this new living not because of his travail of innocence, but only because Mr. Arabin and Archdeacon Grantly are married to sisters.

36. Henry James, *The Portrait of a Lady* (Oxford: Oxford University Press, 2009), 567.

37. Richard Wagner, *Die Walküre*, act 2, scene 2, in *The Ring of the Nibelung*, German text with English translation by Andrew Porter (New York: Norton, 1977). My translation.

38. Lukács, *History and Class Consciousness*, 169, 208.

Bibliography

Adorno, Theodor W. *Negative Dialectics*. Translated by E. B. Ashton. New York: Continuum, 1973.

Agnew, Jean-Christophe. "The Consuming Vision." In *Henry James: A Collection of Critical Essays*, edited by Ruth Bernard Yeazell. New York: Prentice Hall, 1994.

Althusser, Louis. *On the Reproduction of Capitalism*. Translated by G. M. Goshgarian. Brooklyn: Verso, 2014.

Anderson, Amanda. *The Powers of Distance: Cosmopolitanism and the Cultivation of Detachment*. Princeton, NJ: Princeton University Press, 2001.

——. "Trollope's Modernity." *ELH* 74, no. 3 (Fall 2007): 509–34.

Aristotle. *Poetics*. Translated by James Hutton. New York: Norton, 1982.

Auden, W. H. *Selected Poems*. Edited by Edward Mendelson. New York: Vintage, 2007.

Auerbach, Erich. *Mimesis: The Representation of Reality in Western Literature*. Translated by Willard R. Trask. Princeton, NJ: Princeton University Press, 1953.

Balibar, Étienne. *Citizen Subject: Foundations for Philosophical Anthropology*. Translated by Steven Miller. New York: Fordham University Press, 2017.

Balzac, Honoré de. *Le Père Goriot*. Edited by P.-G. Castex. Paris: Garnier Frères, 1963.

Barthes, Roland. *S/Z*. Translated by Richard Miller. New York: Hill & Wang, 1974.

Bayard, Pierre. *Sherlock Holmes Was Wrong: Reopening the Case of* The Hound of the Baskervilles. Translated by Charlotte Mandell. New York: Bloomsbury, 2008.

Belsey, Catherine. *Critical Practice*. London: Routledge, 2002.

Benhabib, Seyla. *Critique, Norm, and Utopia: A Study of the Foundations of Critical Theory*. New York: Columbia University Press, 1986.

Bernstein, J. M. *The Philosophy of the Novel: Lukács, Marxism, and the Dialectics of Form*. Minneapolis: University of Minnesota Press, 1984.

Best, Stephen, and Sharon Marcus. "Surface Reading: An Introduction." *Representations* 108, no. 1 (Fall 2009): 1–21.

Bewes, Timothy. *Reification, or The Anxiety of Late Capitalism*. London: Verso, 2002.

Blackmur, R. P. *Studies in Henry James*. New York: New Directions, 1983.

Blair, Sara. "Henry James and the Paradox of Literary Mastery." *Philosophy and Literature* 15, no. 1 (April 1991): 89–102.

Bloch, Ernst. *The Utopian Function of Art and Literature: Selected Essays*. Translated by Jack Zipes and Frank Mecklenberg. Cambridge, MA: MIT Press, 1988.

Bloom, Harold. "Introduction." In *Henry James*. Edited by Harold Bloom. Broomall, PA: Chelsea House, 2002.

Bollinger, Laurel. "The Ethics of Reading: The Struggle for Subjectivity in *The Portrait of a Lady*." *Criticism* 44, no. 2 (2002): 139–60.

Brandom, Robert. *A Spirit of Trust: A Reading of Hegel's* Phenomenology. Cambridge, MA: Harvard University Press, 2019.

Brantlinger, Patrick. *Fictions of State: Culture and Credit in Britain, 1694–1994.* Ithaca, NY: Cornell University Press, 1996.

Briefel, Aviva. "Tautological Crimes: Why Women Can't Steal Jewels." *Novel: A Forum on Fiction* 37, no. 1/2 (2003): 135–57.

Brooks, Peter. *The Melodramatic Imagination: Balzac, Henry James, and the Mode of Excess.* New Haven, CT: Yale University Press, 1995.

——. *Reading for the Plot.* Cambridge, MA: Harvard University Press, 1992.

Brown, Bill. *A Sense of Things: The Object Matter of American Literature.* Chicago: University of Chicago Press, 2003.

Buck-Morss, Susan. *The Origins of Negative Dialectics: Theodor W. Adorno, Walter Benjamin, and the Frankfurt Institute.* New York: The Free Press, 1977.

Bunyan, John. *The Pilgrim's Progress.* Edited by W. R. Owens. New York: Oxford University Press, 2003.

Burke, Kenneth. *A Grammar of Motives.* New York: Prentice-Hall, 1945.

Butler, Judith. *The Psychic Life of Power: Theories in Subjection.* Stanford, CA: Stanford University Press, 1997.

Cameron, Sharon. *Thinking in Henry James.* Chicago: University of Chicago Press, 1991.

Cave, Terence. *Recognitions.* Oxford: Oxford University Press, 1988.

de Cervantes, Miguel. *The History and Adventures of the Renowned Don Quixote.* Translated by Tobias Smollett. New York: Modern Library, 2001.

Christie, Agatha. *The Murder of Roger Ackroyd.* New York: Harper, 2011.

Cvetkovich, Ann. *Mixed Feelings: Feminism, Mass Culture, and Victorian Sensationalism.* New Brunswick, NJ: Rutgers University Press, 1992.

Dames, Nicholas. "Trollope and the Career: Vocational Trajectories and the Management of Ambition." *Victorian Studies* 45, no. 2 (Winter 2003): 247–78.

Defoe, Daniel. *Robinson Crusoe.* Edited by Michael Shinagel. New York: Norton, 1994.

Dickens, Charles. *Great Expectations.* Oxford: Oxford University Press, 1953.

——. *Little Dorrit.* Oxford: Oxford University Press, 1953.

Doyle, Arthur Conan. *The Complete Sherlock Holmes*, 2 vol. Garden City, NY: Doubleday, 1930.

Duncan, Ian. *Modern Romance and Transformations of the Novel: The Gothic, Scott, Dickens.* Cambridge: Cambridge University Press, 1992.

Eagleton, Terry. *Criticism and Ideology.* London: Verso, 1978.

——. *The English Novel: An Introduction.* Oxford: Blackwell, 2005.

Eco, Umberto, and Thomas A. Sebeok, eds. *The Sign of Three: Dupin, Holmes, Peirce.* Bloomington: Indiana University Press, 1988.

Feenberg, Andrew. *The Philosophy of Praxis: Marx, Lukács, and the Frankfurt School.* Brooklyn: Verso, 2014.

Fielding, Henry. *Tom Jones.* Edited by Sheridan Baker. New York: Norton, 1973.

Fine, Ben, and Alfredo Saad-Filho. *Marx's "Capital."* London: Pluto Press, 2010.

Felski, Rita. *The Limits of Critique.* Chicago: University of Chicago Press, 2015.

Fessenbecker, Patrick. "Freedom, Self-Obligation, and Selfhood in Henry James." *Nineteenth-Century Literature* 66, no. 1 (2011): 69–95.

Foucault, Michel. *L'archéologie du savoir.* Paris: Gallimard, 2008.

Frank, Lawrence. *Victorian Detective Fiction and the Nature of Evidence: The Scientific Investigations of Poe, Dickens, and Doyle*. New York: Palgrave Macmillan, 2003.

Freedman, Jonathan. *Professions of Taste: Henry James, British Aestheticism, and Commodity Culture*. Stanford, CA: Stanford University Press, 1990.

Freud, Sigmund. *Beyond the Pleasure Principle*. In vol. 18 of *The Standard Edition of the Complete Psychological Works of Sigmund Freud*. Translated and edited by James Strachey. London: Vintage, 2001. Hereafter *SE*.

——. "'A Child is Being Beaten': A Contribution to the Study of the Origin of Sexual Perversions." *SE* 17.

——. *Civilization and its Discontents*. *SE* 21.

——. "From the History of an Infantile Neurosis." *SE* 17.

——. *The Interpretation of Dreams*. *SE* 4–5.

——. *Introductory Lectures on Psycho-Analysis*. *SE* 15–6.

——. "Miss Lucy R." In *Studies on Hysteria*. *SE* 2.

——. "Screen Memories." *SE* 3.

Frye, Northrop. *Anatomy of Criticism: Four Essays*. Princeton, NJ: Princeton University Press, 2000.

——. *The Educated Imagination*. Bloomington: Indiana University Press, 1964.

——. *Fables of Identity: Studies in Poetic Mythology*. New York: Harcourt, Brace and World, 1963.

Gallagher, Catherine. *The Body Economic: Life, Death, and Sensation in Political Economy and the Victorian Novel*. Princeton, NJ: Princeton University Press, 2006.

——. "The Duplicity of Doubling in *A Tale of Two Cities*." *Dickens Studies Annual* 12 (1983): 134.

Gilmore, Michael T. "The Commodity World of *The Portrait of a Lady*." *New England Quarterly* 59, no. 1 (1986): 51–74.

Girard, René. *Oedipus Unbound: Selected Writings on Rivalry and Desire*. Translated by Mark R. Anspach. Stanford, CA: Stanford University Press, 2004.

Goethe, Johann Wolfgang von. *Wilhelm Meister's Apprenticeship*. Translated by Thomas Carlyle. New York: Collier, 1962.

Gorra, Michael. *Portrait of a Novel: Henry James and the Making of an American Masterpiece*. New York: Liveright, 2012.

Habermas, Jürgen. *The Theory of Communicative Action*, vol. 1. Translated by Thomas McCarthy. Boston: Beacon, 1984.

Hadley, Elaine. "Nobody, Somebody, and Everybody." *Victorian Studies* 59, no. 1 (Autumn 2016): 83.

Hale, Dorothy. *Social Formalism: The Novel in Theory from Henry James to the Present*. Stanford, CA: Stanford University Press, 1998.

Harris, Susan Cannon. "Pathological Possibilities: Contagion and Empire in Doyle's Sherlock Holmes Stories." *Victorian Literature and Culture* 31, no. 2 (September 2003): 447–66.

Harvey, David. *A Companion to Marx's* Capital. London: Verso, 2010.

——. *Limits to Capital*. London: Verso, 2006.

Heath, Peter, and John Lachs. Preface to *Science of Knowledge*, by J. G. Fichte. Translated by Peter Heath and John Lachs. Cambridge: Cambridge University Press, 1982.

Hegel, G. W. F. *The Phenomenology of Mind*. Translated by J. B. Baillie. New York: Harper & Row, 1967.

Heidegger, Martin. *Being and Time*. Translated by John Macquarrie and Edward Robinson. New York: Harper Collins, 1962.

Hilferding, Rudolf. *Finance Capital: A Study of the Latest Phase of Capitalist Development*. Edited by Tom Bottomore. London: Routledge & Kegan Paul, 1981.

Honneth, Axel. *Reification: A New Look at an Old Idea*. New York: Oxford University Press, 2008.

——. *The Struggle for Recognition: The Moral Grammar of Social Conflicts*. Translated by Joel Anderson. Cambridge, MA: MIT Press, 1995.

House, Humphrey. *The Dickens World*. Oxford: Oxford University Press, 1942.

Jaffe, Audrey. "Trollope in the Stock Market: Irrational Exuberance and *The Prime Minister*." *Victorian Studies* 45, no. 1 (2002): 43–64.

James, Henry. *The Notebooks of Henry James*. Edited by F. O. Matthieson and Kenneth B. Murdock. Chicago: University of Chicago Press, 1981.

——. *The Portable Henry James*. Edited by John Auchard. New York: Penguin, 2004.

——. *The Portrait of a Lady*. Oxford: Oxford University Press, 2009.

Jameson, Fredric. *The Antinomies of Realism*. Brooklyn: Verso, 2013.

——. *The Modernist Papers*. New York: Verso, 2007.

——. *The Political Unconscious: Narrative as a Socially Symbolic Act*. Ithaca, NY: Cornell University Press, 1981.

Jann, Rosemary. "Sherlock Holmes Codes the Social Body," *ELH* 57, no. 3 (Autumn 1990): 685–708.

Johnson, Samuel. *A Dictionary of the English Language*. 1755.

Jottkandt, Sigi. *Acting Beautifully: Henry James and the Ethical Aesthetic*. Albany, NY: SUNY Press, 2005.

Kendrick, Walter. *The Novel-Machine: The Theory and Fiction of Anthony Trollope*. Baltimore: Johns Hopkins University Press, 1980.

Kettle, Arnold. *An Introduction to the English Novel*, 2 vol. New York: Harper, 1960.

Knight, Stephen. *Form and Ideology in Crime Fiction*. London: Macmillan, 1980.

Knox, Bernard. *Oedipus at Thebes: Sophocles' Tragic Hero and His Time*. New Haven, CT: Yale University Press, 1957.

Kojève, Alexandre. *Introduction to the Reading of Hegel*. Translated by James H. Nichols Jr. Ithaca, NY: Cornell University Press, 1980.

Konnikova, Maria. *Mastermind: How to Think Like Sherlock Holmes*. New York: Penguin, 2013.

Kornbluh, Anna. *The Order of Forms: Realism, Formalism, and Social Space*. Chicago: University of Chicago Press, 2019.

——. *Realizing Capital: Financial and Psychic Economies in Victorian Form*. New York: Fordham University Press, 2014.

Krook, Dorothy. *The Ordeal of Consciousness in Henry James*. Cambridge: Cambridge University Press, 1962.

Kucich, John. *The Power of Lies: Transgression in Victorian Fiction*. Ithaca, NY: Cornell University Press, 1994.

——. "Repression and Representation: Dickens's General Economy." *Nineteenth-Century Fiction* 38, no. 1 (June 1983): 62–77.

Kurnick, David. "What Does Jamesian Style Want?" *Henry James Review* 28, no. 3 (2007): 213–22.

Lacan, Jacques. *Écrits*. Translated by Bruce Fink. New York: Norton, 2006.

———. *The Seminar of Jacques Lacan, Book I: Freud's Papers on Technique, 1953–1954*. Translated by John Forrester. New York: Norton, 1991.

Latour, Bruno. "Why Has Critique Run out of Steam?" *Critical Inquiry* 30, no. 2 (Winter 2004).

Leavis, F. R., and Q. D. Leavis. *Dickens the Novelist*. London: Chatto & Windus, 1970.

Levine, George. *Darwin and the Novelists: Patterns of Justice in Victorian Fiction*. Chicago: University of Chicago Press, 1991.

Luckhurst, Roger. Introduction to *The Portrait of a Lady*, by Henry James. Oxford: Oxford University Press, 2009.

Lukács, Georg. *The Historical Novel*. Translated by Hannah Mitchell and Stanley Mitchell. Boston: Beacon Press, 1963.

———. *History and Class Consciousness: Studies in Marxist Dialectics*. Translated by Rodney Livingstone. Cambridge, MA: MIT Press, 1971.

———. "Realism in the Balance." Translated by Rodney Livingstone. In *Aesthetics and Politics*, edited by Ronald Taylor. London: Verso, 2007.

———. *The Theory of the Novel*. Translated by Anna Bostock. Cambridge, MA: MIT Press, 1971.

———. *Writer and Critic and Other Essays*. Edited and translated by Arthur D. Kahn. New York: Grosset & Dunlap, 1970.

Lynch, Deidre. *The Economy of Character: Novels, Market Culture, and the Business of Inner Meaning*. Chicago: University of Chicago Press, 1998.

Mandel, Ernst. Introduction to *Capital*, vol. 3, by Karl Marx. Translated by David Fernbach. London: Penguin, 1991.

Marx, Karl. *Capital*, vol. 1. Translated by Ben Fowkes. New York: Vintage, 1977.

———. *Capital*, vol. 2. Translated by David Fernbach. London: Penguin, 1992.

———. *Capital*, vol. 3. Translated by David Fernbach. London: Penguin, 1991.

———. *Grundrisse*. Translated by Martin Nicolaus. London: Penguin, 1973.

———. *Theories of Surplus Value*, part 1. Translated by Emile Burns. Moscow: Progress Publishers, 1968.

———. *Theories of Surplus Value*, part 2. Translated by S. W. Ryazanskaya. Moscow: Progress Publishers, 1968.

———. *Theories of Surplus Value*, part 3. Translated by Jack Cohen and S. W. Ryazanskaya. Moscow: Progress Publishers, 1971.

McBratney, John. "Racial and Criminal Types: Indian Ethnography and Sir Arthur Conan Doyle's *The Sign of Four*." *Victorian Literature and Culture* 33, no. 1 (March 2005): 149–67.

Messac, Régis. *Le "Detective Novel" et l'influence de la pensée scientifique*. Paris: Honoré Champion, 1929.

Miller, D. A. *The Novel and the Police*. Berkeley: University of California Press, 1988.

Miller, J. Hillis. *Charles Dickens: The World of His Novels*. Bloomington: Indiana University Press, 1969.

———. *Communities in Fiction*. New York: Fordham University Press, 2014.

——. *Literature as Conduct: Speech Acts in Henry James*. New York: Fordham University Press, 2005.

Milton, John. *Paradise Lost*. 1674.

Moretti, Franco. *Signs Taken for Wonders: On the Sociology of Literary Forms*. London: Verso, 2005.

——. "The Slaughterhouse of Literature." *Modern Language Quarterly* 61, no. 1 (2000): 207–27.

Ngai, Sianne. *Theory of the Gimmick: Aesthetic Judgment and Capitalist Form*. Cambridge, MA: Harvard University Press, 2020.

Nunokawa, Jeff. *The Afterlife of Property: Domestic Security and the Victorian Novel*. Princeton, NJ: Princeton University Press, 1994.

Ong, Yi-Ping. *The Art of Being: Poetics of the Novel and Existentialist Philosophy*. Cambridge, MA: Harvard University Press, 2018.

Orwell, George. *Dickens, Dali & Others*. San Diego: Harcourt Brace Jovanovich, 1973.

Pietz, William. *The Problem of the Fetish*. Edited by Francesco Pellizzi, Stefanos Geroulanos, and Ben Kafka. Chicago: University of Chicago Press, 2022.

Pippin, Robert B. *Hegel on Self-Consciousness: Desire and Death in* The Phenomenology of Spirit. Princeton, NJ: Princeton University Press, 2011.

——. *Henry James and Modern Moral Life*. Cambridge: Cambridge University Press, 2000.

Poovey, Mary. *Genres of the Credit Economy: Mediating Value in Eighteenth- and Nineteenth-Century Britain*. Chicago: University of Chicago Press, 2008.

Posnock, Ross. *The Trial of Curiosity: Henry James, William James, and the Challenge of Modernity*. New York: Oxford University Press, 1991.

Postone, Moishe. *Time, Labor, and Social Domination: A Reinterpretation of Marx's Critical Theory*. Cambridge: Cambridge University Press, 1993.

Powell, Michael and Emeric Pressburger, directors. *The Red Shoes*. The Archers, 1948.

Radcliffe, Ann. *The Mysteries of Udolpho*. Edited by Bonamy Dobrée. Oxford: Oxford University Press, 1966.

Rancière, Jacques. *The Edges of Fiction*. Translated by Steve Corcoran. Cambridge, UK: Polity Press, 2020.

Redfield, Marc. *Phantom Formations, Aesthetic Ideology and the Bildungsroman*. Ithaca, NY: Cornell University Press, 1996.

Reinhardt, Karl. *Sophocles*. Translated by Hazel Harvey and David Harvey. New York: Barnes and Noble, 1979.

Ricoeur, Paul. *The Course of Recognition*. Translated by David Pellauer. Cambridge, MA: Harvard University Press, 2005.

Rose, Gillian. *Hegel Contra Sociology*. London: Athlone, 1981.

——. *The Melancholy Science*. London: Verso, 2014.

Schor, Hillary M. *Dickens and the Daughter of the House*. Cambridge: Cambridge University Press, 1999.

Sedgwick, Eve Kosofsky. *Between Men: English Literature and Male Homosocial Desire*. New York: Columbia University Press, 1985.

——. *Touching Feeling: Affect, Pedagogy, Performativity*. Durham, NC: Duke University Press, 2003.

Shaw, George Bernard. *The Quintessence of Ibsenism*. New York: Hill & Wang, 1957.

Shklovsky, Viktor. *Theory of Prose*. Translated by Benjamin Sher. Normal, IL: Dalkey Archive Press, 1991.

Smith, Adam. *The Wealth of Nations*. Edited by Edward Cannan. New York: Random House, 1994.

Sohn-Rethel, Alfred. *Intellectual and Manual Labor: A Critique of Epistemology*. Translated by Martin Sohn-Rethel. Atlantic Highlands, NJ: Humanities Press, 1978.

Sophocles. *Oedipus the King*. Translated by David Grene. Chicago: University of Chicago Press, 2010.

Stephens, Leslie. *George Eliot*. London: Macmillan, 1902.

Stewart, Garrett. "Dickens and the Narratography of Closure." *Critical Inquiry* 34, no. 3 (2008): 509–42.

Tasso, Torquato. *Jerusalem Delivered*. Translated by Edward Fairfax. New York: Capricorn, 1963.

Taylor, Jesse Oak. "Ritual and the Liminality of Sherlock Holmes in *The Hound of the Baskervilles* and *The Sign of Four*." *English Literature in Transition* 48, no. 1 (2005): 55–70.

Thomas, Ronald R. *Detective Fiction and the Rise of Forensic Science*. Cambridge: Cambridge University Press, 1999.

Todorov, Tzvetan. *The Poetics of Prose*. Translated by Richard Howard. Ithaca, NY: Cornell University Press, 1977.

Trilling, Lionel. Introduction to *Little Dorrit*, by Charles Dickens. Oxford: Oxford University Press, 1953.

Trollope, Anthony. *An Autobiography*. London: Penguin, 1996.

——. *Barchester Towers*. Oxford: Oxford University Press, 1989.

——. *The Last Chronicle of Barset*. Edited by Stephen Gill. Oxford: Oxford University Press, 1980.

——. *The Way We Live Now*. Edited by Frank Kermode. London: Penguin, 1994.

Van Ghent, Dorothy. *The English Novel: Form and Function*. New York: Harper & Row, 1961.

Wagner, Richard. *The Ring of the Nibelung*. German text with English translation by Andrew Porter. New York: Norton, 1977.

Weber, Max. *From Max Weber: Essays in Sociology*. Translated by H. H. Gerth and C. Wright Mills. New York: Oxford University Press, 1946.

Williams, Bernard. *Shame and Necessity*. Berkeley: University of California Press, 2008.

Williams, Raymond. *The Country and the City*. New York: Oxford University Press, 1973.

——. *The English Novel from Dickens to Lawrence*. New York: Oxford University Press, 1973.

Wilson, Edmund. *The Wound and the Bow*. New York: Farrar, Straus & Giroux, 1978.

Woloch, Alex. *The One vs. the Many: Minor Characters and the Space of the Protagonist in the Novel*. Princeton, NJ: Princeton University Press, 2003.

Wright, Daniel. "Because I Do: Trollope, Tautology, and Desire." *ELH* 80, no. 4 (Winter 2013): 1121–43.

Yeazell, Ruth Bernard. "Do It or Dorrit." *Novel: A Forum on Fiction* 25, no. 1 (Fall 1991): 33–49.

Žižek, Slavoj. *Living in the End Times*. Brooklyn: Verso, 2010.

——. *The Parallax View*. Cambridge, MA: MIT Press, 2006.

——. *The Sublime Object of Ideology*. London: Verso, 1989.

INDEX

www.ingramcontent.com/pod-product-compliance
Ingram Content Group UK Ltd.
Pitfield, Milton Keynes, MK11 3LW, UK
UKHW040303280125
454147UK00005BA/43/J